THE BOWLES COLLECTION
OF 18TH-CENTURY
ENGLISH AND FRENCH
PORCELAIN

THE BOWLES COLLECTION OF 18TH-CENTURY ENGLISH AND FRENCH PORCELAIN

Simon Spero

Fine Arts Museums of San Francisco

Distributed by the University of Washington Press

The Bowles Collection of 18th-Century English and French Porcelain
is published with the assistance of The Andrew W. Mellon Foundation
Endowment for Publications.

Catalogue photography by Kaz Tsuruta, San Francisco

Produced by the Publications Department of the Fine Arts Museums
of San Francisco: Ann Heath Karlstrom, Director of Publications
and Graphic Design
Editor: Fronia W. Simpson, Bennington, Vermont
Composition: Wilsted & Taylor Publishing Services, Oakland, California
Printed in Hong Kong through Overseas Printing Corporation, San Francisco

ISBN 0-88401-082-1 (soft)
ISBN 0-88401-083-X (hard)

Library of Congress Catalog Card No. 95-61909

Front cover: *Pair of Bow Apple Boxes and Covers*, cat. no. 48
Frontispiece: *Chelsea Botanical Plate*, cat. no. 32
Back cover: *Chelsea Botanical Plate*, cat. no. 31

Distributed by
University of Washington Press
P.O. Box 50096
Seattle, Washington 98145-5096

Printed in Hong Kong

CONTENTS

· DIRECTOR'S FOREWORD ·

WITH THE GIFT OF THE Constance and Henry Bowles Collection of eighteenth-century porcelains, the Fine Arts Museums of San Francisco becomes one of the leading centers in America for the study of fine European ceramics. Newly installed in 1995 in the Bowles Porcelain Gallery at a renovated and greatly expanded California Palace of the Legion of Honor, this distinguished collection of nearly two hundred objects joins the museum's other holdings of European ceramics to constitute a broad-based survey particularly rich in examples of eighteenth-century English manufacture. The present catalogue, fully illustrated with new photography and enlivened with Simon Spero's scholarly yet engaging text, plus contributions by Dr. Bernard Watney and Constance Bowles Peabody, marks this special occasion. It is one of the most important catalogues we have published to date in our ongoing series of books on subsections of the permanent collection.

In a collection as lovingly assembled as that of Constance and Henry Bowles, two different themes reverberate: the connoisseurship and passion of the collectors, and the historical story of eighteenth-century European porcelain, with all it conveys about social customs and taste, stylistic developments, and changes in ceramic technologies.

From the reminiscence provided here by Constance Bowles Peabody we gain a clear impression of the single-minded dedication that she and her husband Henry brought to the quest for fine ceramics during a quarter century of collecting. They decided early to concentrate primarily on English factories and their work from about 1740 to 1775. They could be seduced by other styles, but it is the depth of their holdings of Chelsea, Bow, Worcester, and Longton Hall ceramics, totaling over 150 pieces, that forms the true glory of the collection. Their search for outstanding examples went hand-in-hand with a determination to find out all they could about the technical and historical aspects of European porcelain. It was a shared passion and a source of much mutual pleasure.

Installed at the Bowleses' home, their collection enriched their daily lives and those of appreciative visitors. Now accompanied by several gifts from Henry's brother, George Bowles, it enters the California Palace of the Legion of Honor to become a centerpiece in the museum's distinguished survey of European decorative arts. A total renovation and reinstallation of the Bowles Porcelain Gallery and the addition of a ceramics study room will greatly enhance the presentation and appreciation of ceramics and allow an expanded educational program around them. The museum strives for a position of preeminence among American museums collecting in this field, and the Bowles collection and its new installation are a primary catalyst toward this goal.

This book will provide a lasting scholarly resource and a vehicle for those who cannot visit the museum to enjoy the superb Bowles Collection. We are grateful to all who helped make it possible: our three authors; Lee Hunt Miller, Curator of European Decorative Arts; Ann Heath Karlstrom, Director of Publications and Graphic Design; editor Fronia Simpson; and photographer Kaz Tsuruta. Publication was made possible by The Andrew W. Mellon Foundation Endowment for Publications. We are especially grateful to Constance Bowles Peabody for her continuing generosity to the Fine Arts Museums.

Harry S. Parker III
Director of Museums

· FOREWORD ·

Dr. Bernard Watney

As one of the privileged English ceramicists who used to visit San Francisco twenty years or more ago, I shared with Connie and Henry Bowles their excitement in seeing this collection grow. Between each visit there would be new treasures. "Here," Connie would say, "is our latest Chelsea botanical plate. Last time you came we had just received a Longton leaf-shaped tureen and stand [cat. no. 72]. Do you remember?"

From their elegant house one could look down across the bay from which the mist was just clearing. Fine pieces of Chelsea and Longton Hall displayed around the breakfast room in attractively lit cabinets were most distracting for me at mealtimes. To have seen this collection in the ideal context of the home where it was formed is indeed an unforgettable memory.

When a collection is taken from where it was formed and placed in a museum, it inevitably loses something of its personal significance. However, there are also gains. A splendid illustrated catalogue has been produced, which will take its place in all ceramic libraries and enable the collection to be studied and appreciated far beyond its own country. There is no one who has more knowledge and experience of the particular factories that are best represented here than the author of this catalogue, Simon Spero. He writes with authority and his notes will give readers a new insight into some of the finest porcelain of the eighteenth century.

Looking at the collection as a whole, one can infer the shapes and types of decoration of which Connie and Henry Bowles were especially fond. Foremost among these must be red anchor Chelsea botanical plates and fruit, vegetable, and animal forms. Deserving of special mention are the Bow apples with coddling moth caterpillars as handles (cat. no. 48) and the two delightful peach-shaped wine cups after Fijian originals, one made by Worcester (cat. no. 81) and the other by Longton Hall (cat. no. 76) in the mid-eighteenth century. Chelsea dovecotes as potpourri vases are rare and their large size and intricate modeling always attract attention (cat. no. 42). The design was doubtless based on the substantial architectural dovecotes that were then a common sight all over Europe.

As a collector myself, I inevitably have some favorite pieces in the collection. While sharing in large measure a fondness for vegetable and leaf forms and early botanical painting, I have a special predilection for tall beaker cups, especially early Chelsea examples. In the Bowles Collection there are three superb pieces of this type. Two of them bear the rare underglaze blue mark of a crown and trident, one is a seductive tea-plant molded beaker (cat. no. 2), and the other has the same fluted shape but is enameled with a ho-ho bird in the Kakiemon taste (cat. no. 7). Also in the Japanese style is the third beaker cup; in spite of a crisp leaf molding, it is successfully enameled with a design featuring a tiger (cat. no. 6).

The earliest wares from a factory are often the most attractive, and this is certainly true of the Chelsea triangle-marked strawberry dish (cat. no. 5). The enameled decoration is differently arranged on every polychrome example of these rare vessels, the intention seemingly to have been to disguise firing faults. The primitive painting of insects and sprigs makes me, at any rate, long to know about the artist responsible for the enameling; perhaps he was one of a group of independent London decorators, as he also seems to have worked on some very early Bow.

I cannot resist drawing attention to another, but totally different, type of early piece, the primitive Lund's Bristol blue-and-white mug (cat. no. 156), which is in such marked contrast to the desirable enameled Worcester wine funnel (cat. no. 79) or the exceedingly fine wall vase, or wall pocket (cat. no. 89), lavishly decorated with bunches and sprays of European flowers over a molded country scene of farmhouses, trees, and cattle. The blue-and-white mug is based on a much earlier shape, which probably derives originally from seventeenth-century German stoneware but was later copied in blanc de chine from Fijian. The decoration is a direct copy of a Chinese pattern, even to clusters of three dots in the landscape, a feature that led earlier writers to believe that it was a distinguishing trait of a particular blue-and-white painter on Lund's Bristol and early Worcester.

Now armed with this catalogue, those lucky enough to live within reach of the Fine Arts Museums of San Francisco can visit or revisit the collection to find out which pieces they themselves like the best and perhaps to establish the reasons why they do so. Those who are never able to make the pilgrimage to San Francisco will be even more grateful for the publication of this catalogue.

· AUTHOR'S PREFACE ·

Simon Spero

San Francisco is a city of many collections, and English ceramics feature prominently in many of them. So prominently indeed, that in 1972 Graeme Keith, curator of sculpture and decorative arts at the M. H. de Young Museum, conceived the idea of mounting an exhibition of English pottery and porcelain belonging to collectors in the Bay Area. This event, entitled *Uncommon Clay*, and, more specifically, the buffet supper given for the lenders, proved to be the catalyst from which evolved the San Francisco Ceramic Circle, which thrives to this day.

The range and quality of these local collections became evident for all to see, when in 1980 a further exhibition, *English Ceramics from Northern California Collections*, was organized, and on this occasion it was held at the California Palace of the Legion of Honor. It comprised 288 objects drawn from over thirty private collections, an extraordinary reflection of the enthusiasm for ceramics that exists in the area and that has been nourished and stimulated by the dedication of a small band of local collectors. A prime mover in the planning of both these exhibitions and in the broadly based formation of the San Francisco Ceramic Circle was Henry Bowles who, together with his wife, Constance, have done so much to support the Fine Arts Museums. They were, at that time, in the process of assembling a fine collection of eighteenth-century English and French porcelain, and Henry was one of the first speakers to address the newly formed San Francisco Ceramic Circle. The Bowleses' collection had already become well known to porcelain experts and museum curators visiting San Francisco, both from out-of-state and from Europe, all of whom could be certain of a warm welcome and a taste of the Bowles California hospitality.

Henry Bowles was a mining engineer with a courteous and formal manner, behind which lay a shrewd, brilliant mind. His reserved and often self-effacing exterior served as an ideal counterfoil for Connie's more extrovert personality. Yet if Henry gave a superficial impression of seriousness, his quiet manner concealed a keen sense of humor.

I first met Henry and Connie Bowles while visiting San Francisco for the first time in the autumn of 1976. I was to give a lecture at the California Palace of the Legion of Honor and had been invited to a reception beforehand, at the Bowleses' residence on Jackson Street. I had had an absorbing, though exhausting, day, looking at three collections in differing parts of the city, and my mind was in a whirl as I entered the Bowleses' breakfast-room gallery, lined with china cabinets containing Chelsea, Bow, Worcester, Longton Hall, Meissen, and Chantilly, as well as choice pieces of Derby, Lowestoft, and Lund's Bristol.

The room was already full of local collectors, some of whom I recognized as members of the San Francisco Ceramic Circle and luminaries from the museum. I was introduced to Connie Bowles but had hardly time to take my bearings before Henry advanced upon me and drew me toward a table, around which was clustered a group of collectors, peering intently at a pair of tureens in the form of apples (cat. no. 48). Henry, curious to assess my mettle, explained that these apples had proved a source of mystery and that no one had ever been able to identify them satisfactorily . . . with the solitary exception of Robert Williams, the eminent London dealer. In these unpropitious circumstances, surrounded by a sea of expectant faces, I was obliged to establish my credentials.

Porcelain tureens in the forms of vegetables and fruit can be among the most difficult of all pieces to identify, usually having an overall naturalistic coloring that permits few uncovered areas of paste and glaze for close examination. Nor do they have such helpful clues as typical handle forms, spouts, and so forth. They were made at Meissen, Chelsea, Bow, Derby, and Longton Hall, with early-nineteenth-century copies in Coalport, and have also attracted the attention of fakers in both France and England. Yet Bob Williams had positively identified them, and I was now expected to do likewise. Resolving not to be hurried, and mustering what calmness I could, I examined each tureen carefully. They seemed by the vitality and quality of their modeling, and by their palette, to be genuine eighteenth-century pieces, and I judged the porcelain to be soft paste, thereby eliminating Meissen or any other German factory. The modeling and the tone of yellow were inappropriate for Longton Hall and the glaze too thick and opaque for Chelsea. Were they Derby? Looking up, I became aware that my hesitation was attracting further attention and that more people were crowding around the table. There was an air of expectancy as a growing blur of faces watched me intently. Realizing that I could delay my decision no longer, I resolved to grasp the nettle and was on the point of deciding upon Derby, when some instinctive response, connected to the appearance and texture of the glaze, made me change my mind. "I think that these are probably Bow." There was a long silence as Henry Bowles looked first at me and then at the tureens. The faces around the table awaited his verdict. After what seemed like an age, he smiled at me and remarked laconically, "Well, Simon, that's what Bob Williams thinks, too." Endeavoring to conceal my relief, I was able to relax and enjoy the rest of the evening, my confidence restored. Henry Bowles and I had won one another's respect, but it might so easily have been otherwise.

Just as the personalities of Henry and Connie Bowles perfectly complemented one another, so their tastes in porcelain interacted to produce several separate yet comparable strands in their collection, lending it an enviable sense of breadth and variety. They both loved Chelsea and concentrated principally on the early years of the factory, characterized by fluid shapes and superb fable and landscape decoration, tempered by Connie's fondness for botanical and naturalistic themes. The forty or so pieces that comprise this aspect of the collection reflect nearly every element of the Chelsea production during the factory's first decade and represent a classic bedrock for the collection as a whole. By contrast, the Bow section is far more idiosyncratic and selective, displaying Henry and Connie's personal preferences, with a strong emphasis on Kakiemon themes and in particular for the Quail or Partridge pattern. Seven superb examples of Longton Hall, with their extrovert and uninhibited rococo forms, mirror Connie Bowles's effervescent personality, while Henry's more restrained demeanor is expressed in his admiration for the conventional shapes of Worcester teawares. His preference for patterns rather than diversity of shapes was perhaps an expression of his reserved and formal manner and an engineer's appreciation of orderly repetition. However, another side of his personality was revealed by a fondness for the colored grounds, so vividly represented in the Worcester chapter.

On the face of it, the small section devoted to Chantilly might seem an incongruous embellishment to a collection of early English porcelain. Yet in its decorative idiom it maintains and reinforces the resonant Kakiemon theme that recurs so frequently in the Bowles Collection, as a leitmotiv, adding a sense of style and sophistication. It is a personal touch, instinctive rather than carefully planned, yet it embodies the essence of Henry and Connie Bowleses' shared passion for collecting porcelain.

· ACKNOWLEDGMENTS ·

T HE WRITING OF THIS CATALOGUE has consumed large portions of time that I might otherwise have spent with my family, and I would like to thank my wife, Diane, and my children, Christopher and Miranda, for their patience and understanding. Diane has also been of particular assistance in the research on the decoration of the seven botanical plates, included in the chapter on Chelsea. In this regard, my friend Patrick Synge-Hutchinson has generously lent me his advice and experience, for which I am most grateful. Sir Bruno Welby has helped me greatly in several discussions about fable painting, and I am also indebted to John Sandon for his many astute comments on the complex issue of Worcester decoration and redecoration.

Dr. Bernard Watney has contributed a foreword to this catalogue, with his customary panache and perception, and Corinne Gibbons has succeeded in transforming my draft chapters into a format acceptable for publication. Ann Karlstrom has been a friendly and constant source of support at the Fine Arts Museums of San Francisco, and it has been of solace to me on many occasions to hear her friendly voice on the telephone and to be able to consult her on so many matters. Fronia W. Simpson too has been a pleasure to work with, for her efficiency, thoroughness, and, not least, her sense of humor.

I would also like to thank Mrs. Connie Bowles Peabody for her encouragement and cooperation throughout this project and for her understanding of the difficulties involved. Others who have helped me in many ways are George Cobham, Dr. Brent Elliott, Joseph Handley, Errol Manners, Lee Hunt Miller, Letitia Roberts, Tony Stevenson, Robert Williams, and Raymond and Billie Yarbrough.

· INTRODUCTION ·

Constance Bowles Peabody

LONG BEFORE WE MET, Henry and I were ardent book collectors. For me, the door to book collecting was through fine bindings. When I was in Europe in 1937, and visiting San Francisco friends in Paris, I had the opportunity to observe and learn from Mr. Morgan Gunst, who was making daily forays to purchase modern French bindings. I was a complete novice, and he would show me his treasures and take the time to explain why they were unique. Each one was more beautiful than the last. That interest continued when I returned to San Francisco, although once I started lessons in bookbinding I was overwhelmed and humbled by how exacting the work was, and how expensive!

For Henry, books were part of a family legacy. He had a fine set of original Audubon engravings bound in full red morocco left by his grandmother. In the early years of our marriage we began to collect books together. Living on the East Coast gave us access to small, specialized bookshops, and we made the most of them. Shooting and fishing were such an integral part of our lives that our tastes ran to those subjects. Again, we came to these passions separately. I had always adored fishing — I remember trembling with delight when I caught my first fish, a trout, and the same strong feeling of pleasure comes to me now when I see pieces of porcelain that are part of the collection.

Chelsea Botanical Plate
Cat. no. 33

Henry as a sportsman was a perfectionist, and very much a purist — dry fly-fishing, of course — and he indulged us both in the best equipment, the top English guns, the best fishing rods. So here we were, both admiring beautifully bound leather books, both interested in shooting and fishing, and delighted to find that we could combine the two interests. Having grown up in San Francisco, appreciating the fine printing that flourished here, we had high standards and knew exactly what we liked. In our book collecting, Golden Cockerel, Derrydale, Grabhorn, Arion, Bird and Bull were a few of the presses we favored.

About collecting, there are many things to say, but I have to confess that much of the pleasure has been in finding a bargain, as opposed to spending a large amount of money. In so doing, one is constantly challenged to use one's individual judgment. From collecting books Henry and I developed the desire to delve into a subject vigorously. Each piece of porcelain in our collection was discussed and examined and evaluated on all counts. Beauty, rarity, and fine condition were the criteria we tried to fulfill.

After living in New York, we moved to Chicago — this was wartime and Henry was taking a course in Japanese, preparing to go overseas. It was a time to explore, and for me the opening of a new world of interest. I discovered that Marshall Field's had an antique shop on the fourth floor of the store, which was full of porcelain. Certainly every collector always regrets the pieces overlooked, but this particular episode — painful in hindsight — was attributable to sheer naivety. We were still furnishing our home, and I had always wanted a porcelain tea set. There at Marshall Field's were two quite complete sets, in charming patterns, with the teapot, creamer and sugar, and eight cups. But for me there was one drawback: the cups had no handles, and I couldn't serve tea to my friends in cups like that!

Little did I know then that what I was rejecting was probably First Period Worcester, because the factory added handles only after about 1760. Today, of course, one never sees a whole tea set. I did manage to buy twelve glorious soup plates and twelve dinner plates in Masons ironstone for $4.50 apiece, as well as some wonderful early Crown Derby and a tureen for my sister. But those tea sets remain in my mind as a real opportunity missed through lack of knowledge.

A pastime I had in the early days — one that I still enjoy — was finding out-of-the-way antique shops. Once Henry and I were back in San Francisco I came across a small shop on Clement Street that had an unusually attractive chair in the window. I drove past for many months before one day — the year was 1967 — I found the shop open. Inside was an assortment of curious things, but what really caught my eye was some blue-and-white porcelain, a bowl and a *handleless* cup with saucer in what turned out to be First Period Worcester (Dr. Wall). The shop was Adele Morton's, and although she was not there that day, my saleslady was an elderly woman with tremendous knowledge of porcelain. She fascinated me, and my conversation with her really began my education.

My attention that day was also drawn to some pieces of Chelsea, and two beautiful powder blue Bow platters, about 1760. Henry, immediately intrigued with my tale, told me I could buy the Bow and Chelsea. But what is more important, he chose to come with me to learn, as I had, and to pay for the pieces! By our own doing we were completely captivated.

From the beginning of our collecting we heard about Rea Ashley's shop on Union Street in San Francisco. She was the most charming and handsome woman imaginable. Her shop opened onto a lovely garden, and she held forth every Saturday morning with a discussion of porcelain as though in a salon. Since much of the fascination of eighteenth-century porcelain resides in its identification, she had endless talks with us about quality of painting, translucence, factory methods, firing temperatures, and quality of paste. It all intrigued us. We would leave her shop with a piece or two and go home to talk over the details again. At the same time, we were gradually collecting books of every sort on the subject of porcelain.

Then there was Merryvale, the breathtaking antique shop in the old Pacific Gas and Electric building on the Marina. It was a San Francisco showplace for its beautiful garden and wonderful antiques. The owner, Peggy McDonough, was a woman of great taste. She was not a real scholar — she bought pieces of porcelain for aesthetic reasons only. From her we were able to acquire many rare pieces, which, when we purchased them, no one truly understood. Since then, one of the coffeepots we bought thinking it was Worcester has been determined to be a rare Lowestoft coffeepot (cat. no. 71)!

At first as a collector I felt that nothing could be more attractive than blue-and-white, and it was only gradually that I learned to appreciate polychrome. I always knew I considered figurines too fussy, and I wanted to collect only what the English call "useful wares," and only soft paste. Immersed as we were by this time in the new world of eighteenth-century porcelain, Henry and I decided we would confine our collecting to a certain period to make it more concentrated and interesting. So it was to be 1740–75, and predominantly English, with no Chinese export. This was a deliberate decision, which did not change.

In the 1970s, on our trips to England for the shooting and fishing we loved, there was always time to spend at the Victoria and Albert Museum, where we would study the Schreiber Collection. I read Lady Charlotte Schreiber's *Journal* avidly — vicariously thrilling, full of the daily details of buying and dealing! Prices were reasonable in the day of the Schreibers' collecting, although now I think Henry and I were also rather fortunate in our timing.

As we widened our range of study and collecting, we gradually began to meet the dealers and museum people in the field who were to become good friends. We also met American collectors — from Seattle, Washington, to Tennessee — and from one of them we learned about the English Ceramic Circle and its *Transactions*, published every few months. (Bernard Watney, president of the English Ceramic Circle, has written the foreword to this catalogue.) After we were accepted into that elite organization, Henry decided to start a ceramic circle in San Francisco. From a beginning in 1972 with fifteen members, the San Francisco Ceramic Circle has grown to a membership of 170, twenty-three years later. Henry Bowles, Joe Handley, Raymond Yarbrough, Milford Smith, and Graeme Keith were the founding members.

In writing this introduction and reviewing the past, it seems to me that events unfolded in a quite miraculous way. I don't recall who suggested that we stop at the Antique Porcelain Company on 57th Street in New York City. Our first visit was in 1968. The shop was a dream come true, full of every type of porcelain and a feast of beauty — a bit overwhelming! Fortunately, Mr. Weinberg was there, a lively and delightful person, slight of build, with a heavy German accent. He showed us all around. A lawyer in Germany, he had fled the Nazi regime. He was knowledgeable, clever, and charming, and he was to play a large part in our lives.

That day we were ready to broaden our collection, and a pair of Longton Hall basins caught our attention (cat. no. 77). Somehow we expected Mr. Weinberg to be open to a bit of dickering, but though we tried every method, he did not budge on the price. Our children were waiting for us at the hotel, in disbelief, that we, normally notoriously punctual, could be an hour late. Finally, we did buy the basins, but before doing so we examined them under short-wave black light for possible repairs, and it all took several hours to conclude the purchase.

Hans Weinberg's enthusiasm for porcelain was contagious, and our collecting entered a new phase. Every purchase was an education. Every week, it seemed, a new auction catalogue would arrive in the mail, and we would pore over it carefully, with the confident knowledge that if Mr. Weinberg bid for us at Sotheby's or Christie's in London he would examine the pieces thoroughly before bidding.

By this time George (Corky) Bowles, Henry's brother and wonderful friend as well, was intrigued by our collecting, and he was infected with our auction fever. Often the situation would be this: I would be at home, where I had a large household to run, and Henry and Corky would be at the office, where they would have cleared the desk — as men are able to do — and been talking to dealers. Among the three of us — or four, with Hans — and after many telephone calls, we would decide how we thought the bidding for a particular piece might go.

Naturally, I was delighted that, when Hans came to San Francisco in 1972 to appraise our collection, he stayed with us. He wanted to see the "heart of the house," our breakfast-room gallery. Henry and I had gone back and forth about where to make a room for the porcelain, and we finally took our breakfast room and had it redone with special lighting and shantung silk–lined cabinets. It was a complete joy. We used to have most of our meals there, and it was perfect because we could sit and talk about the collection that was all around us; it was a constant part of all our conversations.

Hans Weinberg was very observant as a houseguest. On our ranch in Los Banos, we were growing excellent Israeli melons, which we brought back to our house in the city. While Hans was staying with us, we gave him one for breakfast. Not only was he enthusiastic about the flavor, he thought the outside color remarkably close to our Chelsea melon tureen. Having eaten the fruit right down to the skin, he popped the intact remains into his briefcase and took them back to New York to show the porcelain world that there was a real model for the piece (cat. no. 39).

In a letter to Hans in 1970 Henry said, "Your unfailing good advice and careful representation of our interests add much to the enjoyment of collecting." We became such fast friends that Hans wanted Henry to open a porcelain shop in San Francisco. Of course, that was out of the question, but for us no trip to New York, or to London, which had a branch of the shop, was complete without a visit to the Antique Porcelain Company. A huge gap opened in our lives when at age seventy-one Hans developed pneumonia and died within a week. One never realizes the true importance of a vital person until they are gone. Simultaneously, the auction market for porcelain also seemed to disappear — no catalogues, no chance to decide if something was going to be too expensive, or even to dream of having something at any price.

We continued to deal with the Antique Porcelain Company and Hans's knowledgeable daughter, Rotrant Beiny. We also had discovered Winifred and Bob Williams, and Amor Ltd., and other dealers in London. Although the rare and unusual find was less frequent, when I walked into Bob's shop at No. 7 Bury Street, in 1976, I was completely overwhelmed by the sight of a most beautiful *gros bleu* background O'Neale fable plate (cat. no. 131). It was perfectly displayed in a case lined with brilliant red silk.

Seeing that plate for the first time was a very emotional moment, and I wish that those who may wonder about the passion of collecting could have that initial experience which I relive every time I look at the plate. I was thrilled by the beauty and the humor and the delicacy of the O'Neale painting of a bear standing to put his paw in a beehive to get the honey, while bees swarm all around him. I was immediately drawn to the image, and I hoped I would own that plate someday. Eventually, we did buy it, and I will always see it as I first saw it that day in Bob's shop.

As I have said, the opportunities to buy became fewer, but we still continued to seek and search. I particularly remember when the very rare, very early Chelsea strawberry dish (cat. no. 5) we had purchased by auction arrived in San Francisco. Henry met with the customs agent and had to unwrap the piece in front of him. When the man looked at this rather stained piece and saw the price we had paid for it, he shook his head in disbelief. He was convinced that Henry was a complete eccentric.

Another find, nearly lost, happened on a trip to Europe with grandchildren. This was after Henry's death in 1981. I was scouting the shops on the Left Bank in Paris. To my utter amazement, I spotted a fabulous Chantilly teapot (cat. no. 175) and sugar bowl with cover (cat. no. 176) decorated in the Kakiemon taste, similar to that of a tureen (cat. no. 172) we had purchased several years before. These pieces were bought and packed for departure on the Orient Express the next day, and we took them along with our luggage. In the confusion of eight suitcases and trying to find the train, our package was missing! I was absolutely frantic when we arrived at the railroad car, but there, a man was holding up my porcelain package and asking, "Has anyone lost this?" Those pieces are now safely in the Porcelain Gallery of the Fine Arts Museums, but it was an alarming experience. I have always felt responsible for the well-being and safekeeping of these singular treasures we undertook to collect.

In writing about or discussing the collection, invariably I find myself explaining about the Chelsea dovecote (cat. no. 42), which we purchased in 1973 from Christie's in London. When we bought it, I was amused to read in *Collectors and Antique Dealers Guide 1973*, "The unusual character of the dovecote one recent morning at Christie's roused the congregation to enthusiasm and was bought for 800 guineas." By us! The writer confesses to be shocked at the high price, though he goes on to say it bears the red anchor mark and comes from Chelsea's finest period (ca. 1754–58), the implication being that some people will buy anything!

The dovecote had an appeal for us because of the hunting theme, the fox and doves, the whimsy of the piece, and its bucolic strength. The piece has a central turret and three smaller ones. The upper part has thirteen doves, and the lower part a rockwork base covered with flowers; a fox looks up hungrily at a single dove perched before a door. I clearly remember that when we gave it to the Fine Arts Museums, Henry delivered it himself, with the covers for the turrets jangling around in his pockets. That distressed me because I was sure they were going to be chipped, but it, and they, arrived safely, and for some the dovecote is their favorite piece in the collection!

Keeping in mind a sense of responsibility for the objects we had collected — and that responsibility certainly must be an important part of the definition of the collector — it became Henry's and my ambition to redo the Porcelain Gallery at the Legion of Honor in order to make it a study collection and to have a library of books nearby and available for students. In a letter to Ian White, then director of the Fine Arts Museums, dated 7 July 1977, Henry said:

> We believe that our collection would be an important part of a general porcelain assemblage which could be enjoyed by scholars and others specifically interested in the subject. Properly housed and displayed, our collection plus the Museum's present holdings would form the nucleus of an important collection which I feel would encourage additional gifts.

With the help of Graeme Keith, curator of sculpture and decorative arts, we redid the gallery and had several intriguing exhibitions there. Now I follow the stages of development of the new Bowles Porcelain Gallery with the greatest interest. The new cases will benefit from state-of-the-art lighting and appropriate background color. The room we have planned should be the best porcelain gallery imaginable, and the separate study room will be unique.

Over the years I have come to feel that porcelain collecting is my subject. I only wish that in every way the pleasure that has been mine in spending hours, days, and years in the presence of this craftsmanship and artistry can be felt by others. Our hope is that in this new gallery we can create, and communicate, something of what thrilled us from the start of our collecting. We always felt that the gallery should be a place to learn. It is the measuring, documenting, and studying of the pieces that began to make them come alive for us. Indeed, the study of eighteenth-century English and French soft-paste porcelain is far from over, in the sense of having all the questions answered and all the parts of the puzzle in place. Dozens of books have been written on the subject, there are constantly fresh discoveries and more books, and in England excavations reveal shards of porcelain from early factory sites to this day. Each theory and speculation seems to produce another book or scholarly paper. The whole subject is a challenge.

For me, the history of the period is engrossing. The industrial revolution had taken place in England, and a new merchant class was born. I think of these people as being much like our early settlers in America, their conservative taste marked by simplicity and restraint. An appreciation of nature was reflected in botanic forms and painting, and a refinement of form expressed in beautifully proportioned tureens. An interesting connection with America was the discovery in Aiken, South Carolina, of a mine with a certain type of clay (kaolin) essential to the manufacture of eighteenth-century porcelain. Barrels of this clay were sent to England to be used as an essential ingredient in Worcester and Bow porcelain.

When asked by friends to "explain" what soft-paste porcelain means to me, there is no simple answer. Yes, of course, it is interesting to know the history, and to know about the clay, and to study the shards. When I am thinking about the collection I find myself transported toward the people for whom the porcelain was made. I would love to have known some of those eighteenth-century people, who lived in a period that reflected the best of French, German, and Japanese design.

To know Henry and me somewhat better as collectors, perhaps it helps to look at the pair of Chelsea beakers (cat. nos. 6 and 7). I think they represent aspects of the differences in our personalities, outlook, and priorities. Henry's Chelsea beaker (cat. no. 7), with the decorative ho-ho bird, has the crown and trident mark — a mark so rare that there are only about thirteen examples known in the world! That was very impressive, and Henry was proud of that mark. It also made his beaker quite a bit more expensive than mine. (Bernard Watney speaks about them in his foreword.)

I bought my beaker a year later. It is flamboyant, flowing, and very intricate in its acanthus design (cat. no. 6). I was perfectly honest in saying to Henry that I thought mine much more beautiful than his. We joked about the fact that whereas his was so rare, mine was by far the prettier. As an anecdote, this indicates the differences between us as collectors, but it also indicates the harmony. The difference was only wide enough to be fun. I should think it would be very hard to collect with someone who didn't more or less agree with one. Anything I wanted, Henry would buy, and anything he wanted, he bought anyway!

Having mentioned the Chelsea melon tureen (cat. no. 39), I cannot finish this introduction without some discussion of the theme of botanicals. The charming pair of Chelsea artichokes (cat. no. 40) was given to me by Henry on our twenty-fifth wedding anniversary. They are among my favorite pieces. Henry had a way of surprising me with presents, and these were the best! I have kept the Chelsea botanical plates in my home for the pleasure of living with them for as long as possible.

Humor and light-heartedness appeal to me — in art as in life. I am drawn to questions of history, too. Among the things undone in my life is a sabbatical I would like to take to study the portfolio of Ehret drawings for the Chelsea Physic Garden, the originals for the Chelsea plates, now to be found in the Botanical Garden of the Natural History Museum, in South Kensington. I am fascinated by my Chelsea plantain plate (cat. no. 33) and by the questions it raises of travel in the eighteenth century to lands where plantains grow. Perhaps I have a fevered imagination, but the pleasure I get from every aspect of each piece is such that I want to know more, and more. And I believe the link with the past, as well as the continuing questions for the future, is the gift I most enjoy giving to the Fine Arts Museums and to the museum-going public.

THE BOWLES COLLECTION

· CHELSEA ·

1745–1769

Founded in 1745, the Chelsea factory was primarily the creation and inspiration of one man, Nicholas Sprimont. He was a second-generation Huguenot from Liège who settled in London in about 1742 to become a silversmith. He was a man of great creative energy — a craftsman, designer, sculptor, and, as he was soon to demonstrate, a shrewd and perceptive businessman. From the start, he perceived the manufacture of porcelain as essentially a luxury market, through the eyes of a silversmith accustomed to catering to the tastes of the wealthy. Indeed, an inveterate promoter, he placed many advertisements that clearly demonstrate his intentions as to where the market for his porcelain should lie. Announcements in the *Daily Advertiser* during the early 1750s are full of references to "The Quality and Gentry" and "The Nobility and Gentry," and this clear priority is emphasized by the luxurious nature of his earliest wares, with their swirling rhythms and fluid rococo themes.

In his avowed intention to appeal to this wealthy and discerning market, Sprimont enjoyed several advantages denied to those manufacturers who were to become his rivals. The pleasant location of the factory, not far from the fashionable Ranelagh pleasure gardens, which had opened to the public in 1742, was well chosen for Sprimont's new enterprise. His background as a silversmith made him well attuned to the tastes and requirements of the upper echelons of society, and he had a number of influential friends and contacts. Among these was Sir Everard Fawkener, secretary to William Augustus, duke of Cumberland and the second surviving son of George II. The duke was believed to be "a great encourager of the Chelsea China,"[1] as well as being a customer, though it is unlikely that he had any financial interest in the factory. However, it is clear that Sir Everard Fawkener was involved in the enterprise, from its early days until his death in 1758.

Recent research, based upon French archives,[2] suggests that Charles Gouyn, a Huguenot jeweler born in Dieppe, may have played a prominent role in the establishment of the Chelsea factory. This appears to confirm the puzzling statement in an advertisement in the *General Advertiser* of 29 January 1750/51, that Charles Gouyn had at one time been "Proprietor and Chief Manager of the Chelsea-House," a possibility largely discounted by scholars. Whatever Gouyn's involvement may have been, it was comparatively short-lived, for as the newly discovered archive reveals, he was by 1749 Sprimont's competitor, responsible for the hitherto mysterious "Girl-in-a-Swing" factory.

Although remaining active as a silversmith, Sprimont was involved in every facet of the management and production at Chelsea, even founding a training school for young painters and designers. Yet his influence found its most enduring expression in the porcelain forms themselves, which drew their inspiration from his own creations in silver. The asymmetrical curves of the marine and shell motifs of much of his earliest porcelain echo the silver dishes, saltcellars, and sauceboats conceived during the same period. Indeed, even those porcelain shapes that have no obvious silver counterpart convey in their linear vitality a sense of caprice and overall sophistication that is quite alien to the functional associations of domestic porcelain.

The output of the Chelsea factory can be conveniently divided into four periods, each corresponding to the marks successively used: the incised triangle (1745–49), the raised anchor (ca. 1750–53), the red anchor (ca. 1754–58), and the gold anchor (ca. 1759–69). Throughout this time there were frequent variations made to the recipe of the porcelain body, but these did not always correspond exactly to the changes in the factory mark.

During the triangle period, the porcelain recipe included a substantial amount of lead in the mixture of both the body and the glaze. The shapes during this early period, derived from both silver and oriental porcelain, were most often sparingly decorated either in the Chinese taste or with European floral designs, though a small number of Japanese Kakiemon patterns were also utilized. Yet much of this triangle period porcelain was left undecorated, allowing the swirling rhythms of the tea-plant and strawberry-leaf molding to sustain the visual impact, much as it would in silver. This effect was enhanced by the rich whiteness of the porcelain body, often covered with a glaze further whitened by the addition of tin oxide. Three beautiful white pieces from this period (cat. nos. 1–3) exemplify these qualities, unalloyed by the distraction of colored decoration.

The impact of these first pieces of English porcelain was immediate. The "London" column of the *Daily Advertiser* on 5 March 1745 noted: "We hear that China made at Chelsea is arriv'd to such Perfection, as to equal if not surpass the finest old Japan, allow'd so by the most approved Judges here; and that the same is in so high Esteem of the Nobility, and the Demand so great, that a sufficient Quantity can hardly be made to answer the Call for it." Whether this earliest of all written records of the factory may be accepted as an objective comment, or whether Sprimont had a hand in its wording, is a matter for conjecture, but the reputation of the factory had spread as far afield as France in this short time. A French document of 1745 refs to the newly established English factory as making porcelain that seemed more beautiful than that of Saxony (that is, Meissen, the envy of Europe).[3]

In March 1749 Sprimont suspended sales of porcelain until the end of the year, while the factory was moved to an adjoining site, in larger premises, at the corner of Lawrence Street. During this period of reorganization and expansion, variations were made to the recipe for the porcelain body, reducing the lead content and correspondingly adding more lime, and using tin oxide on a consistent basis to opacify the glaze. This new body was devised to suit a range of shapes more utilitarian in design than the fanciful rococo forms of the preceding decade. Sprimont announced the relaunching of the factory in a series of newspaper advertisements, in one of which (*The Daily Advertiser*, 9 January 1750) he summarized the new range of shapes soon to be available as "a Variety of Services for Tea, Coffee, Chocolate, Porringers, Sauce-Boats, Basons, and Ewers, Ice-Pails, Terreens, Dishes and Plates of different Forms and Patterns, and of a great variety of Pieces for Ornament in a Taste entirely new."

To coincide with the relaunching of the factory, in May 1750 Sprimont introduced a new mark, an anchor, raised in relief upon a small pad, perhaps symbolizing the new venture. The new porcelain body proved to be one of the most beautiful and tactile ever produced in soft-paste porcelain, with a rich, smooth glaze, a warm texture, sensuous to the touch, and for one writer, "producing an effect of voluptuousness,"[4] an analogy that can perhaps only be fully appreciated by a porcelain collector. Needless to say, the motivation behind this new porcelain recipe was far more prosaic. It perfectly suited the octagonal and fluted tewares, the range of plates, dishes, bowls, and vases that came to characterize the raised anchor period.

The "Taste entirely new," so intriguingly described by Sprimont in his advertisement of January 1750, was either a veiled reference to the new range of octagonal and hexagonal shapes that were about to be revealed, or to the Kakiemon style of decoration derived from late-seventeenth-century Japanese porcelain that was to become so distinctive and resonant a theme of the early 1750s. As the shapes and decoration so often occurred in association with one another, it is possible that both constituted the new taste.

The vogue for Kakiemon porcelain was introduced into England from Holland by Queen Mary, wife of William III. She and the ladies of her court created a demand for the imported Japanese wares during the 1690s, and later, when they were no longer available, English collectors turned to the Meissen imitations of the 1730s. When the Chelsea and Bow versions came into production in the early 1750s, their popularity was therefore assured. These subtle designs — with their allusive symbolism and hint of oriental mystery — were painted in a restricted yet distinctive palette, echoing the carefully composed asymmetry of the finest Japanese porcelain. If the arcane subtleties of this language of symbolism were not always fully understood, it nevertheless engendered a striking effect, animated by the vibrant colors and fluid shapes that so fittingly accompanied it. Some patterns were derived directly from Kakiemon originals, while others were taken from Meissen copies of Japanese porcelain (cat. nos. 9 and 11). The heavily potted porcelain body, angular octagonal forms, and opacified glaze formed a canvas ideally suited to the balance between the sparkling colors and the use of areas of space. Yet successful though these Kakiemon patterns were, both aesthetically and commercially, the vogue was comparatively short-lived. By 1754 all the oriental patterns had disappeared, to be replaced by purely European themes.

The influence of the Meissen factory held sway throughout the early and mid-1750s, both in domestic wares and figures and in ornamental pieces. Through the influence of Sir Everard Fawkener, Sir Charles Hanbury Williams, envoy to the Saxon court in Dresden, made his collection of Meissen available at Holland House in London. Naturalistic flower painting closely followed that of the Meissen *deutsche Blumen*, although some of the earlier examples are reminiscent of Vincennes. Landscape scenes, usually contained within reserved panels, were also inspired by Meissen and were for several years a speciality of Chelsea, without parallel in other English porcelain. The Bowles Collection is rich in decoration of this genre (cat. nos. 14–20), and much speculation surrounds the identity of the several painters responsible.

These adaptations of Meissen forms and painted and molded designs were not only a reflection of the tastes and preferences of the affluent echelons of society but no doubt also a measure of Sprimont's artistic admiration for the German factory. Yet this source, which so fueled his creative imagination and contributed so much to the essential character of Chelsea porcelain during the middle years of the 1750s, was perceived by Sprimont the businessman in an altogether more ambivalent light. In about 1752 he even petitioned the government, anonymously, to prohibit the importation of Meissen porcelain.

The overlapping influences at Chelsea — of Chinese, Japanese, and Meissen porcelain and silver forms, so skillfully absorbed and interposed — were lent an added dimension by their glassy soft-paste porcelain, which induced comparisons with the earliest French factories at St. Cloud, Chantilly, Mennecy, and Vincennes. Yet several elements of the Chelsea production owed little, if anything, to oriental or Continental sources, and it is no coincidence that it is these that have become almost synonymous with the factory and its reputation among collectors and admirers of English porcelain. Decoration derived from Aesop's fables was an original innovation at Chelsea, confined almost entirely to the years between about 1752 and 1756, though the idiom had been used briefly, at Meissen, in the 1720s. Subjects were for the most part derived either from designs engraved by Francis Barlow, first published in 1687, or from Samuel Croxall's edition of

1722, which included many of Barlow's fables as a design source. The Croxall version became widely popular and it is likely that most of Sprimont's customers were familiar with it.

Fable painting itself evolved in three distinct phases. At first, pairs of fantastic and often imaginary animals were painted by "the first fable painter" on small dishes of differing shapes, in the 1750–52 period. Overlapping with this idiom was decoration depicting pairs of domestic animals, such as goats, horses, and cows. From these developed the fable subjects, dependent for their effect upon the skill and subtlety of the painter, in depicting a story with a moral. It has long been a matter of conjecture as to whether one or more painters were responsible for this distinctive decoration of animals and fables, and it may be reasonably argued that all can be credited to one accomplished and prolific hand, Jefferyes Hamett O'Neale. This young Irishman was probably barely twenty years old when he began working at Chelsea, but he immediately established a distinctive style in which he imbued his animals with faintly human postures and expressions, lending the scenes a satirical humor, whimsical, yet capturing the essence of these moral tales, in which the characteristics of animals were used to exemplify human follies and gullibility. O'Neale had access to both Barlow's and Croxall's editions of the fables, yet at heart he was an originator. Much of his work consists of free adaptations, often substituting one animal for another, rather than close copies of design sources. Six examples of his work are in the Bowles Collection (cat. nos. 20–25) and they make a revealing comparison, both between one another and with the Worcester plate (cat. no. 131) painted in O'Neale's later, much heavier, style.

Another resonant and archetypal contribution to English ceramics, inspired by Meissen in this instance, was the introduction at Chelsea of botanical decoration. This was one aspect of a wider movement toward naturalistic themes that found expression in domestic and ornamental pieces, as well as figures, birds, and animals. Specimens of plants, vegetables, flowers, leaves, and insects were laid out on plates and dishes to create an illusion of scientific accuracy, though the primary intentions were purely decorative. An advertisement for the factory in *Faulkner's Dublin Journal* for 1 July 1758 describes a service decorated "in curious Plants, with Table Plates, Soup Plates, and Dessert Plates, enamelled from Sir Hans Sloane's plants." Sir Hans Sloane had leased land to the Society of Apothecaries in 1722 for the Chelsea Physic Garden, and its proximity to the factory served as an inspiration for this most celebrated of all decorative themes on Chelsea porcelain. The depiction of botanical themes on Chelsea porcelain was especially appropriate in view of the nature and reputation of the surrounding area. Pehr Kalm, the Swedish traveler and diarist, described Chelsea as a little village a couple of miles from London, where the Thames ran between nurseries and market gardens, "of which there are a frightful number."[5] Subjects were copied and adapted from botanical illustrations drawn

Detail right:
Chelsea Cream Boat
Cat. no. 21

8

from a variety of sources, including Philip Miller's *Figures of Plants* and botanical illustrations after G. D. Ehret. The decoration, laid out in a manner that echoed contemporary book illustrations, was executed with great spirit and panache, though sometimes with a complete disregard for overall botanical accuracy. Not only was the palette usually conceived in purely decorative terms, but in some instances leaves were depicted attached to completely unrelated plants. Yet the overall effect was entrancing, and it is no wonder that it became such a favorite with Mr. and Mrs. Bowles.

The fashion, and consequent demand, for naturalistic themes so integral a component of the rococo style extended well beyond botanical painting on dessert services. For the wealthy and aristocratic classes who could afford Chelsea porcelain, there existed opportunities to show off both their affluence and their taste. Sprimont introduced a substantial range of dishes and tureens in animal, bird, and vegetable forms with which to embellish the dinner table. All copied closely from Meissen, these pieces were usually listed in the surviving contemporary sale catalogues as being "for desart." In the eighteenth century the dessert course was entirely separate from the rest of the meal, succeeding the two main meat and fish courses, and sometimes even taking place in a separate room. The tablecloth would be removed, and what ensued would be not so much a continuation of the serious matter of eating, as an opportunity for the host to demonstrate the resources of his hospitality. This lavish visual fantasy might include the display of tureens in the guises of cabbages, lettuces, lemons, pineapples, melons, artichokes, and partridges, alongside fig leaves, rose boxes, sunflower dishes, animal tureens, and perhaps models of human subjects. These trompe-l'oeil objects, interspersed among pyramids of sweetmeats, whipped syllabubs, jellies, tarts, and sculptures in sugar, would be viewed in the flickering light of candles, their shadows further animating the illusion of an elaborate tableau vivant. Mr. and Mrs. Bowles acquired several of these evocative manifestations of rococo themes, including a melon tureen (cat. no. 39), a pair of artichoke tureens (cat. no. 40), and a partridge tureen (cat. no. 41), together with a pair of Bow apple boxes (cat. no. 48) and a Longton Hall cos lettuce tureen (cat. no. 72).

From 1755 onward auction sales of the previous year's production of the factory were held intermittently, usually at Mr. Ford's Great Room in St. James', Haymarket. By great good fortune, copies of the complete catalogues for March 1755 and March 1756 have survived, together with a portion of the sale catalogue for April 1761. These lend a revealing insight into the previous year's production prior to each auction, and it is often possible to match surviving pieces with their corresponding counterparts listed in the catalogue. Hence, for example, lot 11, on the fifteenth day's sale, Wednesday, 26 March 1755, is described as "Four fine small melons for desart." The imposing Chelsea dovecote, a ceramic tour de force (cat. no. 42), is described in some detail as lot 73 on 11 March of the 1755 sale.

In about 1754 a red anchor replaced the raised anchor as the factory mark, and two years or so later a variation of the recipe for the porcelain body was introduced. It resulted in a lighter, thinly potted body with a more translucent glaze, lacking the tin oxide that was so associated with the oriental patterns of preceding years. These were now rapidly swept away, along with the octagonal and hexagonal shapes, and replaced by a purely European style of decoration that was still dominated by the fashion for Meissen. This period of prosperity and expansion was interrupted in 1756–57, first by Sprimont's declining health, as a result of which there was no auction sale in 1757, and second by the death in 1758 of Sir Everard Fawkener. This was a grievous blow, for not only was he a crucial source of financial support, but he also had a wide network of influential friends among the aristocracy, diplomats, politicians, and even royalty. Tastes and fashions were changing, and with the onset of the Seven Years' War in 1756, importations of Meissen porcelain ceased and the German factory gave way to Sèvres as the leading arbiter of porcelain taste and style.

Yet Sprimont's resilience and business acumen had not deserted him. A further variation to the porcelain body in about 1759, the introduction of bone ash, strengthened it and greatly facilitated the production of figures and vases. This sturdy new white body was covered by a thick glassy glaze, and though this tended to craze easily and provided a less suitable canvas for the painted decoration, these drawbacks proved irrelevant. A gold anchor mark heralded this new phase of the utmost splendor, with the introduction of colored grounds, a freer use of gilding, and a far more liberal approach to painted decoration. Bird and fruit subjects remained popular, but a less restrained rococo style had come into vogue, which gradually gave way to an equally sumptuous neoclassicism. As he had throughout his career, Sprimont remained perfectly attuned to changing tastes and reacted swiftly, even if he did not actually anticipate them.

Mr. and Mrs. Bowleses' admiration for Chelsea embodies a collecting tradition that stretches back into the lifetime of the factory. Horace Walpole and James West, president of the Royal Society, were among the contemporary collectors, and the reputation and quality of Chelsea porcelain were widely acknowledged even after the factory had closed. Writing in 1783, twelve years after Sprimont's death, Mrs. Papendiek, Assistant Keeper of the Wardrobe to Queen Charlotte, recalled the setting-up of her first home: "Our tea and coffee set were of Common India china, our dinner service of earthenware, to which, for our rank, there was nothing superior, Chelsea porcelain and fine India china being only for the wealthy."[6]

1. Adams, *Chelsea Porcelain*, p. 64.
2. Dragesco, *English Ceramics in French Archives*.
3. Legge, *Flowers and Fables*, p. 14.
4. MacKenna, *Chelsea Porcelain: The Triangle and Raised Anchor Wares*, p. 32.
5. Quoted from Le Rougetel, *The Chelsea Gardener: Philip Miller, 1691–1771*, p. 2.
6. Hillier, *Pottery and Porcelain, 1700–1914*, p. 81.

1

1

Chelsea Coffeepot and Cover, ca. 1745–49

Molded in high relief with flowering tea-plant branches curving upward from an octafoil base, the domed cover with similar molding.

HEIGHT: 9¼ in. (23.5 cm)

MARK: None

LITERATURE: Austin, *Chelsea Porcelain at Colonial Williamsburg*, cat. no. 15

ACCESSION NUMBER: 1991.47.40a–b

This is a classic Chelsea form that probably originated in repoussé silver, though the distinctive stylistic concept also occurs in Hochst faience at very much the same period. The subtlety with which the lobed shape is overlaid with the curving tea-plant molding betrays the eye of the silversmith. It typifies the ambitious and highly sophisticated forms made during the early years of the Chelsea factory, combining a rhythmic silver shape, French in feeling, with chinoiserie elements in the tea-plant molding and branch handle, molded with foliage. This fusion of diverse ideas and designs, drawn together with such confidence, springs from Nicholas Sprimont's experience as a silversmith and also from his Belgian roots. Furthermore, as a silversmith, he did not necessarily envisage porcelain forms as being dependent on coloring for their visual impact. Consequently, not only was a high proportion of his earliest porcelain left free of decoration, but it is likely that much of the earliest floral painting was undertaken outside the factory.

Coffeepots were made at Chelsea during the triangle period (ca. 1745–49) with either tea-plant or strawberry-leaf molding, some examples being decorated in color. Thereafter, no coffeepots were produced at the factory until the 1760s, apart from the occasional replacement for a tea-plant example. It must be presumed that during the 1750s it was the custom for Sprimont's clients to use silver coffeepots, although porcelain examples from this period were made at all the other contemporary English factories with the solitary exception of Longton Hall.

2

Chelsea Beaker, ca. 1748–49

Of lobed form, molded in high relief with flowering tea-plant branches curving upward from the base.

HEIGHT: 3 in. (7.6 cm)
MARK: Crown and trident in underglaze blue
LITERATURE: Austin, *Chelsea Porcelain at Colonial Williamsburg*, cat. no. 19
ACCESSION NUMBER: 1991.47.42

The tea-plant decoration, confined at Chelsea to the triangle period, occurs in conjunction with coffee-pots, sugar boxes, cream jugs, beakers, and saucers. No teapots or coffee cups have been recorded. The crown and trident mark is very rare, known on only a handful of pieces, including two figures. Its signifi-cance is not clear, though it has been suggested that it was used on porcelain sold by Richard Stables at his shop at the corner of Crown-and-Sceptre-Court, in St. James' Street. A notice in the *Daily Adver-tiser* on 18 April 1746 mentions Mr. Stables's shop as a source of Chelsea "for the conveniency of the Pub-lick," though a notice in April 1750 subsequently disclaimed any further connection. At any event, it seems probable that this mark corresponds to pieces dating from the later part of the triangle period.

Examples of this rare crown and trident mark on Chelsea include a figure model of the Rustic Lovers, a model of a greyhound, several white tea-plant beakers of the type illustrated here, two cream jugs, two tea bowls, and three saucers all with strawberry-leaf molding, one beaker painted in underglaze blue, and the Ho-Ho Bird beaker in this collection (cat. no. 7).[1] Although most of these pieces are undecorated, at least two have overglaze painting, one has underglaze blue, and two are figure models. It is therefore not easy to assess the significance of this mark by iden-tifying what the pieces have in common in terms of either form or decoration. To complicate matters still further, the single underglaze blue example bearing this mark, an unmolded beaker, shares many charac-teristics with the small class of wares recorded from the St. James' factory of Charles Gouyn.

1. Legge, *Flowers and Fables*, p. 26.

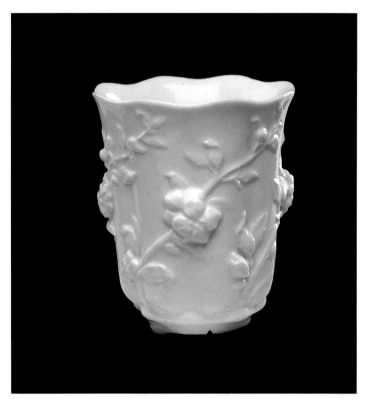

2

3

4

3

Chelsea Goat and Bee Cream Jug, ca. 1745–49

Molded with a pair of goats below flowering branches and a bee in full relief, the handle in the form of a sprouting tree.

HEIGHT: 3¾ in. (9.5 cm)
MARK: Incised triangle
LITERATURE: Austin, *Chelsea Porcelain at Colonial Williamsburg,* cat. no. 5
ACCESSION NUMBER: 1991.47.41

Perhaps the most celebrated of all Chelsea forms, the Goat and Bee cream jug embodies both the frivolity of the rococo style and the essentially luxurious nature of the earliest Chelsea porcelain. With Sprimont's background in a luxury trade and his avowed intention to sell to "The Nobility and Gentry," it was natural that he should envisage porcelain shapes in terms of silver. The Goat and Bee cream jug was conceived by the same creative imagination as the large silver centerpiece that Sprimont made for the earl of Ashburnham in 1747 (London, Victoria and Albert Museum). This was designed in the form of a basket, supported by two goats facing opposite directions. Designing a range of porcelain forms while still active as a silversmith, it was inevitable that there should be an interaction between Sprimont's concepts and ideas for the two materials.

The sophistication and complexity of design of this cream jug convey no hint that it is one of the earliest of all shapes to be produced in English porcelain and the first manifestation of the rococo style in all English ceramics. That so ambitious a rococo form could have been envisaged at this experimental stage of production is a measure of Sprimont's experience, confidence, and skill as a silversmith, allied to a less readily accountable mastery of porcelain technology. However, a newly discovered French archive suggests that Charles Gouyn,[1] who was involved in the inception of the Chelsea factory, employed a "German" chemist, "d'Ostermann." He may possibly be identified as Jean-Baptiste Clostermann, a chemist who joined the Vincennes factory in March 1753.

1. Dragesco, *English Ceramics in French Archives,* p. 14.

14

4

Chelsea Goat and Bee Cream Jug, ca. 1745–49

Molded with a pair of goats below flowering branches and a bee in full relief, the handle in the form of a sprouting tree, all picked out in enamel colors.

HEIGHT: 3¾ in. (9.5 cm)
MARK: Incised triangle
LITERATURE: Austin, *Chelsea Porcelain at Colonial Williamsburg*, cat. no. 6
ACCESSION NUMBER: 1990.51.4

These cream jugs are among the earliest Chelsea forms, several examples bearing the incised date *1745* alongside the triangle mark. They are invariably very thinly potted and generally free of the imperfections that might be expected on so early a form. Indeed, their thin, well-controlled glaze is not entirely typical of other pieces from this period, suggesting that special care may have been taken with these sophisticated cream jugs. The quality of the decoration on the colored examples varies considerably, and it is likely that some had their color added some years later, during the red anchor period (ca. 1754–58). Several of these cream jugs are known with decoration under the glaze, either in blue or manganese, and in some instances the bee is absent. It is a measure of the associations and distinction of these cream jugs that they have been reproduced since the early part of the nineteenth century, in bone china at Coalport and, reputedly, in German hard-paste porcelain. An almost contemporary version was made at Vauxhall in about 1755–60. Painted in underglaze blue, this form was adapted as a vase by omitting the handle.

5

Chelsea Strawberry Dish, ca. 1745–49

Of oval fluted form, painted in the interior with insects, a snail, and flowers, the fluted oval foot applied with strawberries and leaves.

LENGTH: 5 in. (12.7 cm)
MARK: Incised triangle, letter *F*, and numeral *4*
LITERATURE: Austin, *Chelsea Porcelain at Colonial Williamsburg*, cat. no. 12
ACCESSION NUMBER: 1991.47.37

One of the earliest of all Chelsea forms, this strawberry dish was almost certainly inspired by silver, though no silver example has so far been discovered. Certainly, this ambitious design has no precursor in ceramics. The shape occurs both with and without the band of applied strawberries, and the interior decoration is sometimes in the botanical or famille rose taste. Undecorated examples are also known. For the most part, the quality of the decoration does not quite match the sophistication and complexity of the shape, a recurring disparity in the triangle period, born of a greater experience and assuredness of form and line than of painted decoration, though a strong possibility exists that many of these pieces were painted by an independent decorator, outside the factory. Intriguing parallels with Bow are evident here. The painting of insects, flower heads, and scattered sprigs seems more intended to disguise blemishes in the paste than to complement the fluid rhythm of the form.

As with so much of the Chelsea from the triangle period, this form is uncharacteristic of English porcelain as a whole, being conceived with its practical utility subordinate to the contours of its linear rhythm, which is baroque in feeling. Letters and numerals incised into the base of these dishes are recorded on several examples, but their significance is not apparent.

5

6

6

Chelsea Beaker, ca. 1745–49

Of flared shape, with strawberry-leaf molding, painted in the Kakiemon taste with a tiger and bamboo.

HEIGHT: 2¾ in. (7.0 cm)
MARK: None
LITERATURE: MacKenna, *Chelsea Porcelain: The Triangle and Raised Anchor Wares*, pls. 23 and 24
ACCESSION NUMBER: 1991.47.44

Decoration in the Japanese Kakiemon taste is relatively uncommon on Chelsea of the triangle period. Only five beakers in this idiom, with strawberry-leaf molding, are recorded. The pattern shares some elements with the "twisted dragon pattern" referred to in the Chelsea sale catalogue of 14 March 1755, well known during the raised anchor period. In it, the bounding tiger, peering inquisitively upward at the bamboo, adds to the sense of rhythmic energy with which this beaker is imbued. The vibrant colors, too, contribute to the dynamic effect of pattern and form. Yet the palette, in particular the yellow and the brilliant tone of green, is reminiscent of Chantilly. Further associations with the French factory are the use of tin oxide, evident here as an opacifying agent, and the strawberry-leaf or acanthus molding. As with so many of the triangle period forms, the swirling rhythm and fluid movement of the molding draws the eye upward toward an irregular rim with such purpose that the vitality of the painted decoration is absorbed in a natural harmony.

The strawberry-leaf molding was used on a slightly wider range of shapes than the corresponding tea-plant decoration. Coffeepots, teapots, cream jugs, milk jugs, tea bowls, saucers, and cream boats are all recorded, either colored or "in the white." In the case of the cream boats, an exactly similar shape was made at Chantilly, though the potting was thinner and the size slightly smaller.

Beakers with strawberry-leaf molding are less common than those with tea-plant decoration. Beakers, as opposed to tea bowls or coffee cups, represented a significant proportion of the Chelsea output during the years from 1745 to 1752. Their precise function has not been identified, but Sprimont's advertisements frequently refer to "Tea, Coffee, or Chocolate Services," and it is possible that beakers such as this example were intended for the consumption of chocolate.

7

Chelsea Beaker, ca. 1748–49

Of fluted, lobed shape, decorated in the Kakiemon taste, with a pheasant perched upon a rock with flowering branches, and on the reverse a phoenix in flight.

HEIGHT: 2¾ in. (7.0 cm)
MARK: Crown and trident in underglaze blue
LITERATURE: Austin, *Chelsea Porcelain at Colonial Williamsburg,* cat. no. 34
ACCESSION NUMBER: 1991.47.43

Derived from a late-seventeenth-century Japanese version of a Chinese design, the so-called Ho-Ho Bird pattern also occurs on Chelsea of the raised anchor and red anchor periods, on Meissen, Chantilly, and Worcester, where it later became known as the Sir Joshua Reynolds pattern.

The ho-ho bird is a decorative motif on Arita porcelain, painted in the Kakiemon taste, depicting a phoenix, or *ho-o.* The corresponding Chinese bird, from which it was derived, was the *feng huang,* or Red Bird of the South, whose element was fire. The phoenix in Chinese mythology represented the empress, while the tiger stood for the emperor. Like the lion, the dragon, and the tiger, the phoenix is one of the fabulous mythological beasts depicted on both Chinese and Japanese porcelain. A Chantilly saucer decorated in a version of this pattern is catalogue number 177 in this collection.

This lobed, flared form, confined to the triangle period, was the basis for the tea-plant molded wares (cat. no. 2) and occurs on Chelsea only during the triangle period, although a plain outline, molded with prunus decoration after Chinese blanc de chine, was issued during the early part of the raised anchor period, about 1750–52.

7

8

8

Chelsea Coffee Cup, ca. 1750–52

Of fluted form, decorated in the Kakiemon taste, with birds perched and in flight, among trailing flowering branches, the interior with a coiled dragon.

HEIGHT: 2½ in. (6.4 cm)
MARK: None
LITERATURE: Spero, "A Taste entirely new," cat. no. 19
ACCESSION NUMBER: 1991.47.48

This is a relatively uncommon Chelsea pattern, derived from late-seventeenth-century Japanese porcelain and confined at Chelsea to the raised anchor period. It is characterized by brilliant enamel colors and occurs in conjunction with fluted forms. The shape of this coffee cup was inspired by a silver form, though the original would have lacked the scroll handle. A silver beaker of this form, dated 1700, during the reign of Queen Anne, is in the Holburne of Menstrie Museum in Bath.

Chelsea coffee cups from the raised anchor period are comparatively scarce, and only six examples are recorded from the preceding triangle period. At this time, a complete tea set of Chelsea porcelain comprised eight teacups and saucers, eight coffee cups (with handles) and saucers, a teapot and stand, a slop basin, a sugar bowl, a cream jug, a plate, and a spoon tray. Judging from the very few teapot stands and spoon trays that have survived, not all Chelsea tea sets were sold "compleat," possibly because of the existence of silver teapot stands and spoon trays. Sprimont, a silversmith, would have been only too aware of the advantages of porcelain over silver for vessels such as coffee cups and tea bowls, used to contain hot liquids.

Chelsea porcelain was expensive at this period and it is no wonder that Sprimont sought an affluent clientele. A Chelsea "milk pott" cost five shillings in March 1749, whereas a Bow milk jug, four years later, was only one shilling and sixpence.

9

Chelsea Bowl, ca. 1750–52

Of octagonal form, painted in the Japanese taste with flowers and emblems divided by iron red panels and white scrolling foliage with gilt flower heads.

DIAMETER: 6 in. (15.2 cm)

MARK: None

LITERATURE: Austin, *Chelsea Porcelain at Colonial Williamsburg,* cat. no. 44

ACCESSION NUMBER: 1991.47.47

Probably derived from a Meissen version of a Kakiemon or Arita pattern, this design was conceived for use on octagonal forms and was issued in three sizes. It corresponds to the "slop-bason" described in lot 68 of the second day of the sale of Chelsea in March 1755, as "of the fine red pannel pattern." At Chelsea the pattern was principally used on teawares and vases, whereas at Bow (cat. no. 55) it was confined to plates, dishes, and bowls. The Meissen version of the 1730s emphasizes the impact of the interplay between the pattern and the shapes by slightly enlarging the flowers and Precious Objects within the plainer panels. An octagonal cup in this pattern, in Japanese porcelain, is in Burghley House, near Stamford, in Lincolnshire.

Chelsea versions of Japanese Kakiemon patterns first appeared in the late 1740s and the main period of production followed in the early 1750s. Yet by 1754, in common with all oriental themes, the idiom had vanished on Chelsea porcelain, never to reappear, though it remained popular at Bow well into the 1760s (cat. no. 55). By contrast, painted designs in the Chinese taste were generally avoided at Chelsea, possibly because of competition from Bow in this market.

10

Chelsea Plate, ca. 1753–54

Of lobed form, decorated in the Japanese taste with a central mons, insects, flowers, and prunus root.

DIAMETER: 9¼ in. (23.5 cm)

MARK: None

LITERATURE: Austin, *Chelsea Porcelain at Colonial Williamsburg,* cat. no. 51

ACCESSION NUMBER: 1991.47.5

The palette and overall composition of this decoration suggest that it originated in Japanese Imari porcelain of the 1720–40 period. Chelsea examples date from the raised anchor and the early portion of the red anchor periods. On fluted teawares, the central mons was omitted from the design, allowing the pattern to be expanded in a freer manner, with more sense of space. This version of the pattern was adapted on Derby teawares of the late 1750s, though the palette is different.

The pattern on this plate shares some basic elements with that on the "Japan pattern" dish (cat. no. 12). The curving border design has been transferred to the center, and the mons is repeated on the radiating border panels. This reversal, together with a complete change of palette, creates a startlingly different visual impact. The lobed shape, which recurs on plates and dishes of the early 1750s, was described in contemporary records as "scallop'd" and seems not to have been used at any other English factory. Like so many forms of this period, it was developed from Japanese porcelain.

Chelsea Plate, ca. 1753–54

Molded with *Gotzkowsky erhabene Blumen* and painted in the Kakiemon taste with a coiled dragon, the border with Japanese flowers and emblems.

DIAMETER: 9½ in. (24.1 cm)
MARK: None
LITERATURE: MacKenna, *Chelsea Porcelain: The Red Anchor Wares*, pl. 8, fig. 16
ACCESSION NUMBER: 1991.47.4

Although the painted pattern harks back to Kakiemon porcelain, the direct influence is certainly that of the Meissen *indianische Blumen*. The relief-molded decoration of flowers corresponds with the oval "dishes, soup plates and table plates" listed in the Chelsea sale catalogue for 1755 as "damask'd with flowers." The molded decoration was in imitation of a pattern designed by Eberlain, an assistant to Kaendler, the chief modeler of the Meissen factory, for the celebrated Gotzkowsky service, originally made for a Berlin merchant of that name. This molding was commonly used on Chelsea plates and dishes of the 1753–54 period, most often in conjunction with flowers and insects, but occasionally with oriental figures, butterflies, and birds, in all cases painted in the Meissen style. Although in production for only a brief period, dinner plates in this molded design were made in great quantities.

Information relating to all aspects of the manufactory of Meissen, elicited through the agency of Sir Everard Fawkener, was of the greatest interest to Sprimont. In a letter of 12 August 1751 to Sir Charles Hanbury Williams, the envoy to the Saxon court at Dresden, Sir Everard requested details about the pricing of Meissen porcelain, remarking that the newly established Chelsea enterprise was "sensible that the extent and success of their manufacture will depend upon the price."[1]

1. Ilchester, "A Notable Service of Meissen Porcelain," p. 18.

10

11

12

Chelsea Plate, ca. 1754

Of lobed shape, painted in the Japanese Imari taste with a central spray of chrysanthemum and radiating panels of mons and flowering plants, divided by brocade panels.

DIAMETER: 9⅝ in. (24.5 cm)

MARK: None

LITERATURE: Ayers, Impey, and Mallet, *Porcelain for Palaces*, cat. no. 345

ACCESSION NUMBER: 1991.47.11

This probably corresponds with the "rare old Japan pattern blue and gold" listed on the seventh day of the 1756 sale of Chelsea porcelain, lot 23. Derived from Japanese Imari porcelain of about 1720–40, the pattern also occurs on Chinese Imari. It was later adapted at Worcester in the early 1770s and at Derby. The pattern also has strong associations with the Old *Mosaik* on Worcester (cat. nos. 137–140). It is one of a very small range of Chelsea designs that incorporate underglaze blue painting, invariably occurring on lobed plates, dishes, and sometimes tureens. It often is found marked with a blue anchor, also used on the Worcester version.

Plates and dishes of various shapes and sizes constituted a major element in the production of the Chelsea factory from the early 1750s until the factory's closure in 1769. By comparison, tea and coffee services formed a relatively less significant proportion of the output. Yet it was not until the formulation of the new recipe in 1750 that the factory was able to manufacture any plates or dishes at all. Coincidentally, this experience mirrored that of other factories, as it was not until about 1752 that the first Worcester and Bow plates came into production.

13

Chelsea Plate, ca. 1754–55

Painted in underglaze blue with two phoenixes perched upon an overhanging rock in a garden planted with bamboo, the border with a trellis diaper with oriental flowers in reserved panels.

DIAMETER: 9 in. (22.9 cm)

MARK: Anchor in underglaze blue

LITERATURE: Ayers, Impey, and Mallet, *Porcelain for Palaces*, cat. no. 344

ACCESSION NUMBER: 1991.47.8

The pattern is a comparatively unusual instance of an apparently direct copy of Japanese porcelain, since the design is unknown on Meissen. This is the only underglaze blue pattern on Chelsea, inspired by Japanese Kakiemon porcelain, though the diaper trellis design on the border is perhaps Chinese in origin. The pattern occurs only on plates.

Underglaze blue decoration is rare on Chelsea, especially without the addition of any overglaze colors. Fewer than thirty examples are known, including octagonal saucers, two late triangle period beakers of differing shapes, a silver-shaped cream jug, an octagonal bowl, and a Goat and Bee cream jug with a blue bee. No mention was made of underglaze blue decoration in the surviving Chelsea sale catalogues, and it is clear that in contrast to all other English factories of the mid-eighteenth century this decoration formed a very insignificant part of the Chelsea output.

It is perhaps pertinent that underglaze blue decoration is especially associated with Chinese porcelain, and this influence, which was so pervasive at Bow, Worcester, and elsewhere, was comparatively muted at Chelsea and had disappeared completely by about 1754. Indeed, the chinoiserie, so integral an element in the decorative idioms on tin-glazed earthenware, salt-glazed stoneware, and porcelain, was almost totally absent on Chelsea. The neighboring Bow factory made a great speciality of blue-and-white porcelain in imitation of and competition with imported Chinese porcelain. This broader, more widely commercial market was avoided at Chelsea.

12

13

14

Chelsea Bowl, ca. 1753

Of octagonal form, painted with a waterfront scene
of figures in discussion as they handle cargo, with
floral decoration on the reverse and a further harbor
scene in the interior.

DIAMETER: 4¼ in. (10.8 cm)
MARK: None
LITERATURE: Spero, "Chelsea Porcelain, 1744–1769,"
pl. VII
ACCESSION NUMBER: 1991.47.34

Landscape decoration in this idiom, with prominent
figures in the foreground, is one of the rarest of all subjects on Chelsea porcelain. A fluted rectangular dish
in the Katz Collection at the Museum of Fine Arts,
Boston, decorated with a harbor scene, bears a mono-
gram that has been attributed to William Duvivier, a
painter active at Chelsea during the early 1750s.
There are strong similarities between the painting on
the Katz dish and this superb bowl, especially in the
treatment of the figure with the stick, the barrels, and
the details of the sail to the left of the figures in the
foreground. In more general terms, the style of decoration was inspired by Meissen, where J. G. Herold
and C. F. Herold both made a speciality of scenes
with European and Turkish merchants bargaining
over merchandise being unloaded from ships. European figure subjects occur on Worcester, Derby, and
occasionally Vauxhall and Longton Hall during the
mid-1750s, but the wealth of detail and the atmosphere of bustling activity conveyed on Chelsea in this
genre were never attempted elsewhere.

The shape of this bowl was adapted from Meissen,
although it can be traced back to late-seventeenth-
century Japanese porcelain. It was issued in three
sizes and occurs in every style of decoration during
the early 1750s. This size may correspond to the "octagon ... sugar bason" listed several times as part of a
tea set in the 1755 Chelsea sale catalogue. No mention was made of covers, and indeed only one example of a sugar box and cover is recorded from the
raised anchor period.

15

15   *Detail right*

Chelsea Dish, ca. 1754

With a petaled rim, painted with a detailed harbor
scene, with a tower and a tall tree flanking
numerous figures and buildings and mountains in
the distance.

DIAMETER: 8¼ in. (21.0 cm)
MARK: Red anchor
LITERATURE: Legge, *Flowers and Fables*, cat. no. 37,
for a dish of somewhat similar form
ACCESSION NUMBER: 1991.41.23

This bustling harbor scene evokes the style made famous by the German painter C. F. Herold. Yet if the
subject and its detailed depiction are inspired by the
German painter, the softer palette and the overall
composition — framed by the slanting tree and the
tall tower and the loose floral painting on the border — characterize a typically English interpretation
of a Continental scene. However, the scene is unusually detailed for Chelsea painting, especially in its
treatment of the large number of figures. The depth
and sense of perspective conveyed in this landscape
are seldom equaled in early English porcelain and
might almost be likened to that in the finest of Robert
Hancock's printed subjects on Worcester of the early
1760s. The superb accomplishment of the decoration
may be measured by a comparison with the pair of
beakers in the Bowles Collection (cat. no. 18).

A feature of the new porcelain body, introduced
in 1750, was the so-called moons, circular areas of
greater translucency, which were in fact air bubbles
trapped in the porcelain. Following the further variation to the porcelain body in about 1754, these moons
became reduced in size and far less prominent. They
tend to be characteristic of glassy porcelain bodies,
rather than unique to Chelsea, and can be seen
through transmitted light on Derby and Longton
Hall wares.

14

22

16

Chelsea Dish, ca. 1754

Of silver shape, painted in the center with a river landscape including a weir, figures, and two boats, with trees in the foreground and mountains in the distance, the border painted with flowers and insects.

LENGTH: 9½ in. (24.1 cm)
MARK: None
LITERATURE: MacKenna, *Chelsea Porcelain: The Triangle and Raised Anchor Periods*, pl. 49, fig. 97
ACCESSION NUMBER: 1991.47.53

Although Meissen was the primary source for landscape painting in this genre, some Chelsea decoration is strongly reminiscent of Vincennes, especially in its palette. On this dish the tones of brown and green and the treatment of the trees and mountains in the distance echo characteristics of the French factory during the mid-1740s, an impression reinforced by the depth of the landscape and its subtle perspective. Landscape decoration in this style is very unusual on early English porcelain, and Chelsea production of this type far exceeded that of any other factory, even though it was almost entirely restricted to a brief period between about 1752 and 1755. Thereafter, the previously dominant influence of the Meissen factory began to wane, giving way to that of Sèvres.

This magnificent dish, which embodies several diverse influences to great advantage, exemplifies the highly derivative nature of early English porcelain. A shape closely adapted from English Huguenot silver, its fluid rococo molding designed to echo that of a silver sauceboat, has been reinterpreted as a rhythmic canvas for a serene landscape in the manner of Meissen and Vincennes. This, in turn, harks back to the Flemish and German tradition of romantic landscape painting.

The apparently arbitrary placing of the bouquets, floral sprays, and sprigs around the border is accounted for by the necessity to disguise firing flaws and imperfections in the paste. In this endeavor even a caterpillar has been summoned to distract the eye from a minor fault. The perceived need to conceal these blemishes has paradoxically furnished an unintentionally added distinctive flavor to the Chelsea wares of the mid-1750s, which is much admired today.

Chelsea Tea Bowl, Coffee Cup, and Saucer, ca. 1753

Of fluted shape, each painted with a landscape scene, the saucer design being enclosed within a double-line border and the coffee cup having an elaborate scroll handle.

DIAMETER OF SAUCER: 4¾ in. (12.1 cm)
MARK: None
LITERATURE: MacKenna, *Chelsea Porcelain: The Triangle and Raised Anchor Periods*, pl. 49, fig. 98
ACCESSION NUMBER: 1991.47.38a–c

In common with the octagonal teawares of this period, these fluted shapes were produced in two sizes and emerged in 1750 as one of the forms "in a Taste entirely new." The landscape decoration, once again in the Meissen style, lacks the clarity and precision of the harbor scenes and employs a heavier palette, with the colors more thickly applied. Yet the effect is nevertheless delightful. Chelsea decoration in this genre may lack the perfection and fine detail of its Meissen progenitor, but the fluid shapes, soft tactile glaze, and harmonious blend of colors lend it a warmth and serenity that contrasts with the more remote qualities of the German factory. Both coffee cup and tea bowl have a wide margin of white porcelain below their decoration that at first seems incongruous when viewed at eye level. However, it should be remembered that the decoration was designed to be seen from above table level, with the tea bowl or cup standing upon a saucer.

As with the Kakiemon style in production during the same period, the Meissen landscapes occur only in association with the more thickly potted body and waxy, slightly opacified glaze, prior to the variations in the recipe of about 1754–55. As a consequence, these landscapes never occur in conjunction with plain, unmolded teawares or flatwares.

16

18

Pair of Chelsea Beakers, ca. 1753–54

Of fluted form, painted with lakeside landscapes, incorporating towers and other buildings, figures, and sailing ships, within lobed reserved panels.

HEIGHT: 2½ in. (6.4 cm)
MARK: None
LITERATURE: MacKenna, *Chelsea Porcelain: The Red Anchor Wares,* pl. 24, fig. 50
ACCESSION NUMBERS: 1991.47.36.1a, 2a

The decoration on these beakers was strongly influenced by the Meissen landscape style of the 1720s and 1730s, promulgated by painters such as C. F. Herold and J. G. Herold. The fluted shape was in production for much of the 1750s, although most examples seem to be from the 1752–55 period. These two beakers are clearly painted by the same hand, and there has been much speculation in the past as to which Chelsea artists were responsible for the decoration in this idiom.

This shape was derived from silver forms of the Queen Anne period, though it also occurs at Meissen during the early 1730s. Yet while it is entirely probable that many of Sprimont's customers could afford the silver vessels, they might well have preferred to drink from porcelain beakers, which were less liable to retain the heat of hot liquids and to burn the lips. The shape was issued in two sizes, either with or without handles, but seems not to have been in production at any other English factory. Taller than the conventional tea bowls of the period (cat. no. 17), this beaker shape may have been intended for chocolate.

18

19a

19b

19

Pair of Chelsea Dishes, ca. 1753–54

Of fluted oval form, each with two shaped panels containing buildings and figures in landscapes, with double-line borders, the panels divided by floral sprays and insects.

LENGTH: 6⅛ in. (15.6 cm)
MARK: None
LITERATURE: Legge, *Flowers and Fables*, pl. 114
ACCESSION NUMBERS: 1991.47.36.1b, 2b

The decoration on these dishes appears to be by a different and more accomplished hand than on the pair of beakers in catalogue number 18, although the idiom is very similar. The placing of the insects, positioned in order to disguise firing flaws in the glaze, adds a delightful sense of asymmetry to this decoration.

For a factory with so restricted a production of painted decoration prior to 1750, it is astonishing that so high a standard was attained by the early 1750s, when form and decoration had reached a point of equilibrium. The question therefore arises as to where so talented a group of painters had come from. One possibility is that some may have been drawn from the flourishing trade of fan painting, a craft often requiring decoration of the most exacting standards.

This oval shape is confined to the early part of the red anchor period, prior to the changes in recipe for the porcelain body. It occurs in conjunction only with landscape painting, either in polychrome or *puce camaïeu*. Contemporary idioms, such as Kakiemon patterns, fables, floral, and botanical painting, are never associated with this shape, suggesting that there was a coherent correlation at the factory between styles of decoration and potting forms. Alternatively, it is entirely possible that this form of dish, in production for a very brief period, was specifically designed for painted landscapes contained within reserved panels. The shape was issued at no other English factory.

Chelsea Dish, ca. 1753–54

Of fluted rectangular shape painted with, on one side, an extensive landscape with trees, figures, sheep, and a distant cottage and, on the other, figures on the bank of a river, observing ruins.

LENGTH: 8 in. (20.3 cm)

MARK: Red anchor

LITERATURE: Austin, *Chelsea Porcelain at Colonial Williamsburg*, cat. no. 55, illustrates a tea bowl and saucer in this style

ACCESSION NUMBER: 1991.47.46

This fluted rectangular form spans much the same period as the oval dish (cat. no. 19), though it occurs in conjunction with a far wider range of decoration, including Kakiemon designs, floral patterns, landscapes in the Meissen style, and fable subjects. The unusual concept of landscape scenes on opposite sides of dishes and saucers was described in contemporary cat-alogues as "double landskips." These are far rarer than the landscapes contained within reserved panels and are invariably executed with great freedom, individuality, and sense of space. They usually feature "pinhead" figures, tall trees, and rocks, partly in shadow, all characteristic of the work of Jefferyes Hamett O'Neale. Unlike so many china painters, he was sufficiently accomplished to be able to convey a detailed perspective and thus a sense of depth in his landscapes, often attained on Meissen of the later 1720s, but seldom on English porcelain. The palette also resembles that used by O'Neale, and the overall impression of these "double landskips" is of decoration less stylized than those enclosed within reserved panels (cat. no. 19).

An example of O'Neale's fable painting, displaying a similar feeling and atmosphere to this decoration, is catalogue number 24. The treatment of clouds is particularly distinctive, as is the distant tree.

20

Chelsea Cream Boat, ca. 1753

Of octagonal shape, with a flattened scroll handle, painted by Jefferyes Hamett O'Neale with the fable of the Ape and the Fox, the reverse with a floral spray in the Vincennes taste.

DIAMETER: 3¼ in. (8.3 cm)
HEIGHT: 2¼ in. (5.7 cm)
MARK: None
LITERATURE: Legge, *Flowers and Fables*, pl. 90, illustrates a silver-shape dish with this subject; illustrated in Spero, "Chelsea Porcelain, 1744–1769," pl. IX
ACCESSION NUMBER: 1991.47.35

Two versions of this popular fable were used by O'Neale on Chelsea porcelain. In an earlier one, probably derived from Francis Barlow's engravings of Aesop's fables (no. 17; first published in 1687), the ape is seated upon the ground. This version also appears in O'Neale's work at Worcester in about 1768–70. However, for this cream boat O'Neale adapted a version from Samuel Croxall's edition (no. 123; first published in 1722), in which the ape is peering down at the fox from the branch of a tree. The painting embodies many of O'Neale's stylistic attributes, including the slight caricature seen in the features and postures of the animals and the evident whimsical humor. Also characteristic are the somewhat arthritic-looking joints of the fox, who is very much the butt of this moral fable. While the majority of fables on Chelsea are indisputably by the same hand, some authorities have suggested that there was at least one other painter who was responsible for the earlier animal subjects. Alternatively, these too may have been the work of O'Neale, whose versatility was one of his artistic strengths.

The shape of this cream boat was adapted from Meissen and first issued at Chelsea in 1750, to be sold alongside the octagonal tea bowls, saucers, and teapots. It remained in production for about three years, being superseded by the more thinly potted, conventional, upright style of cream jug. The scrolled handle, reminiscent of fretwork, was also used on both sizes of the octagonal coffee cups dating from the same period.

Chelsea Beaker and Saucer, ca. 1752

Of octagonal shape, painted by Jefferyes Hamett O'Neale, with, on the beaker, the fable of the Hunted Beaver and, on the saucer, the Wolf and the Goat.

HEIGHT OF BEAKER: 2¼ in. (7.0 cm)
DIAMETER OF SAUCER: 5¼ in. (13.3 cm)
MARK: Raised anchor on each piece
LITERATURE: MacKenna, *Chelsea Porcelain: The Triangle and Raised Anchor Wares*, pl. 44, fig. 89, illustrates a hexagonal teapot with the Fox and the Goat
ACCESSION NUMBER: 1991.47.32a–b

The beaker is vigorously painted with a continuous landscape in which an angry beaver twists fiercely around to confront two pursuing hounds. This unusually realistic subject was probably derived from Croxall's fable 62, though it also occurs in a slightly different version of fable 19 in Barlow's edition. O'Neale rearranged the principal components of the fable in order to create a continuous scene flowing around the beaker. Yet if his characteristically whimsical humor is noticeably absent in this instance, it is hardly appropriate to the fable. This early example of O'Neale's work on Chelsea depicts animals on a larger scale than he was later to employ and the palette too is more vibrant. Yet there are enough similarities with his more typical work on red anchor period wares to be fairly certain that this hand can be safely attributed to O'Neale.

The saucer, painted in a slightly different palette, was possibly adapted from Croxall's fable 81, in which a lion is depicted conversing with a partially hidden goat. O'Neale may have substituted a wolf for

21

22

a lion to add humor to the scene, and it certainly appears that this arthritic-looking animal might have difficulty in approaching nearer to the well-protected goat. An edition of the famous drawing book, *The Ladies Amusement*, dating from about 1776, contains an engraving of this version of the fable, after a drawing by O'Neale.

In the summer of 1751, at the instigation of Sir Everard Fawkener, a group of Chelsea workers was allowed to visit Holland House, to borrow pieces from the Meissen services kept there, which belonged to Sir Charles Hanbury Williams, the British envoy to Dresden. They were permitted "to copy what they like." This they did, for on 12 September Fawkener reported that "many imitations are made." Among the porcelain at Holland House was a Meissen dinner and dessert service from the 1740s, a diplomatic gift from Augustus III, king of Poland and Elector of Saxony (r. 1733–63), the indolent son of the great porcelain collector, Augustus the Strong. The remarkable

dinner service, now at Alnwick Castle in Northumberland, is superbly painted with large animals, the tureens having knops in the form of birds, designed by Kaendler and his assistant, Reinicke. Some of these were converted into tureens at Chelsea (cat. no. 41). The painted decoration of animals fighting and running was in some instances derived from prints by the Augsburg master Johann Elias Ridinger (1698–1767), celebrated for his hunting scenes. One of the tureen covers,[1] depicting a running dog, displays close similarities with the face and posture of the hound on this Chelsea beaker, an early example of O'Neale's work, probably dating from within a year of the visit to Holland House. This suggests the possibility that O'Neale was among the visitors, and that some of the painting that he saw on those Meissen tureens and plates may have influenced his early style of fable decoration.

1. Clarke, "Sir Charles Hanbury Williams and the Chelsea Factory," pls. 61a and 68a.

22 front

22 back

23

Chelsea Tea Bowl, ca. 1753

Of octagonal shape, painted by Jefferyes Hamett
O'Neale, depicting the fable of the Wolf and the
Dog, within a continuous landscape, incorporating a
stream, mountains, trees, and flights of birds.

DIAMETER: 3½ in. (8.9 cm)

MARK: None

LITERATURE: Spero, *English Porcelain and Enamels, 1745–
1785,* cat. no. 5, illustrates a saucer with a slightly different
version of this fable

ACCESSION NUMBER: 1991.47.33

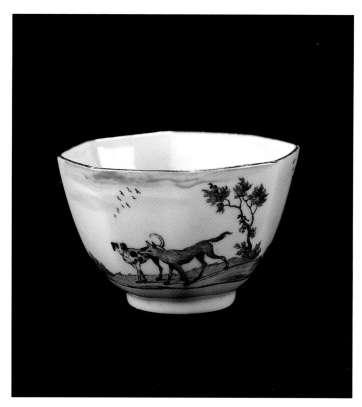

23

The source for this fable may have been number 97
from Francis Barlow's edition of Aesop's fables, first
published in 1687, or Croxall's fable 19, though if this
is correct, O'Neale made substantial alterations to the
original. Alternatively, O'Neale may have used his
own interpretation of the fable, without any direct design source. This theory is lent substance by his inclination to adapt the fable as he repeated the subject.
Among several recurring mannerisms in O'Neale's
style are the treatment of the fox's tail, his arthritic-
looking limbs, and his open mouth. It is characteristic for O'Neale's animals to have their mouths agape,
evident in the wolf, the beaver, and the hound in catalogue number 22 and the tormented bear in catalogue
number 131. Many of these animals, of course, were
engaged in exchanges of conversation.

As the majority of Chelsea decorated with fables
dates from the 1753–54 period, it might be antici-
pated that there would be frequent references in the
Chelsea sale catalogue for March 1755. Yet surprisingly, there are relatively few such references in either catalogue. Lot 62 on the thirteenth day's sale,
24 March 1755, lists "Eight small teacups and saucers,
octagon in flowers, and a teapot in fables," but descriptions of this kind occur only rarely.

O'Neale's fables also appear on Chinese porcelain
decorated in London, and this subject is among those
he painted as an independent decorator. While there
was little fable decoration on domestic wares after
about 1756, pairs of figures and candlesticks repre-
senting fable subjects were made during the gold anchor period and are listed in the final sale of Chelsea,
with the remainder of Sprimont's stock, held at Christie's in London in February 1770.

24

Chelsea Dish, ca. 1753–54

Of fluted rectangular shape, painted by Jefferyes Hamett O'Neale, showing a riverside landscape with a stork swallowing a frog, while other frogs scramble to safety upon a floating log, illustrating the fable of Jupiter and the Frogs.

LENGTH: 8 in. (20.3 cm)

MARK: None

LITERATURE: MacKenna, *Chelsea Porcelain: The Triangle and Raised Anchor Wares*, pl. 45, fig. 91, illustrates this fable on a silver-shape plate

ACCESSION NUMBER: 1991.47.45

Jefferyes Hamett O'Neale freely adapted this subject from Barlow's design of fable 36. Croxall also illustrated this fable under the title "The Frogs Desiring a King." In it, the frogs request Jupiter to send them a king. When he responds by sending them a log, they reject it. In its place, Jupiter sends them a stork who immediately starts devouring his subjects. Panic-stricken, they flee to the protection of the log they had previously rejected. O'Neale has used his wit and imagination to expand upon Barlow's original illustration, imbuing it with his customary vitality and humor, seasoned in this instance with a whiff of pathos.

Fable subjects, as opposed to pairs of animals, first appear on Chelsea in about 1752, and the theme was continued until about 1755–56. Thereafter, examples of this idiom are intermittent. Several references to fables are listed in the Chelsea sale catalogues for both 1755 and 1756. O'Neale's fables recur on Worcester in about 1768–70, often repeating subjects he had painted at Chelsea. His style had become heavier and his compositions much fuller, probably in response to the wide and richly gilded *gros bleu* borders that surround his scenes. Yet a close examination of the facial expressions of his animals, the treatment of their limbs, and their overall postures reveals strong similarities between his work on Chelsea and that on Worcester, some fifteen years later. For instance, the distraught expression of the hound pursuing the beaver (cat. no. 22) is frequently echoed on the faces of his Worcester hounds. A Worcester plate painted with the fable of the Bear and the Beehives is catalogue number 131.

25

25

Chelsea Plate, ca. 1753–54

Painted by Jefferyes Hamett O'Neale with the fable of the Ox and the Toad.

DIAMETER: 9 in. (22.9 cm)
MARK: None
LITERATURE: Austin, *Chelsea Porcelain at Colonial Williamsburg,* cat. no. 61
ACCESSION NUMBER: Promised gift

> . . . *Amongst the belowing Herds, and bleating flocks*
> *The Frog by Chance efpies*
> *Of a prodigious fize*
> *A ftall-fed Ox,*
> *Such Chines and Thighs*
> *Good Ftomachs prize*
> *And Bones with Marrow big as hollow okes:*
> *Wide was his fpreading Horn*
> *As Evening from the Morn*
> *When thus the Frog, in length not half a Span,*
> *Stuff'd up with Envy, and Self-Love, began* . . .

This decoration appears to have derived from Ogilby's *Fables of Aesop* (no. 13; first published in 1665), although the same fable is included in Barlow's *Aesop's Fables with His Life* (no. 26; first published, 1703).

The details of the ox and especially his rather spindly legs, the outcrop of rocks, the wind-blown tree, and the distant river are entirely characteristic of O'Neale's work. The palette, too, is typical. Many of these features are also present in a decagonal saucer or small dish in Colonial Williamsburg (see Literature), marked with a raised anchor and dating from

about 1750–52. A close comparison between this plate and the decagonal saucer suggests that they are probably by the same hand, thus linking O'Neale with the earlier series of fable subjects on Chelsea. The Williamsburg saucer is decorated with the visually somewhat similar fable of the Ox and the Rat, and, even allowing for the earlier palette, there are strong similarities in the treatment of the two oxen, the wind-blown tree, and the overall composition.

This crenellated shape, with three molded cartouche thumbpieces, was adapted from the oval form (cat. no. 27), which was itself inspired by a silver dish of identical shape made by Nicholas Sprimont himself and bearing his hallmark for 1746/47.

26

Pair of Chelsea Saucers, ca. 1752

Of octagonal form, painted with bouquets and sprays of flowers and tiny insects, the rims edged in brown.

DIAMETERS: 4¼ and 4⅜ in. (10.8 and 11.1 cm)
MARK: Raised anchor on each piece
ACCESSION NUMBERS: 1991.47.16.1, 2

Octagonal teawares were introduced at the Chelsea factory in 1750 and advertised as one of the new shapes "in a Taste entirely new." The form, adapted from late-seventeenth-century Japanese porcelain, was in use at Meissen in the 1730s. At Chelsea, "tea cups and saucers, octagon in flowers" are listed many times in Mr. Ford's sale catalogue for March 1755, but they do not occur in the following year's sale. This supports the contention that almost all the octagonal forms at Chelsea were discontinued in about 1754, with the introduction of another recipe for the porcelain body. Coincidentally, the majority of the Worcester octagonal and hexagonal forms disappeared at about this same period, as did those of Longton Hall and Derby. The tiny insects and flower heads on these Chelsea saucers served to disguise tiny blemishes in the paste, a recurring firing fault which was to be largely mitigated by the new thinner glaze.

Before about 1752–53, cups were regularly sold by themselves, lacking saucers, a fact confirmed by contemporary invoices and other documents. At such factories as Bow, Worcester, and Derby, no saucers were made before this period. Only four examples are recorded in triangle period Chelsea. A possible explanation for this lack of saucers, as opposed to tea bowls and coffee cups, might be that whereas Chinese tea bowls and saucers had long been imported into England, coffee cups were less common. Consequently, no traditional imperative existed for coffee cups or beakers to be marketed together with saucers.

27

Chelsea Dish, ca. 1754

Of silver shape, painted with two floral bouquets and scattered sprigs, the crenellated rim outlined in brown.

LENGTH: 9½ in. (24.1 cm)

MARK: Red anchor

LITERATURE: MacKenna, *Chelsea Porcelain: The Red Anchor Wares*, pl. 20, fig. 40 (right)

ACCESSION NUMBER: 1991.47.49

This distinctive form was based upon a silver prototype made by the proprietor of the Chelsea factory, Nicholas Sprimont, bearing his mark and the date letter for 1746/47. It is now in the Sigmund Katz Collection at the Museum of Fine Arts, Boston, together with several other pieces of silver made by Sprimont. In Chelsea porcelain, this shape spans the whole decade of the 1750s and is associated with landscapes, Kakiemon patterns, fables, and bird, flower, and botanical decoration. The shape was also used at Derby on a restricted scale. As a general rule, the earlier examples do not have their rims and handles outlined in brown or gilt. The shape was made in four sizes and also adapted from its basically oval form into a crenellated circular plate shape, in production during approximately the same period (cat. no. 25). Both the oval and the circular shapes occur in conjunction with raised anchor, red anchor, and gold anchor marks.

Writing in 1939, H. Bellamy Gardner identified fifteen known examples of silver made by Nicholas Sprimont, ranging in date from 1743 to 1747.[1] Among these were a pair of shell salts, each flanked by a crayfish, and four stands for sauceboats with shell handles, all foreshadowing forms that were later to be made in Chelsea porcelain. Sprimont's style in silver was innovative and highly distinctive. Its contours and linear rhythms share many similarities with the Chelsea porcelain forms, with their fluid, sweeping curves.

1. "Silvershape in Porcelain."

26

27

28

Chelsea Plate, ca. 1754

Of circular shape with a barbed rim, molded with trellis diaper and reserved with scroll- and feather-molded panels painted with fables, the interior with bouquets and sprays of flowers.

DIAMETER: 9½ in. (24.1 cm)
MARK: Red anchor
LITERATURE: Legge, *Flowers and Fables*, cat. no. 92
ACCESSION NUMBER: 1991.47.3

This shape of dish, with its distinctive floral diaperwork and scroll-molded panels, is associated with Warren Hastings, the great administrator who was one of the prime founders of Britain's Indian empire. A service decorated with fables within the reserved panels was among the effects offered for sale at his family home at Daylesford House in 1818. He may have purchased this service at the time of his first return to England in 1764, when he indulged his taste for fine things. From the style of painting and the palette, the three fables depicted can be safely attributed to Jefferyes Hamett O'Neale, the principal fable painter at Chelsea.

Dinner services with this molding perhaps correspond to the "wrought pattern enamell'd in fables" listed in the 1755 sale catalogue. At any event, these wares seem to have been entirely confined to the 1754–55 period. They occur in conjunction with several decorative idioms within the reserved panels, including birds, figures, Italianate landscapes, and, most rarely, Watteau-like figures in landscapes. The principal decorative themes were thus encompassed within border panels, visible even when the plates were filled with food.

29

29

Chelsea Sauceboat, ca. 1754

The leaf-shaped body molded with strawberry leaves, vines, and berries, supported upon four short leaf-molded feet, with a branch handle entwined with a vine and flowers.

LENGTH: 6¼ in. (15.9 cm)
MARK: None
LITERATURE: Peirce, *English Ceramics: The Frances and Emory Cocke Collection*, cat. no. 75
ACCESSION NUMBER: 1991.41.4

The strawberry-leaf sauceboat, in production from about 1752 to 1756, occurs mainly in conjunction with floral decoration, though several examples are recorded with Kakiemon designs. This example, superbly painted with floral sprays in the interior and with its large flowers in botanical style, corresponds to the "large sauce boats and plates" listed on numerous occasions in the Chelsea sale catalogue for March 1755. By contrast, the slightly later examples, with green branch handles and smaller-scale floral painting, are those described in the Chelsea sale catalogue for March–April 1756 as "large sauce boats and plates with green handles." As the catalogue description implies, these sauceboats were made in two sizes and would originally have had stands, the undersides of which surely echoed the strawberry-leaf molding of the sauceboats.

Considering the quantity and variety of sauceboat shapes produced at such contemporary factories as Limehouse, Bow, Worcester, Longton Hall, Vauxhall, and Derby, it is surprising that the Chelsea output seems to have been almost entirely confined to the 1752–56 period and to this one leaf-molded shape, issued in two sizes. The explanation for this apparent anomaly may lie in the preference of Sprimont's more affluent customers for silver sauceboats, an inclination he would readily have understood.

The contention that the silver-shape dishes (cat. nos. 16 and 27) were intended as stands for these sauceboats is difficult to sustain. Not only do these dishes share no thematic similarities in their molded decoration, but they also span a period of production twice as long as the sauceboats.

From an inscription under the illustration we learn that *Cereus* was "a curious plant sent from the Royal Garden in Paris to the Physic Garden in Chelsea, in 1740. It flowered once in April 1745." Trew mentions in *Plantae selectae* that *Cereus* (a species of cactus) were grown trained against walls in hothouses, and that they bloomed at night. He added that "I have frequently had six or eight flowers open at the same time, which have a most magnificent appearance by candlelight."

The subsidiary plant, next to the caterpillar, resembling a stitchwort, is called *Alsine procumbens Gallii Facie Africana*, known today as *Stellaria alsine*, or bog stitchwort. On the Chelsea plate it appears in pink, whereas Ehret illustrated it in white. Next to the *Cereus*, the blue flower resembles that in plate 14 in Trew's *Plantae rariores* and is a *Sophora caerula*, now also known as *Crotalaria*, or blue broom (*Leguminosae*). The butterfly with the blue and yellow wings is virtually identical in wing coloring to that in Ehret's painting, though the body color has been changed.

In summary, the main components of the decoration on this plate have been faithfully copied from the illustration in Ehret and Trew. However, the pink leaves have been added to the *Cereus* for purely decorative effect and some of the colors have been altered overall.

30

Chelsea Botanical Plate, ca. 1755

Naturalistically painted with a yellow *Cereus* with pink leaves, flanked by two sprays of *Stellaria alsine*, with three insects and a caterpillar painted on the rim.

DIAMETER: 9½ in. (24.1 cm)
MARK: Red anchor and numeral *38*
LITERATURE: Ehret and Trew, *Plantae selectae*, pl. XXX
ACCESSION NUMBER: 1991.41.1

This design source is from *Plantae selectae*, a volume published by Dr. Christopher James Trew of Nuremberg and B. C. Vogel of Augsburg, of paintings by Georg Dionysius Ehret, an immigrant German who had married the sister-in-law of Philip Miller, curator of the Chelsea Physic Garden.

In Ehret's original painting, the principal flower is pink, but on the Chelsea plate it has been altered to yellow. However, the first volume of Philip Miller's *Figures of the most Beautiful, Useful and Uncommon Plants described in the Gardener's Dictionary* (published 1755–60, in two volumes) shows in plate 90 a yellow *Cereus* named *Cereus scandens minor*, and it was perhaps this color that was copied on the plate.

30

31

32

Chelsea Botanical Plate, ca. 1755

Naturalistically painted with a *Cereus*, with pink and yellow petals and blue berry sprays, and a caterpillar and other insects on the rim.

DIAMETER: 9½ in. (24.1 cm)
MARK: Red anchor and numeral *8*
LITERATURE: Ehret and Trew, *Plantae selectae*, pl. XIV
ACCESSION NUMBER: 1991.41.2

The identical flower is illustrated by Ehret and Trew, but the petals have been altered from white, in the original, to pink. It is a *Cereus altiffimus gracilor* (fructus extus), plate 14. On this plate the flower is painted in pink and yellow, with completely different foliage. The blue berry sprays are unidentified but possibly correct for the foliage. The *Cereus* is a flowering cactus, and its sparse, spiky, or nonexistent foliage and juicy stems might not have been considered sufficiently decorative for the composition on a Chelsea plate. The scattered insects, positioned and colored for decorative effect, are generally not accurate representations.

Both this fine plate and the related example (cat. no. 30) have leaves painted in green on their undersides, covering blemishes in the paste. A similar device, utilizing small moths, ladybugs, and other insects, conceals imperfections on the surface of these botanical plates, thereby making a virtue of necessity.

A series of plates with subjects copied directly from Philip Miller's *Figures of Plants*, which was published in separate volumes (1755–60) with original paintings by Ehret, seem always to be botanically accurate. Their decoration of species such as *Acacia, Anthemis, Abrotanum,* and *Antholyza* tends to be wispy, sparse, and restrained in palette,[1] quite unlike the flamboyant and colorful plates in the Bowles Collection, with their extrovert sense of rococo irregularity. Based on an examination of their thinner glaze, with its tendency to craze, this series of plates seems to be slightly later in period, dating from after the changes to the recipe for the Chelsea body.

1. Austin, *Chelsea Porcelain at Colonial Williamsburg,* cat. no. 78.

Chelsea Botanical Plate, ca. 1755

Naturalistically painted with a garden poppy, *Papaver*, a lily of the valley, *Convalaria*, with rose leaves, a small blue flower, asparagus tips, and scattered insects.

DIAMETER: 9¼ in. (23.5 cm)
MARK: Red anchor and letter *j* (or *i*)
LITERATURE: MacKenna, *Chelsea Porcelain: The Red Anchor Wares*, pl. 10, fig. 19, illustrates a botanical plate with similar painting
ACCESSION NUMBER: Promised gift

The garden poppy is accurately represented here, with matching leaves. Attached is a seed pod that appears to have the remains of blue petals. As with other poppies represented on Chelsea plates, this specimen has been viewed from behind. The small blue flowers above the isolated asparagus tip resemble *Anchusa italica*, or borage, depicted in plate 18 of Trew. Alternatively, this could represent a *Myosotis*, or forget-me-not.

Contemporary references in diaries and recipe books confirm the popularity of asparagus in the eighteenth century. The rich soil around the river Thames was ideal for the growing of vegetables. The botanist Richard Bradley (d. 1732) noted kitchen gardens that "exceed all the others in Europe for wholesome Produce." He went on to observe, "tho' Battersea affords the largest natural Asparagus."[1] At Chelsea, tureens and covers were designed as bundles of asparagus. These are listed on many occasions in the Chelsea sale catalogue for March 1756.

The finest and most flamboyant botanical designs, though not the most scientifically accurate, occur in conjunction with the earlier Chelsea plates dating from 1754–55. The decoration was continued for some five or six years into the early part of the gold anchor period, though the later examples are decorated with less freedom and rococo panache. It is perhaps significant that the Chelsea sale catalogue for March 1756 lists far less porcelain decorated with "India plants" than the previous year's catalogue. If this reflected a slackening demand or a change of fashion, it might also account for the advertisement in Faulkner's *Dublin Journal* for 1–4 July 1758, announcing a sale of Chelsea china "to be sold by auction at Mr. Young's Rooms opposite Lucas's on Cork Hill." The advertisement goes on to itemize "a very fine tureen, in curious plants, with table plates, soup plates, and desart plates enamelled from Sir Hans Sloane's plants." Dublin might well have been considered an ideal center for the disposing of some of the factory's stock, which was in a style no longer fashionable in London.

1. Quoted in Le Rougetel, *The Chelsea Gardener: Philip Miller, 1691–1771*, p. 144.

Chelsea Botanical Plate, ca. 1755

Naturalistically painted with a cluster of miniature bananas and a spray of pink flowers, probably a campanula, with scattered insects around the rim.

DIAMETER: 9½ in. (24.1 cm)
MARK: Red anchor and numeral *44*
LITERATURE: Ehret and Trew, *Plantae selectae*, pl. XXIII
ACCESSION NUMBER: Promised gift

This is a plantain, not native to Great Britain. The decoration, illustrated in Ehret and Trew, plate 23, is of *Musae fructi breviori spadicus fructiferi*, or miniature bananas. Sir Hans Sloane, whose name is inextricably associated with Chelsea botanical plates, was a keen plant collector and benefactor of the Physic Garden, who had visited Jamaica, studying and collating the native plants. In 1725 he published a two-volume work, *The Natural History of Jamaica*, in which he recorded his travels, illustrated by etchings in black and white. He would undoubtedly have seen these miniature bananas, although the exact plant does not appear in either volume. However, they would have been one of several ornamental species suitable for growing in hothouses and therefore perhaps available as a design source in the Physic Garden in Chelsea. At this period Jamaica was Britain's most important colony, supplying one-twelfth of its annual imports, and it is likely that interest in the flora and fauna of the island was considerable, especially among those who owed their prosperity to its natural resources.

While Sir Hans Sloane had many connections with the Physic Garden, which was leased upon his land, and had employed artists such as Maria Sibylla Merian, Jan van Huysum, R. Lancake, and possibly Ehret to illustrate specimens from his collections of plants, his association with the Chelsea factory was indirect. He died in January 1752, several years before the first production of porcelain with botanical decoration. His collection of eight hundred species of plants, now dried and preserved, is in the Botanical Department of the Natural History Museum in South Kensington. However, it may have been to the advantage of the Chelsea factory to associate its botanical wares with this prominent figure, well known both in England and abroad, whose name perhaps lent an air of botanical authenticity to this decoration.

This was a period of intense curiosity and learning, especially in all aspects of the sciences. Between 1750 and 1789, nearly nine hundred scientific periodicals were founded, and there was an insatiable demand for illustrated books with colored prints, classifying species of animals, birds, and plants. It was such expressions of learning, displayed to superb decorative effect, that stimulated the production of botanical decoration on Chelsea porcelain.

34

Detail left

34

Chelsea Botanical Dish, ca. 1755

Naturalistically painted with unidentified fruits that resemble tomatoes or ornamental gourds, a floral spray, and a scattering of insects.

DIAMETER: 11 in. (27.9 cm)

MARK: Red anchor

LITERATURE: Legge, *Flowers and Fables*, cat. no. 109, illustrates an oval dish with similar decoration

ACCESSION NUMBER: 1990.51.3

The identity of these fruits is puzzling, especially as they occur on Chelsea plates with some frequency. They may possibly represent ornamental gourds, which are native to tropical America, but which might have been grown in England in hothouses. At any event, the leaves depicted seem to be unrelated to the fruits. Alternatively, they may be tomatoes. Introduced into England in the sixteenth century, the tomato was also known as the love apple and was widely used in soups. Two varieties of wild tomato, grown in Peru, were sent to Philip Miller from the royal garden in Paris, and he named them in his *Gardener's Dictionary*.[1]

Although several books of design sources for Chelsea botanical plates have been identified, G. D. Ehret is the only artist to whom the original designs can be traced with any certainty. An immigrant German, Ehret was an accomplished and talented botanical artist who had worked in Germany, France, and Switzerland. He came to the notice of Dr. Christopher James Trew of Nuremberg, an eminent physician and botanist, who commissioned him to paint as many plants as possible, on "fine large paper." Ehret visited England and settled there in 1736. He met Sir Hans Sloane, who promised him assistance, and also Philip Miller, curator of the Chelsea Physic Garden, later marrying his sister-in-law. He was a prolific artist, and among the works he illustrated were *Plantae et papiliones rariories*, Dr. Pocock's *Descriptions of the East* (1743–45), Dr. Hughes's *History of Barbados* (1750), and Dr. Browne's *History of Jamaica*.

The decoration on this dish is of such quality and has so powerful an impact that the marked warping in the firing is almost entirely offset.

1. Cited in Le Rougetel, *The Chelsea Gardener: Philip Miller, 1691–1771*, p. 54.

35

35

Chelsea Botanical Dish, ca. 1755

Of scalloped shape, naturalistically painted with two melons, together with their related leaves and flowers.

DIAMETER: 9¼ in. (23.5 cm)
MARK: Red anchor
LITERATURE: Spero, "Chelsea Porcelain, 1744–1769," pl. XI
ACCESSION NUMBER: 1991.47.6

In this instance both the flowers and the leaves are accurate representations of those relating to the melon. Melons were a popular decorative theme at this period and were produced in the guise of teapots at Longton Hall (cat. no. 73) and tureens at Chelsea (cat. no. 39). The fruit itself was also popular, although not always readily cultivated. Gilbert White, the author of *The Natural History of Selborne*, had great difficulty, complaining that even "Miller's very fine old seed produced abominable fruit." Philip Miller sent him some cantaloupe seeds from Armenia, together with detailed planting advice. When this too failed to achieve satisfactory results, White visited Miller in Chelsea in order to elicit the correct procedure. Soon afterward, his hot beds at Selborne produced "fine, large, beautiful fruit, just like Miller's."[1]

The Chelsea sale catalogues for 1755 and 1756 contain numerous entries for "Twelve beautiful scollop plates, *India plants*, all different" (March 1755, third day, lot 48), "Three oval dishes of 2 sizes . . . enamel'd in India plants" (March 1756, twelfth day, lot 74), and other entries with similar wording. It seems almost certain that "India plants" correspond to botanical subjects, and the descriptions fully match with the surviving Chelsea shapes decorated in this idiom. The vast majority of these were plates and dishes, though pint and half-pint mugs are known, alongside "basons," finger bowls, and stands, and the component elements of tea services. Yet the layout of these botanical themes, echoing contemporary book illustrations, was less appropriate to these hollow forms, thereby dissipating much of the decorative effect and the teasing sense of trompe l'oeil.

It is likely that plates and dishes were sold as services depicting related themes of fruit, flowers, or vegetables, perhaps mirroring the similarly formed tureens and covers. Certainly the 1755 and 1756 sale catalogues list plates with "India plants," almost invariably in sets of a dozen. This might also account for the puzzling presence of painter's numerals or letters, placed alongside the red anchor mark.

1. Quoted in Le Rougetel, *The Chelsea Gardener: Philip Miller, 1691–1771*, p. 41.

Chelsea Botanical Plate, ca. 1755

Naturalistically painted with a tiger lily, *Lilium tigrinum*, or possibly a martagon lily, *Martagon canadensis*, with scattered insects on the rim.

DIAMETER: 9 in. (22.9 cm)

MARK: Red anchor

LITERATURE: Adams, *Chelsea Porcelain*, pl. 92, illustrates a saucer dish with similar decoration

ACCESSION NUMBER: 1991.47.7

The narrow pointed leaves belong to the lily, a popular and recurring subject on Chelsea botanical plates. However, the larger leaves, unrelated to the lily, closely resemble the mandrake leaves illustrated in Philip Miller's *Figures of Plants*, plate 173. Alternatively, they could be the leaves of an acanthus. Subsidiary leaves, unrelated to the main botanical specimen but included for decorative purposes, may well have been taken from live plants in the Physic Garden, located in convenient proximity to the factory. At any event, these botanical gardens must have stimulated the production of many of the naturalistic themes that had become so popular in ceramics.

It is reasonable to consider that the botanical decoration on Chelsea porcelain was an original contribution to the field of European ceramics. Although probably influenced by the earlier botanically accurate designs on Meissen, painted by J. G. Klinger in the 1740s, the Chelsea decoration was far less stylized and rigid, and the broader palette and freer compositions lent an entirely different atmosphere to the final effect. By contrast to Meissen, blank areas of porcelain were seldom permitted, filled up instead by small sprays of flowers or insects that were sometimes derived from nature but more often from imagination. The success of the Chelsea designs stimulated botanical decoration at Bow, with more variable results, and, to a smaller degree, at Vauxhall, while at Tournai accurate representations of designs derived from Ehret and Trew appeared on services during the 1760s. By the early part of the nineteenth century, botanical decoration was widely used on English ceramics, especially on Derby porcelain and on Wedgwood, Davenport, and Swansea creamware.

36

37

Chelsea Botanical Plate, ca. 1755

Naturalistically painted with a spray of white roses, moths, and a detached floral spray.

DIAMETER: 8½ in. (21.6 cm)
MARK: Red anchor
LITERATURE: Adams, *Chelsea Porcelain*, pl. XII
ACCESSION NUMBER: Promised gift

This less flamboyant botanical design lays out the various elements with a rococo irregularity and a characteristically subtle use of space and placement. The insects are seldom scientifically accurate on Chelsea, and here, the butterfly is edged in shadow, an idiosyncrasy borrowed from Meissen.

The close proximity of the Physic Garden to the Chelsea factory was naturally of great advantage, as it allowed some botanical designs to be copied and adapted from live plants. The association of this decorative idiom with Sir Hans Sloane lent this botanical style an air of authority, and it must surely have brought it to the attention of a wider public. Yet the great botanist's indirect influence extended still further, for it was he who appointed Philip Miller to the Physic Garden in 1722. Miller remained there for nearly fifty years, establishing a reputation as the most distinguished and influential gardener of the eighteenth century.[1]

Widely known throughout Europe and America, Miller's *Gardener's Dictionary* was first published in 1731 and was reprinted many times during the succeeding forty years. A number of botanical designs on Chelsea have been traced to his beautifully illustrated *Figures of Plants,* to which G. D. Ehret contributed drawings. Miller had an especial interest in and fondness for roses, and his many written works testify to his affection for "the most beautiful and fragrant flowers of any kind of shrub yet known."[2]

1. Le Rougetel, *The Chelsea Gardener: Philip Miller, 1691–1771,* p. 9.
2. Ibid., p. 124.

38

Chelsea Rose Dish, ca. 1755–56

Naturalistically molded with a cluster of leaves, three rosebuds, and a branch handle terminating in a rose blossom.

DIAMETER: 7½ in. (19.1 cm)
MARK: None
LITERATURE: MacKenna, *Chelsea Porcelain: The Red Anchor Wares,* pl. 35, fig. 71, for two rose tureens
ACCESSION NUMBER: 1991.41.25

A wide range of naturalistic forms was produced at Chelsea during the mid-1750s, most of which were inspired by Meissen. These included peony dishes, sunflower dishes, and mulberry-leaf dishes, together with tureens in such forms as artichokes (cat. no. 40), melons (cat. no. 39), cabbages, lemons, and roses. It seems likely that this rose dish may have been intended as a stand for the small rose tureen of the same period. This would correspond with the "four small roses and four leaves to ditto for desart" listed in the 1755 sale catalogue and repeated in the following year's auction. Both the rose tureens and the dishes were also produced at Bow, Derby, and Longton Hall during the mid- and late 1750s.

Many of these naturalistic forms, including peony dishes and sunflower dishes, for example, occur only in the more thickly potted body with the heavier, slightly opacified glaze. Yet other forms in a similar idiom, such as this rose dish and the polyanthus dishes, are invariably in the more thinly potted body with the more translucent glaze.

38

39

39

Chelsea Tureen and Cover, ca. 1755–56

Modeled in the form of a melon, naturalistically colored, with a handle in the form of a stalk surrounded by flowers and leaves.

LENGTH: 7 in. (17.8 cm)
WIDTH: 5 in. (12.7 cm)
MARK: Red anchor and numeral *4* on each piece
LITERATURE: MacKenna, *Chelsea Porcelain: The Red Anchor Wares,* pl. 32, fig. 65, illustrates a melon tureen and stand; Spero, "Chelsea Porcelain, 1744–1769," pl. XV
ACCESSION NUMBER: 1991.47.51a–b

This tureen corresponds to the "fine large melons, for desart," listed on numerous occasions in both Chelsea sale catalogues for 1755 and 1756, made in two sizes. In common with the entire range of animal, bird, and vegetable tureens, this Chelsea example was copied directly from Meissen, though it also occurs in both Dutch and French faience. Other fruit and vege-

table tureens made at Chelsea during the red anchor period include cabbages, cauliflowers, artichokes, lettuces, apples, lemons, pineapples, roses, honeycombs, and bundles of asparagus. Melons of this type were also depicted as botanical specimens embellishing Chelsea plates (cat. no. 35). Contemporary factories such as Bow, Derby, and Longton Hall also produced tureens in naturalistic forms, but on a far more restricted scale. A pair of Bow apple boxes (cat. no. 48) and a Longton Hall melon teapot (cat. no. 73) are included in this collection.

This trompe l'oeil, nature in artifice, was an expression of the rococo style, much favored in wealthy society during the mid- and late 1750s and used for the dessert course, after the two main dinner "removes" had been cleared away. Their purpose was primarily as a visual stimulus to conversation, though they no doubt contained great delicacies.

40

Pair of Chelsea Artichoke Tureens and Covers,
ca. 1754–55

Naturalistically molded, with finials formed as
tomtits, pecking at fruit.

HEIGHT: 6½ in. (16.5 cm)
MARK: Red anchor
LITERATURE: Spero, *Twenty-five Years Exhibition,*
cat. no. 7
ACCESSION NUMBER: Promised gifts

These rare tureens correspond to the "Two fine arti-
choaks, second size," listed as lot 47 on the first day of
the sale of Chelsea porcelain held by Mr. Ford on
Monday, 10 March 1755. In the following year's sale
(Tuesday, 30 March 1756, lot 81), they are listed again,
presumably in a larger size, as "Two large artichokes

and leaves." The leaves that originally accompanied
the larger size have never been identified. Artichoke
tureens were occasionally left "in the white," lending
them a greater tactile allure but at the expense of their
teasing sense of trompe l'oeil. This is artfully conveyed by coloring that features the tops of the leaves
painted in puce, as if to emphasize their ripeness.

If the primary purpose of this delightfully inventive shape was the stimulating of conversation during
the dessert course, their practical function was perhaps to contain melted butter sauce or even one of the
popular confections of the period, such as "Barley
cream" or "crisp'd almonds." The charming conceit
of a tomtit, forming the finial, not only enhanced the
naturalistic effect but provided a well-designed and
practical method of lifting the cover.

40

41

41

Chelsea Partridge Tureen, ca. 1754–55

Naturalistically modeled as a partridge roosting upon a nest of applied twigs and leaves, above a basketweave molded base.

LENGTH: 5⅜ in. (13.7 cm)
WIDTH: 3¾ in. (9.5 cm)
MARK: Red anchor and numeral *No 50*
LITERATURE: Austin, *Chelsea Porcelain at Williamsburg,* cat. no. 88; Spero, "Chelsea Porcelain, 1744–1769," pl. X
ACCESSION NUMBER: 1991.47.50a–b

The Meissen prototype for this tureen was first modeled in September 1742 by Johann Joachim Kaendler, who described them as boxes "for butter and the like." They were issued in pairs, each bird being the mirror image of the other. The fashion for partridge tureens may have had its origins in the ancient custom of replacing the plumage on cooked birds, prior to bringing them to the dining table. The Chelsea sale of 1755 lists over one hundred examples of nesting partridges, often "for desart." References in the following year's sale were more infrequent, though lot 54 on 9 April permits a veiled credit to the origins of the tureen: "Two beautiful foreign partridges and two dishes to ditto." Naturally, the two portions of each tureen were fired separately, and in view of the substantial production, it was necessary for the decorator to add a numeral beside the red anchor on each piece so that they could be eventually reunited.

The collection of Meissen at Holland House belonging to Sir Charles Hanbury Williams (1708–1759), British envoy at Dresden, was made available to the Chelsea factory through the agency of the influential Sir Everard Fawkener, "to copy what they like." Among the Meissen was a superb dinner service dating from the 1740s, which included elaborate tureens, the covers of which had knops fashioned as domestic and game birds. The workmen from the factory who visited Holland House in the summer of 1751 were naturally excited by these extraordinarily innovative forms, and in particular by one knop in the form of a partridge and its accompanying vegetables: "Upon the Cover for the handle, a Partridge sitting on asparagus, Colly-flower, Cucumbers & Lemons & Oranges on rileve (in relief)."[1] This solid partridge, duly converted, became the source for the celebrated Chelsea partridge tureen, itself the inspiration for many similar models in English ceramics.

The subject was a very popular one, being produced in French and German faience, in English pottery, and at several other porcelain factories including Bow, Derby, Longton Hall, and Worcester. At Worcester the model was issued in different versions and in differing sizes from the late 1750s until the late 1760s.

1. Clarke, "Sir Charles Hanbury Williams and the Chelsea Factory," p. 110.

Chelsea Dovecote, ca. 1755–56

Modeled in the form of a castle with three turrets, around which are perched fourteen doves. Another dove is perched upon the branches of one of the two trees growing from the rockwork base, while a fox prowls expectantly below.

HEIGHT: 17 in. (43.2 cm)

MARK: Red anchor

LITERATURE: MacKenna, *Chelsea Porcelain: The Red Anchor Wares,* pl. 46, fig. 92

ACCESSION NUMBER: 1986.45a–e

This massive and ambitious example of early English porcelain sculpture corresponds to lot 73, sold on the second day, 11 March, of the 1755 sale of Chelsea porcelain, held by Mr. Ford at his Great Room in the Haymarket. Described in the sale catalogue as "A most beautiful perfume pot, in the form of a pigeon-house, with pigeons, a fox, etc.," it was among the largest objects produced at the factory, echoing the architectural dovecotes which were so popular throughout Europe. The shape, most probably inspired by Meissen, was continued into the gold anchor period, as is exemplified by the fine dovecote resident in the Wrightsman Collection in the Metropolitan Museum of Art in New York. Another dovecote, similarly described, was included in Mr. Ford's sale of April 1756.

A somewhat different model, made at Derby in about 1760, but probably inspired by Chelsea, was even larger, measuring 21½ inches in height. By contrast, the subject was also issued on an altogether smaller scale, as a miniature scent bottle.

The early English factories seldom attempted to compete with the large-scale sculptures and models produced at Meissen and elsewhere. In Germany, France, and Italy, each factory was subsidized by a wealthy aristocratic patron — a nobleman, a duke, a prince, or, as at Sèvres, Meissen, Berlin, and Nymphenburg, even a reigning monarch. In each case, artistic and commercial success of the enterprise reflected directly on the prestige of the patron, and it was therefore in his interests to ensure his factory's financial stability. No such support was available to the English factories, which were dependent entirely upon the business acumen and artistic judgment of their proprietors and the durability and suitability of their porcelain bodies. Only at Chelsea was there any element of the patronage of the sort enjoyed on the Continent, in the person of Sir Everard Fawkener, secretary to the duke of Cumberland and a wealthy and influential man in his own right. As a consequence, Chelsea did from time to time attempt such ambitious and large-scale sculptures as this dovecote.

43

Chelsea Plate, ca. 1755–56

Painted with a large central bouquet of flowers and molded around the rim with strawberry leaves and trailing stems, interspersed with sprigs of strawberries.

DIAMETER: 9 in. (22.9 cm)

MARK: Red anchor

LITERATURE: Cushion and Cushion, *A Collector's History of British Porcelain,* front cover, for the Longton Hall version of this plate

ACCESSION NUMBER: 1991.47.1

Strawberry-leaf plates in Chelsea probably served as the models for the more common Longton Hall examples, though the differing palettes used somewhat mask the similarities. The colors are less vivid and lack the luminosity of the Longton Hall palette or, indeed, that of the raised anchor period. In both instances, the original inspiration can be traced back to Meissen. By the mid-1750s the composition of the floral bouquets had become fuller and the palette had changed, as may be seen by comparing this plate and the silver-shape oval dish (cat. no. 27). Yet the relatively free composition still exhibits a strong Meissen influence. This contrasts vividly with the more stylized and opulent decoration that characterized the later influence of Sèvres (cat. no. 47). From the mid-1750s onward, a high proportion of Chelsea wares had their foot rims ground, leaving them free of glaze, a peculiarity shared with Derby porcelain of the 1755–65 period, but most strongly associated with gold anchor Chelsea wares.

43

44

Chelsea Plate, ca. 1756–57

Decorated on the rim with six exotic birds amid foliage, alternating with panels of ribbed molding, the center with a bouquet of flowers and scattered sprays.

DIAMETER: 8½ in. (21.6 cm)
MARK: Red anchor
LITERATURE: Lippert, *Eighteenth-Century English Porcelain in the Collection of the Indianapolis Museum of Art*, pp. 66–67, cat. no. 3
ACCESSION NUMBER: 1991.47.2

This plate is a relatively late example of the Meissen influence at Chelsea, evident in the free composition of the floral decoration and the somewhat stylized bird painting that was later adapted at Worcester. The relatively thick glaze and overall weight of this plate suggest a bone-ash body, a further modification to the recipe for the porcelain, introduced at Chelsea in about 1756–57 to facilitate the production of figures and vases. The changes in style and palette of floral decoration on Chelsea during the 1750s is illustrated in a comparison between the full floral style on the Bowleses' octagonal saucers (cat. no. 26), echoing the Meissen and Vincennes tradition, the more detailed but sparse style on the silver-shape dish (cat. no. 27), and this plate, which shows a development of the typical red anchor period painting.

44

45

Chelsea Dish, ca. 1756–57

Of octagonal rectangular shape painted with an assortment of bunches and clusters of fruit, flanked by two insects.

LENGTH: 9 in. (22.9 cm)
MARK: Red anchor
ACCESSION NUMBER: 1991.47.52

By the late 1750s the fruit and vegetable decoration at Chelsea no longer aspired to the standard attained on the botanical plates of several years earlier. Nor was that specific style any longer in vogue. Instead, the painting was heavier in both execution and palette, and far more stylized. The influence of Meissen is evident, together with pre-echoes of the style later made famous by the London atelier of James Giles. The slightly dull palette is accentuated by an absence of gilding, which tends to characterize decoration of this type. A comparison with the related decoration on the Worcester plates from the duke of Gloucester service (cat. nos. 97 and 98) exemplifies the decorative impact of gilding. This shape of dish, also used at Bow, became a characteristic Derby form of the 1770s and 1780s.

45

46a

46b

46
Pair of Chelsea Dishes, ca. 1760

Of kidney shape, painted with bunches and clusters of fruit and vegetables, including turnips, peas, and grapes, with narrow brown-line borders.

LENGTH: 10¾ in. (27.3 cm)
MARK: Brown anchor on each piece
LITERATURE: Savage, *Eighteenth-Century English Porcelain*, pl. 34a
ACCESSION NUMBERS: Promised gifts

Although botanical in style, the treatment of the fruit and vegetable theme here is far less detailed and vibrant than on the plates and dishes of the red anchor period. The use of the brown anchor is associated with wares that date from the gold anchor period (ca. 1759–69) but that do not include gilding in their decoration. Gilding was the most expensive process in the manufacture and decoration of porcelain in the eighteenth century, and gilders were the most highly paid workmen.

The kidney-shaped dish, which derived from Meissen, was widely used at the English factories, from the mid-1750s onward. Both the shape and the decoration, palette, and composition on these dishes exerted a strong influence on the London atelier of James Giles. Indeed, his versions of this decorative idiom on Worcester porcelain of the late 1760s are visually hard to distinguish from Chelsea.

The continued popularity of fruit decoration at this period may be judged from the surviving portion of a catalogue of a sale of Chelsea, held by Mr. Burnsall in April–May 1761, devoted to the previous year's production. It contains numerous references to "shell handle baskets, scalloped, oval and square compotiers and tea and coffee services," all "enamelled with fruit." Yet by comparison with the botanical decoration of the red anchor period (cat. nos. 30–37), notions of scientific realism had given way to purely decorative effects.

47

47

Pair of Chelsea Plates, ca. 1762–65

Decorated with large clusters of fruit and insects, with a border with fruit and insects, some painted within molded reserved panels.

DIAMETER: 9 in. (22.9 cm)
MARK: Gold anchor on each piece
LITERATURE: MacKenna, *Chelsea Porcelain: The Gold Anchor Wares,* pl. 4, fig. 8
ACCESSION NUMBERS: 1991.41.3.1, 2

This pair of plates is from a service at one time owned by the duke of Cambridge, one of the grandsons of George II. In its palette and sumptuous decoration, it strongly resembles the slightly later service in Worcester porcelain, said to have been made for his brother, William Henry, duke of Gloucester. The molded panels resemble those on the celebrated service ordered by George III in 1762 as a gift for his brother-in-law, the duke of Mecklenburg-Strelitz. With their rococo overtones and opulent gilding, these plates represent a significant shift in taste from the naturalism of the mid-1750s, exemplified by botanical themes and simple floral designs. This was caused by the preeminent influence of Sèvres, which had largely replaced that of Meissen, as a consequence of the Seven Years' War, which began in 1756. The town was occupied by Prussian troops who caused great disruption, and the factory was never to regain its former influence. However, if the molding, free use of gilding, and overall composition of the decoration on these plates display the influence of Sèvres, the fruit motif is a theme that can be traced back to Meissen. Thus an interaction of different, but not opposing, styles, one French and the other German, was successfully absorbed at an English factory. Two Worcester plates from the related duke of Gloucester service are catalogue numbers 97 and 98 in this collection.

· BOW ·

ca. 1744–1776

THE BOW FACTORY, situated in Stratford in the east of London, was founded in 1747, although the first patent had been taken out in 1744. A second patent was taken out in 1748, by Thomas Frye, who, together with Edward Heylyn, John Weatherby, and John Crowther, was to be the most influential figure in the factory's development over the following twelve years. The Bow factory therefore shared with its metropolitan neighbor, Chelsea, the distinction of becoming one of the first two porcelain manufacturers to be established in England.

The objectives and priorities of the factory were made explicit in the wording of the 1748 patent: "to make, use, exercise and vend my new method of making a certain ware, which is not inferior to . . . China, Japan or porcelain ware." This clearly stated intention was lent graphic substance by the construction of the Bow factory itself, in 1750, the first purpose-built ceramic factory in Britain. The exterior of the building was copied directly from the East India Warehouse in Canton, and the factory was styled in contemporary advertisements and insurance policies as "New Canton." Inkpots decorated in oriental patterns proclaimed their origin, being inscribed MADE AT NEW CANTON 1750. The preoccupation with oriental decorative themes prevailed throughout the 1750s, and it was not until the mid-1760s that European subjects predominated. The bone-ash porcelain body, the precursor to the bone china which was to become the traditional English body, was ideal for the manufacture of figures. It was also well suited to making plates, dishes, and the dinner and dessert services which became a speciality of the factory.

Whereas at Chelsea Nicholas Sprimont intended his porcelain to be purchased by "The Quality and Gentry," Bow sought a far wider market, both for home consumption and export. The factory's success in this endeavor may be judged by the fact that in terms of the insurance policies and the number of workers employed, Bow was by the mid-1750s by far the largest porcelain factory in England and, it has been suggested, in Europe.[1] Yet if their market was wider than that of Worcester, and less elevated than that of Chelsea, it should not be thought that Bow porcelain was anything but a luxury in relative terms. John Bowcock, manager of the warehouse and clerk of the factory from 1753, kept accounts and memoranda that offer illuminating insights into the business methods of the factory and the prices for individual pieces of porcelain. When compared to average wage levels for workers at that time, these prices are anything but inexpensive. The market sought for Bow was what the shrewd Josiah Wedgwood described as "the Middling Class of People — which Class we know are vastly, I had almost said, infinitely superior, in number to the Great."[2]

During the years of the factory's greatest prosperity, from the early 1750s until the early 1760s, there was a deliberate concentration on oriental patterns and motifs, even though many of the potting shapes were adapted from Meissen or from English silver originals. The famille rose idiom derived from Chinese porcelain was absorbed into the Bow factory style, much as chinoiserie was at Worcester. If the decorative effect is less sophisticated, it was ideally suited to the factory's robust and forthright potting shapes. "Sprig'd" decoration of raised prunus blossom applied to porcelain "in the white" was also widely used at this period. Inspired by late-seventeenth-century Chinese porcelain from Fijian province, this style had been popular at St. Cloud, Mennecy, Meissen, and Chelsea. Yet although it had fallen out of fashion elsewhere by the mid-1750s, it remained commercially successful at Bow for a further ten years. Overglaze transfer printing was introduced in about 1754, but as with its underglaze blue counterpart, the technique was not widely used at Bow. Bearing in mind the tremendous commercial success of Worcester in this respect, the failure at Bow to develop transfer-printing techniques may well have made a significant contribution to the factory's eventual decline.

By the late 1750s European themes were becoming gradually more prominent. Botanical decoration, though generally fairly successful, was produced on a more restricted scale than at Chelsea. Floral designs showed a far less direct Meissen influence than at Chelsea or Worcester and often bore a similarity with Mennecy, both in style and palette. Figure models, by contrast, were nearly all derived from Meissen, and a huge range of human and animal subjects was produced. The bone-ash body that made figure modeling so commercially successful was also ideal for the large-scale production of plates and dishes. It gave the Bow factory a crucial advantage over its provincial rival at Worcester, where initially, problems were encountered in the firing of flatware. Conversely, whereas the soapstone body and the hard glaze enabled Worcester to make a speciality of tea-wares, at Bow the impact of boiling water often had dire effects on teapots and tea bowls. Sauceboats and mugs, on the other hand, were a great speciality, often exhibiting the sturdy, confident lines that echoed their silver counterparts.

In common with most other English porcelain factories, a crucial element of the Bow output was devoted to blue-and-white wares. As with all Bow domestic wares, the decoration reflected oriental themes and, in the case of underglaze blue, almost to the exclusion of all other decorative idioms. Perhaps the most characteristic Bow decoration in this style was the powder blue ground, derived from Chinese porcelain of the Kangxi period and usually found in conjunction with Chinese landscapes within fan-shaped reserved panels. The vivid decorative impact of the powder blue grounds evidently appealed to Mr. and Mrs. Bowles, and the collection contains seven examples (cat. nos. 64–70). These include the delightfully artful decoration on catalogue number 70, which shows two Chinamen peering bewilderedly up at a plinth, upon which stands a large and imposing vase inscribed *bow*.

Yet by far the greater representation of Bow in this collection is devoted to the Kakiemon influence, which played so prominent a role in Bow decoration of the 1750s. These Japanese wares, from the last quarter of the seventeenth century, are characterized by a milky white body and brilliant translucent enamel colors. The subtle asymmetrical Kakiemon patterns, replete with symbolism, were seldom fully understood by their European imitators, yet their popularity — especially in England, Germany, and France — was enormous. By 1750 importations of Kakiemon porcelain had ceased, and this opened up a profitable market for the recently founded English porcelain factories at Chelsea and Bow. An illuminating comparison between a Japanese Kakiemon original (cat. no. 54) and a Bow version of the same pattern (cat. no. 52) can be seen in this collection.

However, the particular preference of the Bowleses for Kakiemon themes was still more specific. Their fondness was for the Partridge or Quail pattern, and as many as nine examples of this celebrated design are represented in the collection. The pattern was evidently extremely popular at Bow during the 1750s, and contemporary invoices, account books, and sale catalogues are full of references to such items as "nurl'd open partridge," "octagon nappy plates, partridge pattern," and a "partridge hand'd, cup and saucer." One entry by John Bowcock in his memorandum book for 24 July 1756, "To buy a partridge either alive or dead," may have particularly appealed to Henry Bowles, who was a keen sportsman. Indeed, this enthusiasm was perhaps partly responsible for his fondness for the Quail pattern.

Another preference that finds rich expression in the Chelsea and Longton Hall chapters of this catalogue was for such naturalistic themes as botanical painting and fruit, leaf, and vegetable forms. These exotic manifestations of the rococo style were less prominent in the Bow production than at Chelsea, Longton Hall, and Derby. Yet the relatively few surviving fruit and vegetable forms in Bow lose nothing in comparison. The pair of apple boxes (cat. no. 48), for example, with their handles in the form of arching caterpillars, is a delightfully humorous evocation of the trompe l'oeil that so teasingly refreshed both appetite and conversation for the dessert.

I HAVE INCLUDED the single piece of Lowestoft in the Bowles Collection in this section. Like Bow, this small east coast factory utilized a bone-ash recipe. It catered to a provincial market, primarily local, and much of its decoration was simple and unpretentious, usually in the Chinese taste. The coffeepot (cat. no. 71), purchased in San Francisco, under the misapprehension that it was Worcester, is an exceptionally rare piece, if a little uncharacteristic of its factory.

1. Gabszewicz and Freeman, *Bow Porcelain*, p. 15.
2. Finer and Savage, *The Selected Letters of Josiah Wedgwood*.

Pair of Bow Apple Boxes and Covers, ca. 1756

Each naturalistically modeled, with short brown twigs at one end, with three leaves, and the cover surmounted by a knop in the form of a codling moth caterpillar.

DIAMETER: 4 in. (10.2 cm)

MARK: None

LITERATURE: Peirce, *English Ceramics: The Frances and Emory Cocke Collection,* for a red anchor Chelsea example

ACCESSION NUMBERS: 1991.40.90.1a–b, 2a–b

Contemporary records make it clear that apple boxes were made at Bow, though the surviving examples are far rarer than their Chelsea counterparts. The Bow model follows the Chelsea very closely, but the palette is completely different. It is probably close in date to the "fine large apples and leaves for desart" listed in the 1755 Chelsea sale catalogue.

In the mid-eighteenth century, dessert was regarded as an entirely separate postlude to the main courses of dinner. The elaborate and detailed recipes of the period describe pyramids of sweetmeats and jellies, and this visual dimension to the luxury of the food itself was mirrored by porcelain leaves and tureens in the form of animals, birds, fruit, and vegetables. The majority of these were derived from Meissen, though many forms, including apple boxes, occur in Strasbourg faience. The form was also copied in Chinese export porcelain toward the end of the eighteenth century.

However, the range of fruit and vegetable boxes made at Bow came nowhere near the output of Chelsea during the mid-1750s, in terms of either size or variety. Apart from the apple boxes, surviving papers, accounts, and invoices suggest that Bow also produced "artichoak" cups, rose boxes, and "mellons." The purpose of such trompe-l'oeil, primarily decorative, wares was invariably described in contemporary sale catalogues as "for desart." Yet Benjamin Franklin, writing to his wife in 1758, cast further light on their function. "I send you by Captain Budden a large case and a small box containing some English china, viz: melons and leaves for a dessert of fruit and cream or the like."[1] The pieces itemized were almost certainly of Bow manufacture.

1. Quoted in Adams and Redstone, *Bow Porcelain,* p. 75.

Bow Plate, ca. 1758–60

Of octagonal form, decorated in the famille rose taste, with flowering shrubs, rockwork, bamboo, and insects.

DIAMETER: 8¾ in. (22.2 cm)

MARK: None

LITERATURE: Spero, *The Price Guide to Eighteenth-Century English Porcelain,* p. 41

ACCESSION NUMBER: 1991.40.68

Decoration in the Chinese famille rose taste, named after the predominating palette, was associated with Bow porcelain, from its earliest productions in the late 1740s. Yet whereas at Chelsea this style found little favor, at Bow it was in production for nearly twenty years. The patterns varied considerably, but the principal elements of famille rose flowers and blue rockwork remained much the same. However, the palette altered radically during this period, insofar as the colors became more opaque in the later examples. In the case of this plate, the strong tones of blue and pink lack the translucency and delicacy that are so characteristic of earlier wares in this genre. Overall, the decoration is highly stylized and the border pattern has been compressed into an almost formless assembly of colors. In its avowed intention to imitate imported Chinese porcelain and in its large-scale production, exceeding that of any other factory of the 1750s, Bow did not always succeed in maintaining the consistent standards of its contemporary rivals at Chelsea and Worcester.

49

50

Bow Sugar Bowl, ca. 1753–54

With an everted rim, applied with prunus blossom and painted sprays of flowers and isolated flower heads.

DIAMETER: 4 in. (10.2 cm)

MARK: None

LITERATURE: Gabszewicz and Freeman, *Bow Porcelain,* cat. no. 21

ACCESSION NUMBER: 1991.40.83

This shape originally would have had a lid and been intended as a sugar box. It is one of a large range of forms associated with "sprig'd" decoration, including punch pots, salad bowls, flowerpots, mugs, vases, libation cups, sauceboats, chocolate cups and saucers, tureens, openwork baskets, cutlery, eggcups, cream pots, salts, and ewers, together with a range of dessert and tea services. Most of these were white, though sometimes painted decoration was added, either in the famille rose style or in the Kakiemon taste. Whereas the vogue for this decoration had waned at Chelsea by the early 1750s, it persisted at Bow until the mid-1760s, though by this period the quality of both the porcelain and the applied decoration had deteriorated.

Indeed, Bow was alone among contemporary porcelain factories in persevering with wares bereft of painted decoration beyond the mid-1750s. In the memorandum book kept by John Bowcock, of 1756, 35 percent of the useful wares were "in the white,"[1] an extraordinary proportion for a style of decoration considered no longer fashionable at Meissen, St. Cloud, Mennecy, and Chelsea. Imports from China of these blanc de chine wares had ceased by about 1720, and so it is a little surprising that the demand for them persisted. Conversely, this might perhaps be the very explanation.

1. Cited in Adams and Redstone, *Bow Porcelain,* p. 110.

50

51

Bow Dish, ca. 1754–56

Of rectangular form, the wide rim applied with sprays and sprigs of prunus blossom.

LENGTH: 10¾ in. (27.3 cm)

MARK: None

LITERATURE: Peirce, *English Ceramics: The Frances and Emory Cocke Collection,* cat. no. 94

ACCESSION NUMBER: 1991.40.64

White porcelain with applied prunus and floral decoration formed a major part of the Bow production throughout the 1750s and into the early 1760s. The style originated in the Chinese wares of the late seventeenth century, made at Dehua in Fijian province, opposite present-day Taiwan. Known in Europe as "blanc de chine," these were enthusiastically imitated at St. Cloud, Mennecy, Chelsea, and Meissen. At Bow the decoration was described as "sprig'd" and occurred in many variations, both on oriental forms and English silver shapes, though certain forms were copied from Meissen. John Bowcock, manager and clerk of the factory, refers many times in his memorandum book to these wares, while an invoice dated "16 Ap 1753" for Bow china purchased by the marquis of Rockingham lists "a compleate set White Sp: Tea China £2:2:0." The price mentioned suggests that "sprig'd" wares were considerably less expensive than the Kakiemon designs. Their comparatively low cost may have contributed to what was evidently a very strong demand, which persisted for over half of the factory's lifetime. Intriguingly in commercial terms, Bow was alone among English factories in the large-scale production of these "sprig'd" wares.

51

52

52

Bow Dish, ca. 1755–56

Of rectangular form, decorated in the Kakiemon taste, with pine, prunus, and bamboo, two cranes, a "flaming tortoise," and a curled dragon in the center, all within an iron red border with gilt blossoms.

LENGTH: 11 in. (27.9 cm)

MARK: None

LITERATURE: Ayers, Impey, and Mallet, *Porcelain for Palaces*, cat. no. 330, for a Chelsea bowl in this pattern

ACCESSION NUMBER: 1991.40.69

A comparison between the Bow interpretation of this pattern and the Japanese original (cat. no. 54) is illuminating. The Bow version is laid out in a more elaborate and confusing manner, the overall effect being further muddled by the more detailed border design, the much wider palette, and the addition of extra Kakiemon motifs, such as the large flower head flanking the tortoise. The evident confusion surrounding the tortoise itself, blazing away in every direction, suggests a measure of uncertainty in the painter's understanding of the subject. Yet above all, whereas the Japanese dish shows an appreciation of the rhythm of the design, its restrained asymmetry, and the use of space as an integral element, the Bow painter is more concerned with filling up all available areas of porcelain, thereby creating a loss of focus in a search for decorative effect. However, if the detailed components of the Bow version cannot equal the Japanese in clarity or symbolism, there is instead an infectious exuberance, which pervades so much English porcelain decorated in the Kakiemon idiom.

Aside from the recurrent Quail or Partridge pattern, most of the Bow designs inspired by Japanese Kakiemon wares were issued on plates, dishes, baskets, and forms other than tewares. This perhaps reflected nature and the Kakiemon originals, although none had been exported to Europe since the 1720s. Characteristically, although Bow made gallant if unavailing efforts to imitate Japanese patterns as faithfully as possible, no attempt was made to reproduce the shapes.

53

Bow Dish, ca. 1755–56

Of deep rectangular shape, decorated in the Kakiemon taste with pine, bamboo, prunus, two cranes, and a "flaming tortoise."

LENGTH: 8¼ in. (21.0 cm)
MARK: None
LITERATURE: Spero, "A Taste entirely new," cat. no. 13, for the Chelsea version
ACCESSION NUMBER: 1991.40.70

Derived from a late-seventeenth-century Japanese original (cat. no. 54), this pattern was used at Meissen in the mid-1720s and at Chelsea during the early 1750s. This example is less faithful to the Japanese original, in having a central motif of birds and flowers in place of the curled dragon. This central design, also inspired by Kakiemon porcelain, is an adaptation of a raised anchor period Chelsea pattern that was used in conjunction with fluted tearwares. Yet as on the rectangular dish (cat. no. 52), the Bow decorator was unable to grasp the significance of the value of the space around the decoration, which contributed so greatly to the visual impact of the Kakiemon patterns. At Chantilly, this concept proved far less elusive (see cat. no. 177). This shape of dish was also in production at Chelsea, during the gold anchor period, and at Derby.

While it is likely that many of the Bow patterns in the Kakiemon taste were derived from Meissen, there is evidence that some Japanese originals were obtained for copying. In his memorandum book for 1756, John Bowcock, clerk of the factory, noted, "May 28. Patterns received from Lady Cavendish: a Japan octagonal cup and saucer, Lady pattern . . . a Japan bread and butter plate." These were not returned until the end of the year.

53

54

54

Japanese Dish, ca. 1690

With an everted indented rim, decorated in the Kakiemon taste, with a curled dragon, surrounded by a "flaming tortoise," two cranes, and the Three Friends — pine, prunus, and bamboo.

DIAMETER: 9⅝ in. (24.5 cm)
MARK: None
LITERATURE: Ayers, Impey, and Mallet, *Porcelain for Palaces,* cat. no. 123
ACCESSION NUMBER: 1991.40.7

This Japanese prototype, which inspired patterns at Meissen, Chelsea, and Bow, embodies much of the subtlety and symbolism of the Kakiemon style. By comparison with the Bow interpretations of this design (cat. nos. 52 and 53), here there is an appreciation of the value of the undecorated areas of the porcelain. The simpler palette and more restrained use of gilding lend the design a unity and a clarity lacking on the Bow versions, for all their vitality. As with all Kakiemon porcelain, the visual effect has been achieved in fine translucent enamels, yet in a palette restricted to only four colors, together with a sparing and subtle use of gilding.

Almost every element in this design has a symbolism that was not fully understood by the English painters. The pine is symbolic of longevity, the bamboo of upright character, and the prunus blossom of sweetness. Together they are known as the Three Friends of Winter. The dragon is a benevolent creature, emblematic of fertility, while the crane symbolizes happiness and also literary elegance. The "flaming tortoise" itself, which caused such confusion to the Bow painters, was in reality a Japanese *minogame*, a water creature depicted with seaweed streaming out from its shell. The seaweed emphasizes the connotations of longevity associated with this creature.

The rim of this dish is painted with iron oxide, in a style known as *kuchibeni*, and the milky white glaze, smooth in texture, indicates that it emanates from a good central Kakiemon studio.

55

Bow Dish, ca. 1755

Of octagonal form, painted with alternating panels of emblems and flowers, with iron red panels, with a white whorl pattern.

DIAMETER: 7 in. (17.8 cm)
MARK: None
LITERATURE: Gabszewicz and Freeman, *Bow Porcelain,* cat. no. 57
ACCESSION NUMBER: 1991.40.58

This pattern originated in late-seventeenth-century Kakiemon porcelain and was imitated at Meissen in about 1730. The queen of Prussia was reputed to have presented an entire service of this pattern to Queen Caroline, wife of George II. The Chelsea version, made during the raised anchor period (ca. 1750–53), was known as the "red pannel" pattern, the panels being known as *karakusa* scrolls in Kakiemon porcelain, but the design is altogether rarer on Bow. Devised to suit octagonal shapes, this pattern seldom, if ever, is found on circular forms. In Meissen and Chelsea the pattern is associated with teawares, but the Bow version is mainly confined to plates and dishes. A Chelsea bowl decorated in this design is number 9 in this catalogue. Unlike Chelsea, devoted to luxury wares, Bow sought a middle-class market, with an emphasis on utility and practicality in its porcelain. In its large production of Kakiemon porcelain, it made available to a wider public wares that had previously been within the reach only of the wealthy, able to afford Meissen, Chelsea, and, when possible, the original Japanese porcelain. The "Middling Class of People," who had barely existed in the previous century, were to form the basis for the Bow factory's prosperity throughout the 1750s.

55

56

56

Pair of Bow Sauceboats, ca. 1755–56

Of leaf shape, with irregularly fluted sides and stalk handle, floral-molded on the underside and supported upon four stub feet, and painted with flowers and sprigs below an iron red border heightened with gilt.

LENGTH: 5½ in. (14.0 cm)

MARK: None

ACCESSION NUMBERS: 1991.40.61.1, 2

This is a rare shape, faintly echoing the Chelsea strawberry-leaf sauceboats of the red anchor period. The floral sprigs are slightly reminiscent of the style of James Welch, a painter active at Bow during the middle and late 1750s, though they lack both the detail and the substance associated with that hand. The iron red and gilt floral border is generally linked with Kakiemon patterns, especially the Quail. Yet it sometimes occurs in conjunction with European flower painting and, more surprisingly, overglaze transfer-printed designs. This border design seems to have originated at Bow.

Sauceboats were an important part of the output of the Bow factory, and at least twenty separate models were produced, although after about 1760 the range became far more restricted. Issued in pairs, they were among the earliest of all forms made at the factory, some examples dating before 1750. Sauceboats featured prominently in the output of all the early factories during the late 1740s and early 1750s, including Limehouse, Longton Hall, Lund's Bristol, Vauxhall, and Worcester. Silver sauceboats, which naturally conducted heat, were only suited to cold or warm sauces. Porcelain models therefore had the advantage of being able to contain hot sauces, such as the melted butter sauce. In her book *The art of cookery made plain and easy* (1747), Hannah Glasse, describing the recipe for this usual sauce for vegetables, twice adds the injunction, "without allowing it to boil."

John Bowcock's memorandum book for 1756 includes the entry, "1 pr. large rib'd boats 4s," a description that could correspond to this pair of sauceboats.

57

57

Pair of Bow Plates, ca. 1756–58

Of octagonal shape, painted in the Kakiemon taste, with two quail between a flowering plant and a stylized prunus tree, with scattered floral sprigs and an iron red border, heightened with gilt blossoms.

DIAMETER: 8¾ in. (22.2 cm)

MARK: None

LITERATURE: Spero, *The Price Guide to Eighteenth-Century English Porcelain*, p. 42

ACCESSION NUMBERS: 1991.40.71.1, 2

The Quail or Partridge pattern originated in early-eighteenth-century Japanese Kakiemon porcelain. This motif (*uzura*, in Japanese) was a popular idiom in Japanese paintings, pattern books, and scrolls during the seventeenth century, but it did not appear upon porcelain until the early 1700s. It immediately captured the European imagination, being enthusiastically copied, first at Meissen and Chantilly and then during the 1750s and 1760s at Chelsea, Bow, Worcester, and, to a very limited extent, at Lowestoft,

Liverpool, Plymouth, and West Pans. However, the production at Bow by far exceeded that at any other European factory, with a vast output, especially of plates and dishes.

This pair of plates corresponds exactly to those in John Bowcock's memorandum book for 15 May 1756, "Lady Stairs, partridge octagon plates" and a later entry, "Mr. Fogg, octagon dysart partridge plate 3s 6d." This price seems high when compared to "1 pair sauce-boats Mr Vere's pattern 4s" in March 1756. It seems higher still when put into a social context for the 1750s, when a laborer in London could expect to earn approximately nine shillings a week. Outside London, his wages would be reduced to five shillings a week.[1] A more likely customer for Bow, a gentleman able to live in some style, might have an income of about three hundred pounds a year, at this period.

1. Figures taken from Porter, *English Society in the Eighteenth Century*, p. 387.

58

58

Pair of Bow Dishes, ca. 1756–58

Formed as two overlapping leaves with well-defined veins, painted in the Kakiemon taste, with two quail between a flowering plant and a stylized prunus tree, with scattered floral sprigs and an iron red border, heightened with gilt blossoms.

LENGTH: 12 in. (30.5 cm)

MARKS: None

LITERATURE: Ayers, Impey, and Mallet, *Porcelain for Palaces*, cat. no. 338

ACCESSION NUMBERS: 1991.41.22.1, 2

The Quail pattern was adapted on a large variety of Bow shapes. These dishes were derived from a Meissen form of the early 1730s, which itself was copied from a late-seventeenth-century Japanese original, made for export to the Dutch market. The shape was also issued at Chelsea during the raised anchor period and at Derby. These dishes were almost certainly painted by the same hand, whereas the pair of plates (cat. no. 57) were clearly not.

The range of forms associated with the Quail pattern on Bow was enormous and included tea and coffee services, vases, bottles, openwork baskets, shell centerpieces, leaf-shaped dishes, cider jugs, butter tubs, large tureens, tankards, cutlery, chocolate cups and saucers, inkpots, beakers, sauceboats, coffee cans, shell-shaped dishes, and eggcups, together with a substantial range of plates and dishes of differing shapes. It might therefore be claimed as the single most popular pattern in mid-eighteenth-century English porcelain and would have figured prominently in the thriving export market which had been built up in America. It also represented a style of decoration that for seventy years had been out of reach of all but the wealthy and discerning classes of society. Known today as the Quail pattern, it was described at Bow as the "fine old Partridge and Wheat sheaf pattern" and was essentially an adaptation of a Meissen copy of a Kakiemon design, rather than an exact imitation. Just as the English painters mistook quail for partridges, they also confused wheat sheaves for banded hedges, though it is unlikely that such distinctions would have been either apparent or of any importance to purchasers of Bow porcelain. As at Chelsea, the word "old" seems to have been understood to refer to a Japanese pattern.

59

Bow Openwork Basket, ca. 1754–55

Painted in the Kakiemon taste, with two quail beside a stylized prunus tree and a hovering insect, within an iron red border, heightened with gilt blossoms.

DIAMETER: 4⅝ in. (11.7 cm)
MARK: None
LITERATURE: Adams and Redstone, *Bow Porcelain*, pl. 55
ACCESSION NUMBER: 1991.40.63

Although the pattern itself underwent hardly any variations in design, layout, or palette, the Quail pattern was sometimes painted with particular care and attention to detail. On these occasions the blue quail is executed in a lighter, more grayish tone, and the definition of its markings is clearer. This openwork basket, together with the leaf-shaped dish (cat. no. 61), illustrates the greater care and sensitivity of this decoration and may indicate an example of the earlier pieces in this genre. Conversely, poor quality decoration usually coincides with a later porcelain body.

One of the earliest of the many versions of this pattern at Worcester, introduced in the early 1760s on tea-wares, follows this Bow design very closely, even imitating the distinctive border motif. However, the Worcester version can be distinguished by its paste, its harder glaze, and by the fluted form invariably utilized. Nothing is more symptomatic of the priorities of the two factories, resulting from the differences between the bone-ash and soapstone bodies, than the fact that whereas all but one of the ten Worcester Quail patterns are confined to teawares, the Bow output in this design concentrated principally on dessert services.

Bow baskets in this pattern were issued in three sizes, of which this example is the smallest. The shape was derived from Meissen.

60

60

Bow Dish, ca. 1756–58

Of lobed oval form, painted in the Kakiemon taste, with two quail between a flowering plant and a stylized prunus tree, within an iron red border, heightened with gilt blossoms.

LENGTH: 7¼ in. (18.4 cm)
MARK: Painter's mark *m* in red
LITERATURE: Adams and Redstone, *Bow Porcelain*, color pl. P, illustrate the shape
ACCESSION NUMBER: 1991.47.21

The vast majority of the Quail pattern that appears on Bow is confined to a single version of the design, which employs two quail, one in blue and one in red, and a border of iron red foliage with gilt blossoms, a feature of the Bow version that does not occur at Meissen, Chantilly, or on the Kakiemon originals. The quail themselves symbolize autumn and moonlight in Japanese art.

A version of the pattern derived from Chelsea and featuring larger quail and an altogether more elaborate and freely drawn design occurs on Bow bottles and vases of the mid-1750s, and several examples are known with pink and blue quail, which presumably echo a Meissen version. There was also a Bow Quail pattern in underglaze blue. Yet for the most part, there was no attempt to parallel the increasingly elaborate variations on this theme devised at Worcester during the 1760s and 1770s, several of which strayed far from the formalized motifs of Japanese Kakiemon wares (cat. no. 152).

This shape, strongly associated with the Bow factory and apparently not used elsewhere, is often described as a spoon tray. Yet it is considerably larger than other porcelain spoon trays of the period and conforms neither to the established Worcester shape nor to the silver form from which it was derived. Furthermore, it is never found as a component of Bow tea services yet is often found among dinner wares. A possible explanation for its function is as a stand for a sauceboat. Introduced in the early 1750s, this shape also occurs in a European floral pattern and, less often, in underglaze blue.

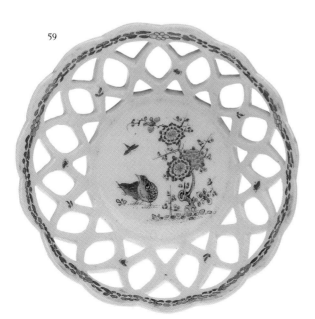

59

61

61

Bow Leaf-Shaped Dish, ca. 1755–56

Of irregular fluted form, leaf-molded on the underside and supported upon six stub feet, painted in the Kakiemon taste with two quail between a flowering plant and a stylized prunus tree, with scattered floral sprigs and an iron red border, heightened with gilt blossoms.

WIDTH: 5½ in. (14.0 cm)

MARK: None

LITERATURE: Hurlbutt, *Bow Porcelain*, pl. 23b (right-hand side)

ACCESSION NUMBER: 1991.40.59

The many contemporary references at Bow to this pattern, in invoices, accounts, and in the Bowcock memorandum books, invariably describe it as the "Partridge pattern," perhaps because the larger birds would be more familiar to prospective purchasers. Thus, John Bowcock's memorandum book for 1756 mentions "octagon nappy plates, partridge pattern," "nurl'd open partridge," and still more cryptically, a note, "To buy a partridge either alive or dead."

It is significant that whereas Chinese porcelain was being imported into England in large quantities during the mid-eighteenth century, the importation of Japanese wares, especially in the Kakiemon taste, had declined sharply by the 1720s and entirely ceased by the 1750s. Neither was Meissen in the Kakiemon taste readily available in England. These circumstances may account for the huge demand for these wares and the consequently large production at Bow, which so fueled the increasing prosperity of the factory throughout the 1750s. While at Chelsea the Kakiemon style had passed out of fashion by the mid-1750s, at Bow it remained popular well into the following decade. A notice in the *Public Advertiser* for February 1758, advertising Bow, stated, "some part of this Porcelain is very little inferior to the fine old brown edge Japan," a reference to such highly esteemed wares as the Japanese plate in the Bowles Collection (cat. no. 54), which was by this time being collected by connoisseurs of old china.

62

62

Bow Teapot, ca. 1752–54

Of lobed oval shape, painted in the Kakiemon taste, with two quail between a flowering plant and a stylized prunus tree, with scattered floral sprigs and an iron red border, heightened with gilt blossoms.

HEIGHT: 2³/₈ in. (6.0 cm)

MARK: None

LITERATURE: Gabszewicz and Freeman, *Bow Porcelain*, color pl. III, no. 51, illustrate the shape

ACCESSION NUMBER: 1991.40.60a–b

This is an extremely rare shape that originated in Japanese Kakiemon porcelain of the 1680–1700 period, though the form was probably suggested by a European design.

The Quail pattern spanned a period of at least ten or twelve years at the Bow factory. Production had begun as early as 1753. An invoice dated 5 March 1753, to the "Honb' Gen Clayton," includes "6 fine Parteridge handled Cups," costing twelve shillings and sixpence and "1 fine Parteridge Tea pot" at five shillings and sixpence, high prices at a time when such craftsmen as printers and Spitalfields silk weavers were earning two to three pounds a week.[1] Yet judging from surviving examples of this pattern, the bulk of the production dates from the 1755–65 period. John Crowther, a partner at the factory, was obliged to sell up his stock in 1764, including "beautiful deserts of the fine old partridge and wheatsheaf patterns."[2] This

teapot is likely to represent the earliest Bow examples of the Quail pattern and probably corresponds to the type of vessel ordered by General Clayton. The "handled Cups" mentioned would almost certainly have been coffee cups with the familiar Bow crabstock handle of the early 1750s. The distinction between Japanese and Chinese origins would not have seemed important to the designers of Bow, if indeed they were even aware of them. It would therefore not have seemed in any way incongruous that this Japanese-inspired shape should have been occasionally decorated in the Chinese famille rose taste.

For a factory that had perhaps the largest output of any porcelain manufactory in Europe during the 1750s and early 1760s, it is extraordinary how few teapots from Bow have survived in undamaged condition. By comparison, Worcester seems to have been a smaller-scale enterprise. Yet from this same period at least a hundred times as many Worcester teapots have survived in perfect condition. More than anything else, this comparison exemplifies the advantages of a soapstone recipe, over that of bone ash, in devising a porcelain body resistant to hot liquids.

1. Figures taken from Porter, *English Society in the Eighteenth Century*, p. 235.

2. Quoted by Mallet, in Ayers, Impey, and Mallet, *Porcelain for Palaces*, p. 54.

63

Bow Small Dish, ca. 1756–58

Of lobed oval shape, painted in the Kakiemon taste,
with two quail beside a stylized prunus tree, within
an iron red border, heightened with gilt blossoms.

WIDTH: 4 in. (10.2 cm)

MARK: None

LITERATURE: Gabszewicz and Freeman, *Bow Porcelain,*
cat. no. 64

ACCESSION NUMBER: 1991.40.60c

63

The intended function for this small dish is not clear.
It is too small for a teapot stand or for a sauceboat. A
more feasible explanation is that it was used as a
spoon tray, though this form has no counterpart in
the output of any other contemporary factory. Alternatively, it may simply have been a component part of
a large dessert service. The shape also occurs in the
Image pattern.

For a factory almost entirely preoccupied with the
manufacture of porcelain in competition with imported oriental wares, it might seem remarkable that
so little effort was made to imitate oriental shapes. Yet
to the public able to afford fine porcelain, there was
no contradiction in shapes reflecting silver or Meissen
being decorated with the fashionable oriental motifs
of the period.

The cost of Bow porcelain in the Partridge or
Quail pattern is well documented. A coffeepot cost
nine shillings in May 1756 and an "octagon dysart partridge plate, 3s 6d" later on, the same year. Prices
were apparently higher than for the white "sprig'd"
ware. Whereas a teapot such as catalogue number 62
cost five shillings and sixpence in 1753, a "sprig'd upright teapot" was priced at only three shillings in
1756. Yet these seemingly low prices, to modern eyes,
should be seen in the context of the wages of that era.
Broadly speaking, prior to 1765, laborers' wages varied from about nine to twelve shillings per week in
London, less in rural areas, while several years later,
in 1770, china painters earned ten to twelve shillings
per week.

64

Pair of Bow Dishes, ca. 1758–62

Of rectangular octagonal form, each painted with a
Chinese landscape within an oval reserved panel,
surrounded by fan-shaped and circular panels, upon
a powder blue ground.

LENGTH: 10¾ in. (27.3 cm)
MARKS: Pseudo-Chinese characters on each
LITERATURE: Adams and Redstone, *Bow Porcelain*, pl. 92
ACCESSION NUMBERS: 1991.47.30.1, 2

The powder blue ground was derived from Chinese
porcelain, where it was known as *chui qing*. It was
used at Meissen by J. G. Herold and later on at Sèvres,
where it was known as *bleu soufflé*. In England it was
produced in great quantities at Bow and at Worcester,
though in the latter factory it is most often found in
conjunction with overglaze colors (cat. no. 126). On a
smaller scale, the powder blue ground was used at
West Pans, Lowestoft, and Caughley, and, in addition, several pieces attributed to Derby have recently
been discovered. An account dated 5 March 1753 lists
"4 fine Blue Oblong Dishes" at four shillings each,[1] at
a time when a loaf of bread cost 5d. [approx. 2 pence
in today's currency].

The mottled effect achieved by the powder blue
ground was also imitated on early English pottery,
where the technique was known as "sponging." This
was attempted by Wedgwood on his bone-china
body, between about 1812 and 1820.

1. Adams and Redstone, *Bow Porcelain*, p. 85.

65

Pair of Bow Plates, ca. 1760–65

Of circular form, each painted with a Chinese
landscape within a circular reserved panel,
surrounded by fan-shaped and smaller circular
panels, upon a powder blue ground.

DIAMETER: 7½ in. (19.1 cm)
MARKS: Pseudo-Chinese characters on each
LITERATURE: Honey, *Old English Porcelain*, pl. 42C
ACCESSION NUMBERS: 1991.47.28.1, 2

The technique of the powder blue ground was first
used in China during the Kangxi period of the Qing
dynasty (1662–1722). The method involved the cobalt
blue being sprinkled onto the biscuit body, prior to
glazing. The reserved panels were masked, and the
pigment was blown through a tube, closed at the end
with gauze. The objective of this process was the
well-defined powdered ground achieved on Chinese
wares. For successful results, it was crucial that the
pigment be evenly distributed in exactly the correct
quantity.

It is generally considered that the powder blue
ground was introduced at Bow in about 1759, which
is the date noted upon the base of the celebrated bowl
inscribed, *JOHN & ANN BOWCOCK, 1759*. This bowl is
decorated on its exterior with chinoiserie scenes
within elaborate rococo reserved panels upon a powder blue ground. However, there seems no cogent reason for supposing that this bowl is proof of the exact
date for the introduction of powder blue decoration.
In the absence of any firm information one might suggest a period of production from the late 1750s until
about 1770. Judging from the large output of these
wares and some discernible changes in paste, glaze,
and overall quality, a production span of some twelve
years seems a reasonable speculation.

66

Bow Plate, ca. 1762–65

Of circular form, with a fluted rim, painted with a Chinese landscape, within a circular reserved panel, surrounded by fan-shaped and smaller circular panels, upon a powder blue ground.

DIAMETER: 8¾ in. (22.2 cm)

MARK: None

LITERATURE: Spero, *The Price Guide to Eighteenth-Century English Porcelain,* p. 58

ACCESSION NUMBER: 1991.47.20

The output of powder blue decoration at Bow was prodigious. The definition and tone of the ground color, determined by the evenness of the distribution of the pigment, varied considerably. Most often it was a rich, full tone of underglaze blue, brighter and more intense than the tone employed at Worcester. This difference in ground color between the two factories would have been deliberate. For whereas Worcester used it in conjunction with overglaze colors and would not have employed a heavy or overpowering tone of blue, the Bow powder blue was generally devised in monochrome, and therefore the strength and depth of the blue determined the visual impact.

The richness and depth of the finest Bow grounds contrast starkly with the poorly defined and much darker powder blue of later examples and underline the likelihood of a ten- or twelve-year production span for this decoration.

67

Bow Dish, ca. 1760–65

Of lobed square shape, painted with a Chinese landscape within a circular reserved panel, surrounded by fan-shaped and smaller circular panels, upon a powder blue ground.

WIDTH: 8 in. (20.3 cm)

MARK: None

LITERATURE: Adams and Redstone, *Bow Porcelain,* pl. 92

ACCESSION NUMBER: 1991.47.15

In general terms, the Bow powder blue was a richer, more vibrant tone than that of Worcester or Caughley, although it was generally a less well defined powdered ground. Lowestoft was altogether less successful in both definition and tone. The inky tone of underglaze blue made the Lowestoft version seem very dark and heavy, and it sometimes had an almost solid appearance, far removed from the Chinese originals. While some shapes decorated in this idiom were limited only to Bow, others, such as kidney-shaped dishes, octagonal plates, and the fluted bordered form (cat. no. 66), were produced both at Worcester and Caughley.

The fan-shaped reserved panels associated with the powder blue ground also occur on Worcester and Caughley, but in the case of Lowestoft, the panels are of irregular form, resembling billowing clouds.

66

67

68

Bow Teapot and Cover, ca. 1760–65

Painted with two Chinese landscapes within fan-shaped reserved panels, upon a powder blue ground, the cover similarly decorated.

HEIGHT: 4¾ in. (12.1 cm)
MARK: Pseudo-Chinese characters
LITERATURE: Gabszewicz and Freeman, *Bow Porcelain,* cat. no. 104
ACCESSION NUMBER: 1991.40.81a–b

The powder blue ground is relatively uncommon in conjunction with tewares. This teapot displays the rich, vivid ground color often associated with the mid-1760s. Another feature suggestive of this period is the somewhat small loop handle.

While the bulk of this decoration at Bow was confined to dessert wares, the powder blue ground does occur on a wide range of utilitarian forms. These include eggcups, mugs, coffee cans, tureens and ladles, openwork baskets, guglets, vases of various forms, bowls, tewares, and jardinieres.

The first newspaper advertisement for tea appeared in 1658, in *Mercurius Politicus,* announcing the arrival of "that excellent and by all Physitians approved China drink, called by the Chineans Tcha, by other nations Tay, alias Tee." The earliest English porcelain teapots tended to be of relatively small size, reflecting the high cost of tea, and to be decorated in the Chinese taste, which was so firmly associated with the habit of tea drinking.

69

Bow Plate, ca. 1758–60

Decorated with a large central panel and four smaller panels of lobed rectangular shape, containing the Hundred Antiques, and four small circular panels of insects, all reserved upon a powder blue ground.

DIAMETER: 9¼ in. (23.5 cm)
MARK: Pseudo-Meissen crossed swords in underglaze blue
LITERATURE: Spelman, *Lowestoft China,* pl. LXIV, fig. 1, wrongly attributed
ACCESSION NUMBER: 1991.40.67

Perhaps surprisingly, there is comparatively little variation in the scenes within the central panels of Bow powder blue dessert wares. This example affords a refreshing contrast and is much closer in feeling to its Chinese counterpart, although the presence of a pseudo-Meissen mark suggests associations with Meissen in either pattern or shape, although the forms can be traced back to Chinese Kangxi porcelain. At any event, this relatively rare design is particularly successful. So too is the equally unusual "solid" powder blue ground, which, like the design illustrated here, principally occurs on plates.

An extremely rare variation on this theme was the powder manganese ground, which is known on several Bow tea bowls and saucers. Manganese was the only color, other than blue, to be successfully used in Europe underglaze. The few examples recorded are all marked with crossed swords, once again suggesting a derivation from Meissen. An underglaze manganese was also used, experimentally, on triangle period Chelsea and early Worcester.

69

Bow Plate, ca. 1758–60

Of octagonal shape, painted with a central quatrefoil panel enclosing two Chinamen in a landscape, one of them pointing to a large vase mounted upon a pedestal and inscribed BOW on the base, surrounded by panels containing Buddhist emblems, all upon a powder blue ground.

DIAMETER: 8½ in. (21.6 cm)
MARK: None
LITERATURE: Adams and Redstone, *Bow Porcelain,* color pl. M
ACCESSION NUMBER: 1991.47.9

Twelve plates from this service are recorded, one of which is in the Victoria and Albert Museum. The humorous and somewhat cryptic scene depicted is open to a certain degree of interpretation as it contains a delightful element of self-mockery. However, the likely intention was to convey the astonishment and admiration of the two Chinamen on seeing so fine a "Chinese" vase, inscribed BOW. In this light the plates might have been intended as a humorous advertisement for a factory much preoccupied with the production of porcelain in the Chinese taste.

Whereas Bow was very successful in the manufacture of plates and dishes, as is evident from the examples in the Bowles Collection, its main competitor, Worcester, was not able fully to overcome the difficulties in firing such pieces until the 1760s and did not engage in the large-scale production of dinner services for a further ten years, allowing Bow a crucial commercial advantage in this important aspect of production.

Lowestoft Coffeepot and Cover, ca. 1768–70

Decorated with panels of underglaze blue scale, alternating with panels of oriental figures, flowering plants, and quail, in the Kakiemon taste.

HEIGHT: 8¾ in. (22.2 cm)
MARK: None
LITERATURE: Corson, *Variety in Lowestoft Porcelain,* cat. no. 117
ACCESSION NUMBER: 1986.87.2a–b

This is a very rare pattern, known only on Lowestoft coffeepots. It combines the underglaze blue scale, from the Robert Browne pattern, with three pseudo-Kakiemon designs, a form of decoration otherwise unrecorded on Lowestoft. During the late 1760s, the Lowestoft factory expanded its output to include overglaze decoration, and for several years much of the painting was of high quality and the ambitious and enterprising patterns seemed set to compete with such factories as Bow, Christian's Liverpool, and even Worcester. However, by the mid-1770s the range of patterns had narrowed and the standard of painting had declined, as the factory began to concentrate on the simple, repetitive Chinese-style designs that were to characterize production during the 1780s. The contours of the spout, the handle form, low domed cover, and the overall shape are all typical features of Lowestoft coffeepots of the late 1760s and early 1770s.

71

70

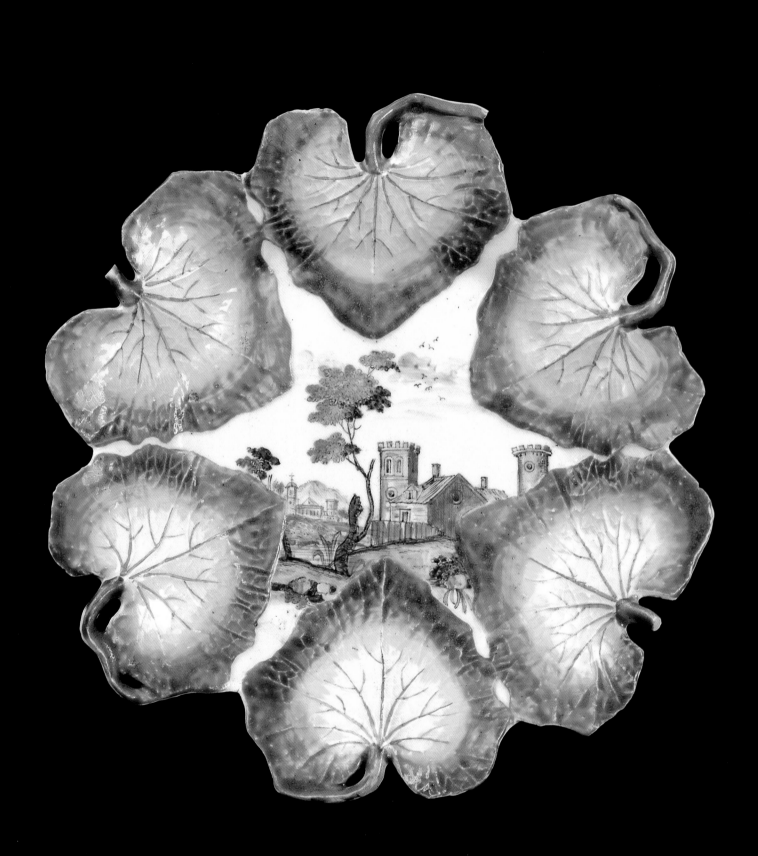

· LONGTON HALL ·

1750–1760

Longton Hall
Leaf-Molded Dish
Cat. no. 74

L ONGTON HALL, founded in 1750, was the first commercially successful Staffordshire porcelain factory, thereby initiating in its brief lifetime a
proud tradition that prevails to the present day. The principal figures were
William Jenkinson, William Nicklin, and William Littler. Of these, it was
Littler, an experienced potter, who became the motivating force at the factory, providing a crucial link with Staffordshire pottery and, in particular,
salt-glazed stoneware.

The earliest productions consisted almost exclusively of figures, a curious departure from convention, which finds parallels only with Derby,
among other early English porcelain factories. These early figure models,
with their thick glaze, glassy paste, and poorly defined features, have become known as the Snowman family. There followed a brief period from
about 1752–53, when almost every single factory shape, together with most
of the decoration, showed an overriding Meissen influence. Whereas some
shapes, such as the leaf-shaped sauceboats (cat. no. 75), were adopted at
other English factories, several others were not attempted elsewhere. From
about 1754 onward the distinctive Longton Hall style began to emerge,
which by April 1757 was being described in the London *Public Advertiser*
as "new and curious Porcelain or China . . . of the LONGTON HALL MANUFAC-
TORY." The advertisement went on to elaborate on the wares, "consisting of
Tureens, Covers and Dishes, large Cups and Covers, Jars and Beakers, with
beautiful Sprigs of Flowers, open-work'd Fruit Baskets and Plates, Variety
of Services for Deserts, Tea and Coffee Equipages, Sauce Boats, leaf Basons
and Plates, Melons, Colliflowers, elegant Epargnes and other ornamental
and useful Porcelain, both white and enamell'd."

Unlike at Bow and Worcester, the oriental influence at Longton Hall
was restricted to underglaze blue decoration, together with a relatively
small range of polychrome patterns. The Kakiemon idiom, so important
an element on Chelsea and Bow, was almost completely absent on Longton
Hall porcelain. Instead, a style was developed that incorporated shapes and
motifs derived from Meissen, augmented by a free and at times capricious
interpretation of the rococo, which had its roots in the contemporary Staffordshire potteries. Here was a truly original ceramic style, suggested by

the severe rococo shapes of Meissen, yet entirely transformed by idiosyncratic adaptations, uninhibited modeling, and an exuberant palette into what was perhaps the most unself-consciously English of all classes of eighteenth-century porcelain. From this emerged the range of naturalistic forms with which the factory is so much associated. These leaf-molded forms often mirrored Chelsea counterparts, themselves derived from Meissen. Yet just as many of the Longton Hall figures, with their awkward rococo scroll bases, were original creations, so too were some of the domestic wares. Both the swirling asymmetrical spoon tray (cat. no. 78) and the melon-shaped teapot (cat. no. 73) come into this category. The teapot, an extreme expression of the rococo style, appears wildly impractical, even by the standards of this vogue for naturalism. The spout and handle seem especially unsuited to the functions of a teapot, and the overall design seems to have been determined by an intention to startle, or even deceive, in the manner of trompe l'oeil. Its origins owe something to contemporary Staffordshire potteries, such as Fenton, and possibly in its leaf-molded feet, to rococo silver. It represents an extreme embodiment of a defining mid-eighteenth-century characteristic, in which purely functional, utilitarian objects became vehicles for exotic designs. At Longton Hall, the rococo style was interpreted with more spirit and panache than understanding, and it was this element of naivety that contributed to the freshness and originality of the factory's production.

It was these spirited and uninhibited rococo forms that especially appealed to Mr. and Mrs. Bowles. They are unlike anything else in early English porcelain, an individuality reinforced by their distinctive palette with its shades of green, either bright or yellowish in tone. At their best and most extrovert, they represent an original contribution to the field of eighteenth-century ceramics, in what might be termed "country rococo."

72

72

Longton Hall Tureen and Stand, ca. 1756

Naturalistically modeled in the form of a cos lettuce, the oval body molded with overlapping leaves and the stand similarly decorated and molded.

LENGTH OF STAND: 12¼ in. (31.1 cm)

MARK: None

LITERATURE: Peirce, *English Ceramics: The Frances and Emory Cocke Collection,* cat. no. 142

ACCESSION NUMBER: 1991.40.1a–c

An advertisement in *Aris's Birmingham Gazette* in June 1757, for the "new and curious Porcelain or China . . . of the LONGTON HALL MANUFACTORY," describes a "Variety of Services for Deserts with Figures and flowers of all Sorts made exactly to Nature." This last phrase embodies a claim that was fully justified by the range of vegetable tureens, fruit boxes, leaf-molded wares, and leaf-shaped dishes made at the Staffordshire factory during the mid-1750s. At their best they excelled even their Chelsea counterparts, and the potters had sufficient confidence in the plastic-ity of their material to leave substantial areas of porcelain free of painted embellishment. Yet the problems experienced in manufacture are evident in the interior of this tureen, with painted leaves placed in such a manner as to disguise firing blemishes.

This particular model was also made at Chelsea and is described in the 1755 Chelsea sale catalogue for the fifteenth day's sale, on Wednesday, 26 March, lot 31: "Two fine coss lettices and two leaves." Whether the Longton Hall version was inspired by Chelsea or taken directly from the Meissen original is uncertain and may never be proven either way. That a demand existed so far from the metropolis for such ambitious and frivolous trompe l'oeil is perhaps a measure of the wealth and taste of the local landowners who most surely would have numbered among Littler's customers. Indeed, the advertisement in the London *Public Advertiser* of the previous month claimed that the china had been "recommended by several of the Nobility."

73

73

Longton Hall Teapot and Cover, ca. 1756

In the form of a melon, naturalistically modeled and colored, supported upon triangular leaf feet, with a spout formed by two leaves and a rustic stalk handle.

HEIGHT: 4½ in. (11.4 cm)

MARK: None

LITERATURE: Watney, "A Study of Longton Hall Teapots," fig. 7

ACCESSION NUMBER: 1991.40.3a–b

An extraordinary range of teapots was devised at Longton Hall, modeled in the guises of cabbages, melons, pineapples, and even tulips. The handles, and in particular the spouts, were often designed more for visual effect than for practicality. These daring expressions of the rococo style are without parallel in early English porcelain, and it is surprising, to say the least, that they spring from a Staffordshire factory, remote from metropolitan centers of fashion. That Meissen was a potent inspiration on the Longton Hall potters

is evident from such shapes as the cos lettuce–leaf sauceboat (cat. no. 75), but whether the whole corpus of leaf-molded vegetable forms can be ascribed to this influence is quite another matter. Just as many Longton Hall figures were original creations, it is likely that some of the more fanciful naturalistic forms echo Meissen porcelain and German faience in spirit, rather than in substance. This melon form was clearly popular, for it occurs with a powder blue ground, on West Pan's porcelain, and also "in the white." Needless to say, both versions look startlingly different from this example, swathed in naturalistic colors.

At Chelsea, trompe l'oeil of this kind was almost invariably intended "for desart," and it is difficult to envisage this vessel, startling in its appearance, as being a dependable conduit for the pouring of tea. More probably, it too was principally designed for visual rather than gastronomic stimulation.

Longton Hall Leaf-Molded Dish, ca. 1756

Molded in relief with six hollyhock leaves, pointing inward toward a central landscape incorporating turreted buildings and a church in the background.

DIAMETER: 8½ in. (21.6 cm)

MARK: None

LITERATURE: Watney, *Longton Hall Porcelain*, pl. 36A

ACCESSION NUMBER: 1991.40.2

A characteristic Longton Hall shape, this dish is similar in form to a Chelsea model of the same period, both inspired by Meissen. Yet the typical Longton Hall palette, especially its tones of green, sets it apart from its Chelsea counterparts and imbues it with greater vitality, wholehearted and uninhibited, with no hint of restraint. The decoration by the "Castle Painter" strongly resembles that on the spoon tray (cat. no. 78) in subject, palette, and in the treatment of the buildings and trees. This distinctive form seems to have been confined at Longton Hall to the mid-1750s and was not made at West Pans in Scotland, where Littler opened a new factory in 1764. Five glazed fragments from this shape of dish were discovered during excavations on the Longton Hall factory site carried out between 1955 and 1971. Two of these fragments were decorated with colored enamels.

Longton Hall Sauceboat, ca. 1753–54

Of cos lettuce–leaf form, with a branch handle and modeled with bunches of figs and flowers, painted with bouquets of flowers.

LENGTH: 5½ in. (14.0 cm)

MARK: Script *P* in puce

LITERATURE: Watney, *Longton Hall Porcelain*, pl. 28A

ACCESSION NUMBER: 1986.87.1

The cos lettuce–leaf shape of sauceboat spans the entire period of production of Longton Hall domestic wares, in both color and underglaze blue. The basic shape, derived from Meissen, was also used at Worcester and, in somewhat differing adaptations, at Derby, Champion's Bristol, and West Pans.

This particular example is transitional, between the Snowman period of the early 1750s and the middle period (1754–57). It is a peculiarity of these wares that not only do all the shapes echo Meissen originals, but the decoration, too, is strongly inspired by the German factory. Naturally, this Meissen influence is overlaid by a rustic naivety emphasized by the thick glaze and lumpy potting. Yet the individuality of these pieces is heightened by a palette reminiscent of Staffordshire salt glaze. The comparatively early period of this sauceboat is evident from the palette of the floral bouquet, from the distinctive tone of pink on the figs, and from the tone of green, a little paler than on most wares of several years later. This fusion of Meissen shapes and decorative motifs, absorbed into Staffordshire traditions and colors, makes this brief period in the factory's production unique in the early years of Britain's porcelain industry.

75

76

76

Pair of Longton Hall Wine Tasters, ca. 1755–56

Of peach shape, the exteriors modeled in high relief with flowers, buds, and leaves, an entwined branch forming the handle and feet, and decorated in the interior, in *puce camaïeu*, with houses and trees in landscapes.

DIAMETER: 4¾ in. (12.1 cm)
MARK: None
LITERATURE: Watney, *Longton Hall Porcelain*, pl. 67A
ACCESSION NUMBERS: 1991.40.5.1, 2

Derived from an early-eighteenth-century Kangxi bridal cup, or libation cup, this distinctive form occurs at Longton Hall with differing molded designs on the exterior, though the basic shape remains the same. This rare form was also made at Worcester (cat. no. 81) in a smaller diameter and in salt-glaze stoneware and redware. While the colored examples all seem to date from the mid-1750s, those with underglaze blue decoration span almost the entire period of the factory's production. The interior scenes are painted by an anonymous hand known as the "Castle Painter," tentatively ascribed by Dr. Bernard Watney to John Hayfield. Hayfield, who seems to have made

a speciality of landscapes and buildings in the Continental style, was named in the Third Agreement, dated 1 September 1755, a lengthy legal document between Littler and the factory's other proprietors. In it, Hayfield is identified as being paid one guinea a week. He was apparently the only painter at the factory at that time, for the agreement enjoined Littler, the manager, to employ "one painter and no more at the same time," a curious and somewhat unlikely injunction. In the light of the probable size of production at Longton Hall in the mid-1750s, it seems hardly possible that the agreement was fully adhered to in this instance. Indeed, an advertisement concerning Longton Hall in the *Daily Advertiser* in January and February 1758 noted, "Skilful China Painters in the Dresden and Roman Taste will meet with great Encouragement." At Bow, admittedly a much larger factory, Thomas Craft, one of the principal decorators, recalled in a written testimony that in about 1760, the factory employed "300 persons; about 90 painters."[1]

1. Quoted in Adams and Redstone, *Bow Porcelain*, p. 46.

77

77

Pair of Longton Hall Basins, ca. 1758

Of leaf-molded form, molded in high relief on the exterior with pansies and strawberry leaves and painted in the interior with bouquets of flowers and scattered sprigs.

DIAMETER: 8¾ in. (22.2 cm)
MARK: None
LITERATURE: Watney, *Longton Hall Porcelain*, pl. 58A, for a pair of basins with their stands
ACCESSION NUMBERS: 1991.40.6.1, 2

These characteristic Longton Hall forms, echoed in cream jugs and cider jugs, were designed to have leaf-shaped stands, painted with either flowers or birds. The shape appears to be unique to the factory and does not occur with underglaze blue decoration. The floral decoration in the interior owes something to Meissen and perhaps also to red anchor period Chelsea, but the slightly hesitant style and the purplish pink tone are typical of Longton Hall; this painting recurs frequently on teawares of the late 1750s. Pansies and strawberry-leaf molding were characteristic motifs on Longton Hall plates, dishes, and tureens during the later 1750s. The overall design of these basins exemplifies the imagination and inventiveness of the factory with a distinctive rococo flamboyance, which has no parallels in any other English porcelain. The resonance of the vivid Longton Hall palette, with its unexpected juxtaposition of colors, made an enormous contribution to the artistic style of the factory, and its importance is emphasized by the parallels with Littler's porcelain made at West Pans, in Scotland, from 1764 to 1777. Although Littler reissued many of his distinctive leaf-molded shapes, including stands for these basins, their dull and restrained palette and poor-quality glaze utterly changed their aesthetic impact. This particular shape surely corresponds to the "leaf Basons" itemized in the London *Public Advertiser* in April 1757.

78

Longton Hall Spoon Tray, ca. 1756–58

Of asymmetrical star shape, painted with a turreted edifice, flanked by a church and a sailing boat, in a wooded landscape.

DIAMETER: 8½ in. (21.6 cm)
MARK: None
LITERATURE: Watney, *Longton Hall Porcelain*, pl. 65A
ACCESSION NUMBER: 1991.40.4

Both the shape of this spoon tray and the decoration are facets of the Longton Hall production that do not occur at any other factory. The country scene, with its castellated building, church, and boat, typifies the style associated with the "Castle Painter," whose work occurs on teawares, leaf dishes, and sauceboats. His predilection for landscapes in the Continental taste, seldom including figures, is evident here, especially in the smaller turreted building. The swirling form, with its restless energy, is one of the factory's most adventurous essays into the rococo style, and the faintly rustic, unsophisticated element of the design adds a refreshing measure of individuality. These flowing curves are distantly evocative of the bases of Nymphenburg figures, though the linear rhythm and asymmetric balance have not been fully mastered. The same basic form in Longton Hall was adapted in a more elongated version, and it occurs in various styles of decoration, including underglaze blue. Often described as a teapot stand, it is more likely to have been an alternative form of spoon tray.

78

· WORCESTER ·

1751–present

Worcester Wall Pocket
Cat. no. 89

THE WORCESTER FACTORY was founded by deed of partnership in June 1751 and has continued in an unbroken period of production until the present day. The measure of this astonishing achievement may be judged by the experiences of other contemporaneous factories, seeking to establish themselves artistically and commercially in the porcelain industry, which had begun to emerge in England in the late 1740s.

Some factories, such as Limehouse and Plymouth, survived for fewer than three years, while others, including Longton Hall and Richard Champion's Bristol factory, barely reached a ten-year span of production. Even the great metropolitan factories at Chelsea and Bow, established in the 1740s, had closed within thirty years. Indeed, of more than a dozen porcelain factories established in those first years of the industry, from the late 1740s until the mid-1750s, only two, Worcester and Derby, survived into the nineteenth century.

The reasons for the success of the Worcester factory, in the face of so many obstacles and so much competition at home and abroad, are inextricably bound up with the history and production of those first twenty-five years of the factory, known to collectors as the First Period, or the Dr. Wall Period. In February 1752, soon after the establishment of the Worcester partnership, the Bristol factory at Redcliffe Backs, on the River Avon, was united with Worcester. Benjamin Lund, the proprietor at Bristol, sold the lease of his soaprock mine to Richard Holdship, one of the Worcester partners, and not only were his materials and machinery sent up the river to Worcester, but he himself remained in the city for a year, enabling the partners at Warmstry House to have the benefit of his expertise and experience. This was of crucial importance, as Lund had been making porcelain for some two years, using a soapstone formula, with the aid of workmen who had previously been employed at Limehouse, in London, during the late 1740s.

By these means, the period of trial and experimentation, so essential in the early stages of porcelain manufacture, was hardly necessary at Worcester. It was this that accounted for the extraordinary degree of sophistication in terms of firing, potting, and decoration, which was achieved almost from the start of production. A further advantage for Worcester over its rival manufactories lay in the employment of the soapstone recipe, which enabled the use of a hard, close-grained body with a high, durable glaze. This was ideally suited to the manufacture of teawares, which, unlike those of other factories, could really withstand the impact of boiling water.

An anonymous contributor to the *Annual Register* in 1768 reported:

I have seen porcelain of all manufactures in Europe. Those of Dresden in Poland, and Chatillon [*sic*] in France, are well-known for their elegance and beauty, — with these I may class our own of Chelsea, which is scarce inferior to any of the others, but these are calculated rather for ornament than use, and if they were equally useful with the Oriental china, they could yet be used but by few, because they are sold at high prices. We have indeed, here, many other manufactories of porcelain, which are sold at a cheaper rate than any that is imported; but except the Worcester, they all wear brown, and are subject to crack, especially the glazing, by boiling water; the Worcester has a good body, scarce inferior to that of Eastern china; it is equally tough, and its glazing never cracks or scales off.[1]

These perceptive observations embody three of the main contributions to the commercial success of the Worcester factory: the relatively low cost, the resistance of its durable body and glaze to hot liquids, and the concentration on useful and domestic wares, rather than the more restricted market for ornamental wares and figures. To these commercial virtues should be added an acute awareness and understanding of changing fashions and styles, augmented by an unmatched ability to assimilate and absorb designs from oriental and Continental sources. The recognition of the crucial importance of transfer printing and its imaginative development was also a key factor in the continued success of the factory, especially during the 1760s.

In this way, at different periods during the first twenty-five years of production, the factory reflected the changing tastes of the times in the decorative idioms of chinoiserie, Meissen, colored grounds, Sèvres, and neoclassicism. So well designed were the Worcester shapes, and so well defined was the factory style, that these successive influences seemed almost to be a natural progression.

Alongside the vogue for porcelain was the tremendous popularity of tea drinking, which, in the eighteenth century, by virtue of its high cost and social implications, took the form of a ceremony that enabled the hostess to show off her fine china. Whereas before 1750 this china was for the most part oriental, it soon became a speciality of the Worcester factory. The beautifully designed teaware forms, practical and resistant to hot liquids, were unrivaled in English porcelain. By contrast, it was not until the late 1760s that the large-scale production of dinner services was introduced.

It is characteristic of the early years of the Worcester factory that whereas many of the shapes echoed silver models, the decoration was principally in the oriental taste, especially the Chinese famille verte and famille rose. The graceful wine funnel in this collection (cat. no. 79) illustrates this dichotomy, wherein a fine silver form is embellished with a chinoiserie theme. Far from being in any way incongruous, this affords an ideal fusion of the arts of the designer, the potter, and the decorator.

The cross-fertilization of disparate influences creating a strong visual impact upon a single piece can be traced back to the Lund's Bristol factory, the forerunner of Worcester. The Lund's mug (cat. no. 156) is a distinctive form derived from German stoneware. Thus, a German pottery shape appears in an English porcelain mug, painted in the Chinese taste. This element of paradox, involving interrelated decorative influences, recurs frequently in the Worcester section of the Bowles Collection.

While the main strength of the collection lies in the wealth of decorative styles and patterns, mainly on teawares and dessert wares, there is also a seasoning of rare forms. The elegant wine taster (cat. no. 81) is a classic shape derived from Chinese famille verte, while the extremely rare cornucopia wall pocket (cat. no. 89) represents in its serpentine contours a hint of rococo flamboyance. The soapstone body, so crucial to Worcester's success in the manufacture of domestic wares, was less suited than the bone-ash body of Bow or the glassy body of Derby to the manufacture of figures. Consequently, figures in Worcester porcelain are exceedingly rare and only a handful of models is known. The candlestick group of canaries (cat. no. 96) is one of the models only recently discovered, and in the modeling of the flowers on its bocage reveals intriguing links with the floral modeling around the handles of Worcester openwork baskets (cat. nos. 108 and 110).

The enchanting pair of plates decorated with cranes in subtle and tranquil colors (cat. no. 87) lies outside the conventional Worcester style, and indeed they may have been made as replacements for Japanese or even Meissen originals. Yet for all that, they have a slightly exotic visual impact, all the more refreshing for being unlike any other Worcester of the period. Similarly atypical of the factory is a delightful plate painted with butterflies (cat. no. 88), though in this case it is the palette, rather than the composition itself, that draws the eye. Indeed, it is perhaps the very absence of a pattern linking the butterflies, and the use of space, that is so startling.

During the late 1760s and early 1770s a significant proportion of the finest decoration on Worcester porcelain was done at the London atelier of James Giles. He was an independent decorator who had entered into an agreement with the Worcester factory, which undertook to supply him with white porcelain for him to decorate in the latest "London taste." The Giles style tended to be more flamboyant than that of the Worcester factory and also more adventurous. At its best, it was of superb quality and embellished with *ciselé* gilding. Two examples from the Bowles Collection illustrate Giles's work at its finest. The milk jug and cover (cat. no. 92) are decorated with children in the manner of David Teniers the Younger, an extremely rare style of painting not undertaken at the factory. Nor did the factory attempt the *Mosaik* borders that evolved at Meissen in about 1760–61 and were reputedly inspired by the enthusiasm of Frederick the Great.

The magnificent pair of plates (cat. no. 119) decorated in this idiom display the Giles style at its most resplendent. The sliced fruit and the pink scale *Mosaik* border echo Meissen themes of the Academic Period (1763–74), while the cornucopia-shape border, a rococo conceit, harks back to Vincennes. Yet this is an assimilation of European influences, rather than an imitation. The vibrant palette, the gilding, and the overall composition of the fruit and floral sprays convey a distinctive character and individuality that are unique to the Giles atelier.

An advertisement in the *Public Advertiser* for the sale of Worcester held in London in May 1769 lists porcelain decorated "in the beautiful colors of Mazarine Blue and Gold, Sky Blue, Pea Green, French Green, Sea Green, Purple, Scarlet and Gold," and a sale catalogue for December of the same year mentions yellow ground sauceboats. Some Worcester decorated with a yellow ground had been in production during the late 1750s, on a very limited scale, but it was not until the late 1760s that the colored grounds for which the factory became so celebrated came into prominence, a period that coincided with the closure of the Chelsea factory.

The yellow scale seems to have been derived from Meissen, although it was also used at Sèvres. The Worcester version, confined mainly to tea services, combined two separate elements, both inspired by Meissen: the yellow scale ground and exotic birds within mirror-shaped panels. The effect was extraordinarily successful, as can be seen from the examples in this collection (cat. nos. 99–101). The solid yellow, solid turquoise, and apple green grounds are more likely to have been influenced by Sèvres, and these too are all well represented in the Bowles Collection. By contrast, the direct inspiration for the claret ground tea bowl and saucer (cat. no. 118) was probably Chelsea, where the color had been firmly established by the early 1760s. The Chelsea tradition of that period is also echoed by two sumptuous plates from the famous duke of Gloucester service (cat. nos. 97 and 98), with their vivid and colorful renderings of fruit and insects.

The underglaze blue grounds, which have become almost synonymous with the First Period of the Worcester factory and contributed so much to its prosperity, were clearly admired by Mr. and Mrs. Bowles. One example of each of the three categories of blue ground will serve to illustrate the reason for the success of this decoration during the 1760s and 1770s and for its popularity among collectors today. The powder blue coffeepot (cat. no. 126), a noble and well-designed form, displays this subtle ground color to splendid effect, the ground itself acting as a backdrop to heighten the dramatic impact of the alert and fierce-looking birds. The *gros bleu*, or "wet blue," ground probably corresponds to the "Mazarine Blue and gold" of the May 1769 advertisement and was derived from Sèvres. It was regularly used as a background to offset the fable subjects painted by Jefferyes Hamett O'Neale, as on the fine plate (cat. no. 131) painted with the Bear and the Beehives. The torment and frustration of the unfortunate beast are vividly conveyed, and it is hardly necessary to be acquainted with the fable to understand the story.

Yet the underglaze blue ground most associated with Worcester is undoubtedly the blue scale. This justly famous decoration, if not literally invented at the factory, was certainly refined there to perfection. Strangely, this ground was not mentioned in the advertisement of May 1769 possibly because the ground was already in production and well known to the public. It is seen to great advantage on the broth bowl and cover (cat. no. 129), the symmetry of its outline emphasizing the richness of the decoration.

Patterns adapted from Japanese Imari are also well represented in the Bowles Collection, and it is informative to compare and contrast them with one another. For instance, one single design, with radiating panels in underglaze blue (or orange) and with a central circle of white prunus blossom, served as a basis for a whole range of "Japan" patterns (cat. nos. 143–148). Nor were the Japan patterns limited always to a purely oriental influence. The leaf-shaped dish (cat. no. 136) is decorated with a Japanese-style pattern, upon a blue scale ground, derived in part from Meissen and embellished with the lapis *caillouté* gilding of Sèvres. Thus, decorative idioms from four different countries are combined in harmony upon one single piece of porcelain.

This same cross-fertilization that might be seen as an analogue for the derivative nature of early English porcelain is also evident in the Worcester teapot (cat. no. 152). Originating in Japan, the Quail pattern had undergone a process of transformation and elaboration through its interpretation at Meissen, together with some sparkling variations on a rococo theme to its border design. Conversely, the fluted form, ear-shaped handle, and inset cover mirror the pervasive Sèvres taste which had become preeminent at Worcester by the late 1770s and which epitomized the neoclassical influence on porcelain. The pattern itself recurs on many pieces in the Bowles Collection, in the various guises adopted at Bow, Lowestoft, and Chantilly, yet it was at Worcester that this subtle Kakiemon design reached its furthest point of departure.

1. Quoted in Barrett, *Worcester Porcelain and Lund's Bristol*, p. 14.

79

Worcester Wine Funnel, ca. 1754

Of accentuated trumpet shape, painted in a brilliant famille rose palette, with flowering peony branches growing from hollow rocks and bamboo, with insects above and further flowering branches on the interior rim.

HEIGHT: 4½ in. (11.4 cm)
DIAMETER: 4¼ in. (10.8 cm)
MARK: None
LITERATURE: Spero, *Worcester Porcelain: The Klepser Collection*, color pl. 12, cat. no. 31
ACCESSION NUMBER: 1991.40.39

Derived from a George II silver original, this rare form is known in only two polychrome patterns, although this root design sometimes occurs with the principal colors reversed. The manner in which oriental themes were absorbed into the established factory style, reflecting such diverse influences as the enameled opaque white glass of South Staffordshire, Chinese famille rose, and the *indianische Blumen* of Meissen, was an achievement unique to the early years at Worcester. This multifaceted idiom, used to embellish the fluid and rhythmic contours and the eccentric rococo forms of English silver, contributed still further to the originality of these early wares. Wine funnels were issued in three basic sizes — four inches, four and a half inches, and five inches high — and some fourteen examples are known, all dating from about 1754. In addition, four blue-and-white Worcester wine funnels are recorded, two hand-painted and two larger transfer-printed examples. The shape appears not to have been made at any other factory, possibly reflecting the intrinsic unsuitability of using a porcelain vessel for this function. Indeed, the rarity of wine funnels today may be in part a consequence of their vulnerability to damage while being used. Since they were hand thrown, no regular size became standardized and the dimensions vary in both height and diameter.

Although all Worcester porcelain from the first two or three years of the factory's existence is very scarce today, the initial production was on a reasonably substantial scale. An advertisement in the *Public Advertiser* on 1 March 1754 states:

> For SALE by the CANDLE, At the Royal Exchange Coffee-house, Threadneedle-Street, On Friday the 15th Inst. at Five in the Afternoon, ABOUT 40,000 Pieces of China Ware of the Worcester Manufactory; the Commodity will speak for itself. They will be shewn at London House in Aldersgate-Street.

79

80

Worcester Sauceboat, ca. 1753–54

Of molded form, with a flat base, painted in a bright famille rose palette with floral sprays and insects and an interior border of flowers and leaves.

LENGTH: 5 in. (12.7 cm)

MARK: Painter's mark in black

LITERATURE: Spero, *Worcester Porcelain: The Klepser Collection,* cat. no. 26

ACCESSION NUMBER: 1991.47.56

This Worcester form evolved from a Lund's Bristol sauceboat, though the thumb rest on the handle has become less prominent and the handle itself less flattened in its inner surface. At Worcester the shape spans a brief period from about 1753 to 1756 and occurs in conjunction with polychrome, underglaze blue, and, less often, "pencilled" decoration. The form is considerably rarer than the pedestal-footed sauceboat produced over much the same period. At this time Worcester sauceboats were press-molded in block molds, and consequently, the molded decoration on the sides did not necessarily always correspond to that on the other half exactly. Whereas at Lowestoft and Longton Hall, for example, many molded designs lack sharpness in their contours, suggesting worn molds and consequent loss of detail, this fault is rarely, if ever, evident on Worcester. Indeed, such was the care and pride taken in this aspect

of production that the quality and intricacy of the Worcester molding were unequaled at any other English porcelain factory. This innovative form of decoration on porcelain, inspired by rococo silver, is strongly indicative of the presence of modelers from Staffordshire, working on salt-glazed stoneware. The molded and embossed designs of the 1750s served a further purpose, which was functional rather than decorative, in disguising the distortions experienced in the biscuit kiln, which afflicted such shapes as sauceboats, vases, cider jugs, and butter tubs. Thus, the Worcester designers, with typical pragmatism, made a virtue out of necessity.

Referring to the establishment of the Worcester factory in 1751, the bankruptcy papers of Richard Holdship, one of the original partners, state that the manufactory had been set up to imitate "Dresden Ware," the contemporary term for Meissen.[1] This was achieved not in the direct manner employed at Chelsea but by the more oblique means of interleaving the Chinese famille rose idiom with the *indianische Blumen* of Meissen, thereby creating an entirely innovative style with which to embellish forms primarily European in origin.

1. Watney, *English Blue-and-White Porcelain of the Eighteenth Century,* p. 36.

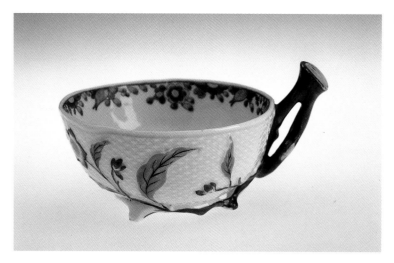

81

Worcester Wine Taster, ca. 1765

Of peach shape, with an interior famille rose border, the basket-molded exterior modeled in high relief with flowers, birds, and leaves, and an entwined branch forming the handle and feet.

DIAMETER: 3 in. (7.6 cm)

MARK: None

LITERATURE: Spero and J. Sandon, *Eighteenth-Century Worcester Porcelain: The Zorensky Collection*, chap. 2

ACCESSION NUMBER: 1991.40.21

This rare form derives from a Chinese famille verte libation cup of the early eighteenth century. Judging from the strong similarities between the known examples, these were made over a very brief period during the mid-1760s. The molded decoration and palette seem to show no variations, although two examples painted in underglaze blue came to light in the 1970s, an uncharacteristic reversal of the factory's treatment of utilitarian shapes.

The only other English factories to produce this form were Bow and Longton Hall. The Longton Hall examples are larger in diameter and tend to be more shallow (cat. no. 76). However, the shape occurs in both salt-glazed stoneware and redware. The exact function of these pieces is uncertain, but the shape in English porcelain was confined entirely to 1752–65.

82

Worcester Teapot and Cover, ca. 1760–62

Of widely fluted form, painted with a prominent Chinese figure in a long purple robe, his hand raised, and, on the reverse, a lady holding a fan, accompanied by a child, flanked by rocks, a tree, and famille rose flowers.

HEIGHT: 6 in. (15.2 cm)

MARK: None

LITERATURE: Spero and J. Sandon, *Eighteenth-Century Worcester Porcelain: The Zorensky Collection*, chap. 3

ACCESSION NUMBER: 1991.41.20a–b

82

This distinctive pattern, the Beckoning Chinaman, is principally confined to Worcester mugs, teapots, and cider jugs, though it is occasionally found on other tea-wares. The design on the reverse, of a lady and child, is often omitted on mugs and jugs and replaced by a large spray of flowers, usually painted in a brilliant famille rose palette, somewhat in the style of Meissen. Indeed, the parallels with Meissen extend to the pattern as a whole, with the tall robed figure, freely drawn rockwork, and the lady and child on the reverse all evoking Meissen themes of the late 1720s. The pattern seems to have evolved from earlier Worcester designs in this idiom and was one of the first in polychrome to become established at the factory. It spans a period from about 1755 until the mid-1760s. A version was also produced at Christian's Liverpool factory, where it seems only to have been issued on teapots. In many respects these closely resemble their Worcester counterparts but may be distinguished by the differences in palette, tone of glaze, and a marked tendency to show glaze imperfections.

Up until the late 1760s, the undersides of the flanges of Worcester teapot lids were fully glazed. Thereafter, these areas were unglazed, like their Caughley counterparts. This rule of thumb applies also to the lids of Worcester milk jugs, tea cannisters, sucriers, and coffeepots.

The habit of tea drinking was introduced into England in the mid-seventeenth century, but due to high taxation, first levied in 1698, it was not until the end of the eighteenth century that it became widespread among all classes of society. Initially, tea was imported mainly from China, and only later did the varieties from India and Ceylon become readily available.

83

Worcester Teapot and Cover, ca. 1760–62

Transfer printed in black and painted in enamel colors with oriental figures and two bulls within a landscape.

HEIGHT: 4 3/8 in. (11.1 cm)
MARK: None
LITERATURE: Spero and J. Sandon, *Eighteenth-Century Worcester Porcelain: The Zorensky Collection,* chap. 13
ACCESSION NUMBER: 1991.40.36a–b

This well-known pattern, the Red Bull, derived from the Yongzheng period Chinese porcelain, occurs only with the addition of overglaze enamel colors. It was in production from about 1754 until about 1765 and appears on a wide range of forms. Among the earliest of these are octagonal teawares in two sizes, mustard pots — both "wet" and "dry" — finger bowls and stands, deep pickle-leaf dishes, and flared hexagonal bowls. A fragment of this pattern, fully colored, was discovered among biscuit wasters of early Worcester wares in the grounds of the King's School in Diglis, Worcester, in 1973.[1] A related pattern, in underglaze blue, was used at Bow and Derby.

Throughout the first thirty or more years of the factory's existence, the vast majority of the output was of utilitarian domestic wares. Consequently, for all their enticing molded forms and chinoiserie patterns, the reputation of the factory depended upon the practicality of the various shapes. In this respect, Worcester was preeminently successful. Teapots and sauceboats poured well, tea bowls and coffee cups withstood high temperatures, and robustly potted tankards were formed with a satisfyingly low center of gravity. Furthermore, the durable glaze avoided the tendency to chip, a fault experienced at Bow and Vauxhall and endemic to tin-glazed earthenware. These factors, along with the introduction and imaginative development of overglaze transfer printing, were crucial ingredients to the prosperity and commercial security of the Worcester factory throughout the 1760s.

1. J. Sandon, *The Dictionary of Worcester Porcelain, 1751–1851,* p. 275.

83

84

84

Worcester Bowl, ca. 1762–65

Transfer printed in black and painted in enamel colors with oriental figures and two bulls within a landscape.

DIAMETER: 5 in. (12.7 cm)
MARK: None
LITERATURE: Spero, *Worcester Porcelain: The Klepser Collection*, cat. no. 190
ACCESSION NUMBER: 1991.41.26

The advantage of the technique of transfer-printed outlines was that it required far less skill and experience on the part of the painter than did purely hand-painted patterns. In addition to this, the printing process encouraged the use of detailed designs, such as this, the Red Bull pattern. In these circumstances, it is surprising that the vast majority of colored Worcester porcelain of the First Period is purely hand painted.

This size of bowl would have been a component of a tea service, but it is likely that some of the larger sizes were sold separately. The wholesale price list of about 1755–56, which has survived from the factory's London warehouse, cites bowls (described as "Basons") in half-pint, pint, and quart sizes, all priced per dozen. The likelihood that many bowls were available separately is reinforced by the many patterns, both overglaze and in underglaze blue, that occur only on bowls.

85

Worcester Bowl, ca. 1768–70

Decorated with groups of oriental figures and furniture, transfer printed in outline and filled in with enamel colors.

DIAMETER: 7½ in. (19.1 cm)
MARK: None
LITERATURE: Spero, *Worcester Porcelain: The Klepser Collection*, cat. no. 82
ACCESSION NUMBER: 1991.40.32

The technique of oriental figures transfer printed in outline and filled in with enamel colors was limited at Worcester to a small range of patterns, though several were produced in large quantities. The best-known examples are the one illustrated here and the Red Bull pattern (cat. nos. 83 and 84), dating from several years earlier. A similar style of decoration was in use at Bow during approximately the same period, though with far less successful results. The patterns incorporating Chinese figures, which came into vogue at Worcester in the 1760s, were often almost literal copies of oriental originals, whereas the chinoiserie designs of the 1750s owe more to an interpretation through the medium of delftware and, occasionally, Meissen. Here, the decoration includes no fewer than nine Chinese figures, two of whom are pointing at a monkey, while in the interior other figures are smoking pipes. The precise function of the various sizes of "bason," sold by the dozen, is uncertain and was probably left to the discretion of the customer.

85

Worcester Cream Jug, ca. 1768

Painted in the famille rose taste with an oriental lady seated at an elaborate loom, with flowering plants growing from rockwork on the reverse.

HEIGHT: 3¾ in. (9.5 cm)

MARK: None

LITERATURE: Spero and J. Sandon, *Eighteenth-Century Worcester Porcelain: The Zorensky Collection,* chap. 4

ACCESSION NUMBER: 1991.40.78

This cream jug displays one of two delightful patterns that share the theme of the Spinning Maiden. Although this version seems to be an exact copy of Chinese export porcelain, an earlier one is clearly influenced by the Meissen chinoiseries of the 1730s. Following the standard practice on nearly all early English porcelain, the principal portion of the decoration, incorporating the main decorative motif, is placed to the left of the handle. By comparison with the slightly later cream jug (cat. no. 91), the curve of the body is lower down, thereby balancing the weight of the handle. The handle itself is more generously proportioned than on the later cream jug.

The undated price card from the Worcester factory's London warehouse, most probably drawn up in about 1755–56, lists "Milk jugs, round and press'd" at eight and twelve shillings per dozen and "Cream ewers, ribb'd and pannel'd" at nine shillings, thus making a distinction between vessels for milk and cream. It was not until the early 1760s that "milk-pots and covers" (cat. nos. 92 and 138) were introduced. As a general rule, whereas milk jugs, milk pots, and upright cream jugs were sold as components of tea and coffee services, cream boats (or ewers) were sold separately or in pairs.

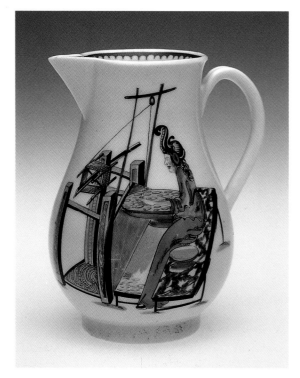

86

87

87

Pair of Worcester Plates, ca. 1770

Decorated with two cranes, one standing and the other in flight, surrounded by flowering trees, prunus, and bamboo, within a narrow plain gilt border.

DIAMETER: 9 in. (22.9 cm)

MARK: None

LITERATURE: Spero and J. Sandon, *Eighteenth-Century Worcester Porcelain: The Zorensky Collection*, chap. 7

ACCESSION NUMBERS: 1991.40.15.1, 2

One of the finest of all the Worcester interpretations of an oriental design, this pattern was inspired by a Japanese Arita original, although the shape echoes that of Meissen. On Worcester the pattern is known only on plates in two shapes, and it is likely that some were made as replacements. Their comparative rarity would certainly support this contention. Both the style of painting and the palette are remarkably faithful to the Japanese original. It is notable that the gild-

ing is used not only as a highlight but as an integral part of the decoration. The design itself, allusive, yet somewhat altered from the Japanese original, depicts the *sochikubai*, or the Three Friends of Winter, the pine, bamboo, and prunus blossom. The delightful, if somewhat puzzling, green fan-shaped objects have been misinterpreted as stylized pine needles, rather than the trefoils of the Japanese original.

Imports of Japanese porcelain had been suspended during the early part of the eighteenth century and consequently neither the Kakiemon nor the Imari wares were available in England. These were highly prized, and at Meissen, Chelsea, and Worcester the styles were imitated enthusiastically. However, it was at Worcester and at Derby that exact replacements for Chinese and Japanese originals became a speciality, and during the 1770s especially both factories responded positively to this demanding challenge.

Worcester Plate, ca. 1770–72

Of fluted form painted in the Kakiemon taste with stylized butterflies, five around the rim and two facing one another in the center.

DIAMETER: 8¼ in. (21.0 cm)

MARK: None

LITERATURE: Ayers, Impey, and Mallet, *Porcelain for Palaces*, cat. no. 334, for a Chelsea example

ACCESSION NUMBER: 1991.40.46

This is an extraordinary pattern that derived originally from Japanese Kakiemon porcelain of the late seventeenth century. It was used at Chantilly in the late 1730s to a most delightful effect, an example of which is a five-lobed tea bowl and saucer in the Metropolitan Museum of Art in New York. In England it occurs on Chelsea of the red anchor period, dating from 1753–54, and at Worcester during the early 1770s. Although the design itself remains unaltered through these various transitions, apart from variations in palette, the effect achieved is startlingly different. While the use of space and lack of distraction in the design is characteristic of Kakiemon and Chantilly porcelain, the symmetry is most unexpected. The Chelsea and Worcester examples are of such rarity as to give rise to the possibility that they are replacements for Japanese or Chantilly originals. However, both the Chelsea and Worcester versions occur on shapes that are absolutely typical of their factory and period.

88

89   *Ill. p. 82*

Worcester Wall Pocket, ca. 1756–58

Of cornucopia form, molded with cows grazing before a church in a rocky wooded landscape, and painted with a large bouquet of flowers and scattered sprays.

HEIGHT: 9½ in. (24.1 cm)

MARK: None

LITERATURE: Wills, *English Pottery and Porcelain*, color pl. 36, illustrates a slightly different model

ACCESSION NUMBER: 1991.40.53

Worcester wall pockets, sold in pairs and known in some five different molded designs, were almost entirely confined to the 1756–62 period. This form, derived from salt-glazed stoneware, is the rarest of the models. All examples are more commonly decorated in underglaze blue, and indeed overglaze painting occurs on only three of the molds. This rare wall pocket is well modeled and superbly painted, though the painted decoration shows little regard for the subtleties of the relief molding. By contrast, the underglaze blue version of this mold perfectly complements the superbly modeled pastoral scene. Wall pockets of cornucopia shape were also made at Bow, Derby, Vauxhall, Lowestoft, and Gilbody's Liverpool factory, as well as in delft creamware and salt-glaze stoneware. The shape seems to have fallen out of fashion by about 1770, and Worcester examples almost all date from before 1765. Indeed, the popularity of the form in all ceramic factories waned during the 1770s, as rococo forms yielded to the neoclassical style. An undated price card for the Worcester factory's London warehouse in Aldergate Street, listing wholesale prices, quotes "cornucopias 1st and 2nd" at "2/3 and 2/6" depending on size. Judging from the shapes listed, the price card probably dates from about 1755–56.

Worcester Teapot and Cover, ca. 1770

Of globular form, decorated with a large bouquet of flowers and scattered sprays, the cover having a floral knop.

HEIGHT: 4½ in. (11.4 cm)

MARK: None

LITERATURE: Spero, *Worcester Porcelain: The Klepser Collection*, cat. no. 72

ACCESSION NUMBER: 1991.40.86a–b

By comparison with the cream jug (cat. no. 91), the floral decoration on this piece shows no oriental influence. In this instance, it is a generalized Meissen style that has been assimilated, evolving through the tradition of floral decoration established at Chelsea during the red anchor period. The compact and dense floral bouquet is typical of the Factory style and contrasts with the looser and freer bouquets that characterize the work of the London atelier of James Giles. This form became an established standard shape at Worcester from the late 1750s until the introduction of the Sèvres shapes in the 1770s (cat. no. 152). Its longevity is a tribute to the simple yet practical design, which poured well and never cracked on the impact of boiling water, and its success enabled Worcester to lead the market in the manufacture of teawares for almost the whole of the second half of the eighteenth century. The anonymous contribution to the *Annual Register* in 1768, stating that Worcester "never cracks or scales off," is literally true of the teapots. Whereas at least three-quarters of all surviving Chelsea and Bow teapots, and a far higher proportion of Derby examples, have been cracked, Worcester teapots are seldom encountered in cracked condition, especially those from the late 1750s onward. Worcester teapots during the 1760s and 1770s were made in three sizes and, when sold separately from tea services, cost fifteen, twenty-one, and twenty-seven shillings per dozen, according to size.

90

91

Worcester Cream Jug, ca. 1772–75

Painted with stylized floral sprays and with an inner border in reddish brown.

HEIGHT: 3¾ in. (9.5 cm)

MARK: None

LITERATURE: Spero, *The Price Guide to Eighteenth-Century English Porcelain*, p. 69, illustrates a coffeepot in this pattern

ACCESSION NUMBER: 1991.40.79

The decoration on this cream jug demonstrates the manner in which the Chinese famille rose idiom was simplified and assimilated into the Worcester factory style. The relatively small size of the handle and the curve of its upper terminal are features that help to determine its period. By the mid-1770s the oriental patterns at Worcester, so popular during the two previous decades, were giving way to the more fashionable neoclassical patterns derived from Sèvres and Derby. However, the oriental patterns of this period were simple in style and less expensive in cost, and therefore a ready market was maintained. This shape of cream jug, loosely adapted from silver, was the established standard shape at every English porcelain factory, from the early 1750s until the 1790s. Its popular sobriquet, "sparrow beak," stems from the V-shaped lip, and the overall shape displays little variation from one factory to another. The presence of the inner border serves to confirm that this is a cream jug and therefore would not have needed a cover.

91

92

92

Worcester Milk Jug and Cover, ca. 1770–72

Painted in the atelier of James Giles, in the manner of David Teniers the Younger, with two children in a rural landscape, flanked by trees.

HEIGHT: 5½ in. (14.0 cm)

MARK: None

LITERATURE: Amor, *James Giles: China Painter, 1718–1780,* cat. no. 47

ACCESSION NUMBER: 1991.40.37a–b

The attribution to the Giles studio is partially based upon the figure decoration on two Worcester blue scale tea cannisters, reputed to have been painted by Giles himself and sold in 1952 by a descendant, Mrs. Dora Edgell Grubbe. The figure painting of children on those tea cannisters strongly resembles that on this milk jug. Characteristics of the Giles atelier present here include the style and quality of the gilding, especially on the handle and lip. The solid gilt border on the foot rim is another typical feature, derived from Meissen, which was also the direct source of the decoration, popular during the 1740s.

A ledger itemizing many of Giles's financial transactions and accounts covering the years 1771 to 1776 makes it clear that he purchased oriental porcelain. Mixed services of Chinese and Worcester porcelain are known, usually decorated at the Giles studio, with either exotic birds or figures, superbly executed in the Teniers style. Lot 51, on the second day of a sale at Christie's in March 1774, entirely devoted to Giles's stock, lists "a pair of jonquil jars in figures after Tenier." This style of decoration, which is sometimes controversially accompanied by a pink scale border, was not done at the Factory.

Jugs of this form with covers were intended for hot milk rather than for cream, as was the case with the smaller, more slender form (cat. no. 91). Whereas the cream jug, developed from a silver model, was issued from the factory's earliest days, the milk jug was not introduced until the early 1760s, and even then, it was a component only of the "full" service.

Worcester Dish, ca. 1778–82

Of lobed square form with an osier-molded rim picked out in gilding, decorated with a group of animals including a bear, a monkey, an elephant, a horse, a leopard, and a hare playing a drum.

WIDTH: 9½ in. (24.1 cm)

MARK: None

LITERATURE: Spero and J. Sandon, *Eighteenth-Century Worcester Porcelain: The Zorensky Collection*, chap. 5

ACCESSION NUMBER: 1991.40.41

Although this style of decoration has in the past been attributed to Jefferyes Hamett O'Neale, perhaps because of its humorous and whimsical quality, a comparison with undisputed examples of his work on Worcester *gros bleu* plates (cat. no. 131) clearly contradicts this contention. More recently, Franklin Barrett and other writers have speculated that the painter might be Fidèle Duvivier, pointing to comparisons with Tournai porcelain attributed to him. This attribution too seems unconvincing, and it is hard to envisage Duvivier painting animals in so idiosyncratic a palette. The background vegetation and trees, far from evoking the distinctive style of either O'Neale or Duvivier, is reminiscent instead of that which accompanies the typical Worcester Fancy Birds in landscapes. What is certain is that these osier-bordered dishes are invariably at least ten years later than O'Neale's *gros bleu* plates. The artist was influenced by O'Neale but was far less accomplished, and lacked the ironic sense of human caricature and vitality that distinguish O'Neale's work. The painter of this dish was certainly responsible for fable subjects and often exhibits a fondness for animals grouped closely together, as if about to be photographed. His humor is here exemplified by a doleful pink horse, a musical hare, an argumentative bear, and a monkey in apparent dispute with a leopard, the whole tableau presided over by a corpulent elephant.

93

94

Worcester Plate, ca. 1772

Molded in relief with a spray of rose leaves, buds, and a brown stalk, and decorated in the atelier of James Giles with a large rose and a gilt rim.

DIAMETER: 7½ in. (19.1 cm)

MARK: None

LITERATURE: Spero and J. Sandon, *Eighteenth-Century Worcester Porcelain: The Zorensky Collection*, chap. 12

ACCESSION NUMBER: 1991.40.31

The attribution of this plate to the London studio of James Giles is based upon the palette, which is paler than the Factory colors, together with the loosely composed rose, painted in a typically deep shade of pink. This celebrated embossed pattern, known as the Blind Earl, occurs on plates, sweetmeat dishes, and small oval trays and was introduced at Worcester in the late 1750s. It was made in conjunction with a wide range of patterns including underglaze blue and overglaze transfer prints. It takes its name from associations with the earl of Coventry, who, blinded in a hunting accident in 1780, was able to feel, but not see, the pattern. However, this romantic association seems to have been made some years later, with the benefit of hindsight, as the earl's accident occurred over twenty years after the introduction of the molded design. The molded design itself was derived from Chelsea originals of the red anchor period, and it remains in production at the Royal Worcester factory.

94

95

Worcester Cauliflower Tureen and Stand,
ca. 1758–60

The tureen painted in naturalistic colors and the stand transfer printed in outline with butterflies and insects and hand painted in color.

LENGTH OF TUREEN: 4 in. (10.2 cm)

LENGTH OF STAND: 8 in. (20.3 cm)

MARK: Script *W* in brownish black

LITERATURE: Spero and J. Sandon, *Eighteenth-Century Worcester Porcelain: The Zorensky Collection*, chap. 2

ACCESSION NUMBER: Promised gifts

Tureens in the naturalistic guise of vegetables were produced at Worcester on a far more restricted scale than their slightly earlier Chelsea counterparts. Yet paradoxically, this cauliflower tureen is more common than any of the comparable Chelsea shapes. Inspired by Meissen, but possibly imitating Chelsea, the Worcester version, press-molded and sometimes misshapen, lacks both the intoxicating tactile dimension and the innate sense of frivolity that characterize Chelsea and Longton Hall vegetable tureens. The palette, too, fails to convey the deceptive sense of trompe l'oeil that so distinguishes such pieces as the Chelsea artichoke tureens (cat. no. 40). The leaf-shape stand is far more common than the tureen itself and was probably sold separately in some instances, or in pairs. Some were outline printed in monochrome, and others, as here, filled in with enamel colors.

For contemporary factories, Worcester and Chelsea, sharing the prevailing widespread Meissen influence and a desire to adapt and interpret silver forms and to express rococo themes, it is remarkable that two such entirely separate paths were followed. The cauliflower tureen represents a rare instance of the paths coinciding and at the same time demonstrates the wisdom of the Worcester factory's independent approach to porcelain design and decoration.

95

96

96

Worcester Candlestick, ca. 1772–75

Modeled in the form of a pair of canaries perched upon tree stumps among flowering bocage, below a molded sconce, all supported upon a scrollwork base enriched in gilt.

HEIGHT: 9¼ in. (23.5 cm)

MARK: None

LITERATURE: Spero and J. Sandon, *Eighteenth-Century Worcester Porcelain: The Zorensky Collection*, chap. 11

ACCESSION NUMBER: 1991.40.48

Fewer than a dozen figure models are known in Worcester, and indeed it is only in the last seventy years that any models have been positively identified. An entry in the *Public Advertiser* in December 1769 referred to "Jars, and Beakers, Figures," and this reference was supported by Mrs. Lybbe Powys and Captain Joseph Roche, both writing in August 1771. The latter, recording a visit to Worcester on 21 August, noted that "they make very fine figures or ornamental china, it being done much better and also cheaper at Derby." However, it was not until the analyses carried out by Herbert Eccles in the early 1920s that the presence of magnesia from soapstone was identified in certain figures, in amounts consistent with an attribution to Worcester.

Although there is an insufficient range of Worcester models to enable a coherent factory style to be recognized, there are several characteristics that most of the models share and that set them apart from other English porcelain figures. Foremost among these are the flower buds and the modeling of the green leaves, both of which correspond closely to the flowers and leaves around the handles of openwork baskets (cat. nos. 108 and 110). In the case of this candlestick, both the palette and the gilding are typical of Worcester, and the slightly blue tinge to the glaze in places is strongly indicative of a soapstone body. The model as a whole might be compared in composition to the well-known Bow "Birds in Branchis" candlesticks of the late 1750s. Although bearing no mark, this candlestick group is typical of the work of a modeler who used an impressed letter *T* or *To* on the underside of the bases of figures. He has been identified as John Toulouse, and it is likely that he was responsible for many of the Worcester figures and vases of the late 1760s and early 1770s. He had previously worked at Bow, and his impressed mark also occurs on pieces of Champion's Bristol, Caughley, and Chamberlain's Worcester porcelain. His work at Worcester, on figures, vases, and shell centerpieces, shares many features with Bow models of the late 1750s and early 1760s.

97

97

Worcester Plate, ca. 1775–78

Sumptuously painted with a central cluster of fruit surrounded by small insects and with smaller groups of fruit and larger insects within a turquoise rim edged in gilt.

DIAMETER: 8¾ in. (22.2 cm)

MARK: Crescent in gold

LITERATURE: Spero, *Worcester Porcelain: The Klepser Collection*, color pl. 19, cat. no. 64

ACCESSION NUMBER: 1991.41.8

This celebrated service is reputed to have been designed for William Henry, duke of Gloucester (1743–1805), the third son of Frederick, Prince of Wales, and his wife, Princess Augusta of Saxe-Gotha. The elaborate style of decoration was derived directly from a Chelsea service made during the gold anchor period, in about 1765, for the duke of Cambridge. Indeed, these two services share so many decorative motifs that it is entirely reasonable to speculate that the Worcester pieces may have been made as replacements for the earlier Chelsea service. This theory is somewhat supported by the sale at Christie's in June 1904 of seventy pieces from the Worcester service, owned by a subsequent duke of Cambridge. A plate from the Chelsea service is catalogue number 47 in this collection.

As can be noted from a comparison with catalogue number 98, plates from this service were made in two shapes, though all examples were marked with a crescent in gold. This established factory mark, painted overglaze, is further confirmation that the decoration was undertaken at Worcester rather than in London. The opulence of this decoration was unprecedented at this period, as might befit the first royal service commissioned from Worcester.

98

98

Worcester Plate, ca. 1775–78

Elaborately decorated with an extensive cluster of fruit surrounded by small insects and with smaller groups of fruit and larger insects within a turquoise rim edged in gilt.

DIAMETER: 9⅝ in. (24.4 cm)

MARK: Crescent in gold

LITERATURE: H. Sandon, *The Illustrated Guide to Worcester Porcelain, 1751–1793,* color pl. IV

ACCESSION NUMBER: 1991.40.33

This decoration has in the past been attributed to the London atelier of James Giles, and it is clearly evident that it represents a departure from the Factory style of the 1770s. However, as Gerald Coke has pointed out in his book *In Search of James Giles,* the decoration is uncharacteristically ornate for the Giles studio. Furthermore, neither the style of gilding nor the gilding itself corresponds to the richly laid on *ciselé*

gilding of Giles. The overall composition of the decoration is laid out for maximum effect with little evidence of the looser and more restrained style often associated with the London atelier.

From this somewhat contradictory evidence, Coke suggests that this Worcester service, made for the duke of Gloucester, may have been decorated by former Chelsea painters who were employed at the Worcester factory after the closure of the Giles studio in London in 1776. The similarities with the decoration on the Chelsea service made for the duke of Cambridge in the mid-1760s are certainly very close, as can be seen by a comparison with the example in this collection (cat. no. 47). The more informal and relaxed treatment of decoration in this idiom from the Giles atelier is exemplified on the fine pair of plates (cat. no. 119).

99

Worcester Tea Cannister and Cover,
ca. 1768–70

Of ovoid shape, painted with disheveled birds
within gilt-edged mirror-shaped panels,
interspersed wth insects, upon a yellow scale
ground.

HEIGHT: 6½ in. (16.5 cm)
MARK: None
LITERATURE: Barrett, *Worcester Porcelain*, pl. 52A
ACCESSION NUMBER: 1991.41.5a–b

The yellow scale on Worcester is considerably rarer
than the solid yellow ground and is associated with a
Meissen influence. Whereas the solid yellow was in
intermittent production for some fifteen years or so,
the yellow scale spans a far shorter period, from
about 1765 to 1770. This form of tea cannister, echoing a Meissen shape of the mid-1730s which was also
used in Chinese export porcelain, was introduced at
Worcester in about 1765. It remained in production
until about 1780, by which time it had been gradually replaced by a cylindrical form. This later shape,
with its larger capacity, reflected the reduced cost of
tea, caused by progressively lower taxation. As with
spoon trays and teapot stands, cannisters were an optional component of tea services and were sometimes
sold in pairs, presumably for "Green" and "Bohea"
teas. They are considerably more common in polychrome than in underglaze blue. A fluted form of tea
cannister, dating from the following decade, is catalogue number 124 in this collection.

Despite its high cost, due mainly to taxation, the
habit of tea drinking was firmly established by the
middle of the eighteenth century among the upper
and middle classes, though not everyone approved of
its extravagant nature. In his *Farmer's Letters* for
1767, Arthur Young complained that "as much super-
fluous money is expended on tea and sugar as would
maintain four millions more subjects on bread," an
observation that would become still more relevant as
the century progressed.

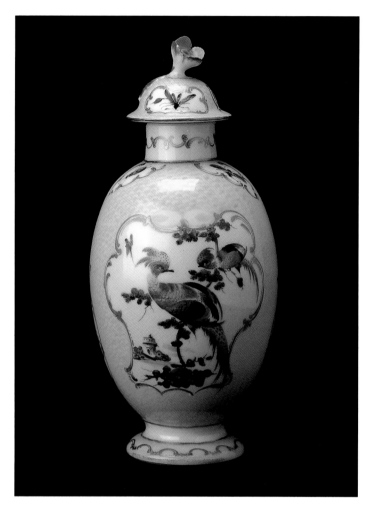

99

100

Worcester Bowl, ca. 1768–70

Painted with disheveled birds within mirror-shaped panels edged in gilt, interspersed with insects, upon a yellow scale ground.

DIAMETER: 6½ in. (16.5 cm)
MARK: Crossed swords and numeral 9
LITERATURE: Tilley, *Teapots and Tea,* color frontispiece, illustrates a teapot and stand
ACCESSION NUMBER: 1991.40.28

The yellow ground, traditionally the most prized ground color among collectors of Worcester, was inspired by the two great Continental factories at Meissen and Sèvres. A yellow ground was in use at Meissen by 1730, and at Sèvres it was gradually introduced from about 1753 onward. The first yellow grounds appeared on Worcester in the mid-1750s, all clearly showing a Meissen influence. By the late 1760s the yellow scale designs were established, also derived from Meissen. Thereafter the majority of yellow grounds were inspired by Sèvres. This example demonstrates, in its clarity and color, the yellow scale ground at its most impressive. By contrast with the solid yellow, which is generally associated with floral decoration, the yellow scale is almost invariably found in conjunction with bird painting. This combination of idioms, while aesthetically pleasing, was produced at Worcester on a restricted scale, suggesting that it was not fully appreciated by the contemporary public.

101

Worcester Teacup and Saucer, ca. 1770

Painted with disheveled birds within gilt-edged mirror-shaped panels, interspersed with insects, upon a yellow scale ground.

DIAMETER OF SAUCER: 5 in. (12.7 cm)
MARK: Crossed swords and numeral 9
LITERATURE: Spero, *Worcester Porcelain: The Klepser Collection,* color pl. 26, cat. no. 93, illustrates a milk jug and cover
ACCESSION NUMBER: 1991.41.10a–b

The inspiration for this classic Worcester decoration can be traced to Meissen, both in terms of the yellow scale ground and the concept of the exotic birds within elaborate panels. This motif was also adopted at Chelsea. Unlike the solid yellow, the scale ground was principally confined to tea and coffee services and two-handled caudle cups and saucers. It does not appear on tankards and cider jugs. A distinctive style of bird painting occurs in the panels of yellow scale wares, featuring a disheveled bird with a brilliant blue crest. Although this painter also worked on blue scale teawares, his hand is especially associated with the yellow scale ground. The pseudo-Meissen crossed swords, with which this is marked, refer to the shape of cup and saucer rather than to its decoration, though both reflect the influence of the German factory. The numeral 9 is recorded on Meissen, in conjunction with the factory mark, and it is possible that someone at Worcester had seen a piece marked in this manner. In any event, throughout the 1760s and early 1770s, it was regularly employed on teawares, especially in those services which included teacups.

102

Worcester Junket Bowl, ca. 1762–65

Of basket-weave molded form, painted with bouquets of flowers within cartouches edged in puce, upon a yellow ground with a floral chain border.

DIAMETER: 9 in. (22.9 cm)

MARK: None

LITERATURE: H. Sandon, *The Illustrated Guide to Worcester Porcelain, 1751–1793*, pl. 65, illustrates a junket dish, alongside an unglazed waster

ACCESSION NUMBER: 1991.40.45

A superb illustration of the dramatic effect of the yellow ground upon a molded shape, the form was first produced at Worcester in the late 1750s and occurs in a variety of overglaze patterns and in underglaze blue painted and printed subjects. An identical shape was also made in underglaze blue Chinese porcelain, for the export market. Junket, or curds and whey, was a popular dish in the eighteenth century, though it gradually lost favor as the century progressed. An alternative use for this dish might be salad. Somewhat similar forms, made in underglaze blue at Worcester and Caughley, are printed on their outer sides with fruit and vegetable motifs, suggesting clear evidence for their possible use. Another shape of junket dish, in underglaze blue, is catalogue number 157. The solid yellow ground, introduced at Worcester in about 1756–57, predates the yellow scale, which was chiefly confined to tewares. It is characterized by a puce scrollwork border around the reserved panels and the rim, and this feature is a reliable indication that the decoration is contemporary with the porcelain.

102

103
Worcester Mask Jug, ca. 1768

Of cabbage leaf–molded form, transfer printed and colored with milking scenes, within puce scroll cartouches, upon a yellow ground enriched with scattered insects and a floral band.

HEIGHT: 8¾ in. (22.2 cm)

MARK: None

LITERATURE: Marshall, *Coloured Worcester Porcelain of the First Period*, pl. 29, no. 651; Spero and J. Sandon, *Eighteenth-Century Worcester Porcelain: The Zorensky Collection*, chap. 6

ACCESSION NUMBER: 1990.51.2

This classic Worcester form occurs in a wide range of decoration, including the blue scale and apple green grounds (cat. no. 112), various oriental designs, overglaze transfer prints, and underglaze blue painting and printing. It evolved from a Worcester form that lacked the mask spout and that came into production in the late 1750s. By the mid-1760s the masked version was firmly established, and it remained popular well into the following two decades.

These jugs were made in at least three sizes and almost certainly correspond to the "Dutch Jugs" described in the factory's price lists. So successful was this Worcester design that it was copied at several contemporary factories, including Lowestoft, Caughley, and Christian's Liverpool factory, and remains in production at the Royal Worcester factory. The molded mask lips, which characterize these jugs, varied according to factory. At Worcester, the mask resembles a bearded man with narrowed eyes, which appear closed.

The decoration combines the dramatic yellow ground of Meissen and touches of the *indianische Blumen* with overglaze transfer printing, a purely English innovation. The printed designs were embellished with additional hand painting to create an effect more sympathetic to the yellow ground. The transfer prints themselves are *The Rural Lovers,* from an engraving by Francis Vivares, published in 1760, after a painting by Thomas Gainsborough; *Milking Scene, No. 1* was copied by Robert Hancock from an engraving by Luke Sullivan, published in 1759, of a view of Woobourn in Surrey, the seat of Philip Southcote, Esq.; and *The Milkmaids,* after an engraving by Robert Sayer, published in 1766.

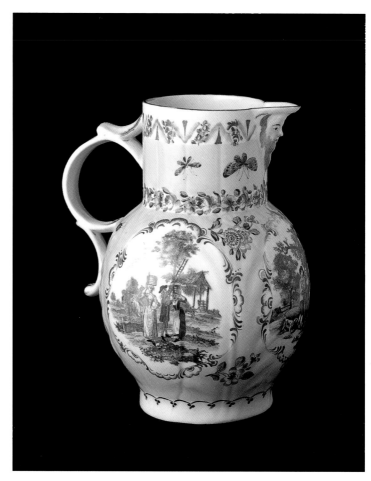

103

104

Worcester Mug, ca. 1765–68

Of bell shape, painted with two large bouquets of flowers and a butterfly, upon a solid yellow ground, within a narrow gilt band border.

HEIGHT: 6 in. (15.2 cm)

MARK: None

EXHIBITED: Birmingham City Art Gallery

ACCESSION NUMBER: 1991.40.29

Mugs of this form were one of the most elegant and satisfactory shapes produced at Worcester. Introduced during the late 1750s, this bell-shaped mug remained popular for almost twenty years, although the later examples are slightly more bulbous in outline. Issued in three sizes, this form occurs in a wide variety of patterns and was used as a model at other English factories, including Derby, Caughley, Lowestoft, and Champion's Bristol.

The floral decoration in this instance is of excellent quality, though some authorities have questioned whether the yellow ground is contemporary with the porcelain.[1] The tone of yellow on Worcester varies considerably, from a pale yellow ground, often on the earlier examples, to a strong sulphur tone. After about 1770 the yellow ground fell out of fashion at Worcester, until its reintroduction in the 1790s. As a ground color, yellow was comparatively little used on English porcelain during the third quarter of the eighteenth century, perhaps because it was difficult to control. It was produced at Chelsea and at Derby in the mid-1750s, but an even distribution of tone was not always achieved and the style was short-lived.

1. J. Sandon, *The Dictionary of Worcester Porcelain, 1751–1851,* p. 277.

105

Worcester Plate, ca. 1770–72

Decorated with a central cluster of fruit, flanked by bouquets and sprays of flowers, upon a solid yellow ground with a narrow gilt border.

DIAMETER: 8¼ in. (21.0 cm)

MARK: None

LITERATURE: Coke, *In Search of James Giles,* color pl. XVIII

ACCESSION NUMBER: 1991.41.15

The distinctive style of floral painting, especially in the main bouquet, and the palette itself strongly suggest that the flowers and fruit on this plate were the work of the London atelier of James Giles. The period of the yellow ground is slightly questionable, though it may well correspond to the decoration on one single piece in the Christie's sale of Worcester porcelain in December 1769. This was described as having a "yellow ground enamell'd in flowers." However, no other lot in this sale appears to have been decorated in this idiom. The comparative scarcity of the yellow ground, more successfully mastered at Worcester than at Chelsea or Derby, is paradoxically a measure of its relative lack of popularity at the time. Much admired today for its dramatic impact, it did not find favor with earlier collectors of Worcester porcelain until the second half of the nineteenth century.

It is perhaps no mere chance that the large-scale introduction of colored grounds at Worcester coincided with the decline and closure of the Chelsea factory. The London factory had been very much the leader of fashion and had made a speciality of ground colors, especially mazarine blue, turquoise, and claret. A yellow was attempted during the mid-1750s with uneven results, and consequently it never became one of the established ground colors at Chelsea.

105

106

106

Worcester Plate, ca. 1770

Painted with a large bouquet of flowers, together with smaller sprays, upon a yellow ground with a narrow gilt border.

DIAMETER: 8¼ in. (21.0 cm)

MARK: None

ACCESSION NUMBER: 1991.40.18

A comparison of the plate decorated in the Giles atelier (cat. no. 105) with this example reveals that here the palette is entirely different, featuring a distinctive "dry blue" and a style of painting that is far more akin to the conventional Worcester Factory decoration. As with the Giles decorated plate, there are reservations about the date at which the yellow ground was applied. A very similar yellow ground plate was exhibited at the Art Institute of Chicago, 7 May–3 November 1947, as catalogue number 132. The catalogue entry noted, "Ground color re-decorated in nineteenth century. Rim of base has been ground down to obviate refiring."

The "solid" yellow ground on Worcester seems, for the most part, to postdate the introduction of the yellow scale. Paradoxically, the reverse was true at Meissen, where the ground colors originated. The solid yellow was in production by the early 1730s, whereas the scale yellow did not appear until the 1750s. The color had originated in Chinese porcelain and first appeared on Meissen in the early 1720s, one piece being dated 11 January 1726.[1] At Sèvres, it was first recorded in 1751, when it was termed *à fond jaune.*

1. Cited in Pietsch, *Early Meissen Porcelain*, pl. 76.

107

Worcester Circular Basket, ca. 1765–68

Of openwork form, painted in the interior with a bouquet and scattered flowers, and on the exterior with a yellow ground.

DIAMETER: 6½ in. (16.5 cm)

MARK: None

LITERATURE: Marshall, *Coloured Worcester Porcelain of the First Period*, no. 232; Spero and J. Sandon, *Eighteenth-Century Worcester Porcelain: The Zorensky Collection*, chap. 6

ACCESSION NUMBER: 1991.41.18

This steep-sided form of basket, issued in three sizes, was probably the earliest shape of openwork basket produced at Worcester, though it was not mentioned in the price list of the factory's London warehouse, dating from about 1755–56. Introduced in about 1760, it became progressively more flared in its outline, before being replaced in the early 1770s by baskets with two twig handles. The earlier examples tend to lack the molded flower heads on the exterior intersections. The overall shape was probably derived from Chelsea porcelain of the red anchor period, itself harking back to a Meissen form of the late 1740s. The shape was later copied at Caughley in the 1770s and early 1780s. From about 1780 onward, baskets became less fashionable as a ceramic form, though they remained popular in the less costly creamware.

The method of production for this shape of basket involved cutting out the interlaced circles in the construction while the clay was still wet. The outlines to be followed were drawn with a compass, the marks of which are still discernible. The floral buds on the exterior were employed to strengthen the intersections, where firing faults were most likely to occur. They also served to disguise any such flaws.

107

Worcester Oval Basket, ca. 1768–70

Of openwork form, with twig handles, painted in the interior with a large bouquet of flowers, and on the exterior with puce flower heads upon a yellow ground.

LENGTH: 8¼ in. (21.0 cm)

MARK: None

LITERATURE: Spero, *Worcester Porcelain: The Klepser Collection,* cat. no. 73

ACCESSION NUMBER: 1991.40.19

The painting on colored Worcester openwork baskets of this type is often characterized by the free use of a pinkish puce color. A wide range of decoration occurs on this form, including bird and fruit patterns, underglaze and overglaze ground colors, and underglaze blue painting and printing. Issued in three sizes, this form of basket was introduced in about 1768–70 and continued in production until the late 1770s. A blue-and-white example bears the incised date *1772.* This shape was also made at Lowestoft, Caughley, and, to a lesser extent, at Bow and Champion's Bristol factory. It is likely that this shape was introduced at the time of John Toulouse's arrival at Worcester in the late 1760s, and it largely replaced the more steep-sided circular form that had been in production for about ten years (cat. no. 107).

Worcester Circular Basket, ca. 1770–72

Of openwork form, painted in the interior with a bouquet and scattered flowers, and on the exterior with puce flower heads, modeled upon a yellow ground.

DIAMETER (handles missing): 8⅝ in. (21.9 cm)

MARK: None

LITERATURE: Spero, *Worcester Porcelain: The Klepser Collection,* cat. no. 132, illustrates this shape decorated with the Sir Joshua Reynolds pattern, upon a *gros bleu* ground

ACCESSION NUMBER: 1991.40.20

By comparison with the oval form of openwork basket (cat. no. 108), this shape occurs in a slightly more restricted range of patterns, though in this instance they include overglaze transfer prints. As with the oval basket, the palette is vivid and features the distinctive pinkish puce tone. Although the yellow ground is comparatively rare on Worcester and, it must be assumed, did not meet with the full approval of the public, it was regularly employed on the exterior of openwork baskets. The interior decoration was in a sense of secondary importance, since it was obscured by the contents of the basket. This shape of basket remained in production until the early 1780s and was probably made as a component of a dessert service. In most instances molded florettes were applied to the intersections of the basketwork sides, and compass marks can often be observed, drawn to indicate where the shapes should be cut out. The shape also occurs in tin-glazed earthenware and salt-glazed stoneware.

108

109

Worcester Chestnut Basket, Cover, and Stand,
ca. 1770

With twig handles, the exterior with a yellow
ground and puce flower heads, and the interior
decorated with the Bengal Tiger pattern.

LENGTH: 8½ in. (21.6 cm)

MARK: None

LITERATURE: H. Sandon, *The Illustrated Guide to
Worcester Porcelain, 1751–1793*, color pl. VII

ACCESSION NUMBER: 1991.41.12a–b

This is a classic Worcester form, whose production
spanned the early 1770s and inspired copies made at
Derby, Lowestoft, and Caughley. The shape occurs in
a wide range of decoration, including blue scale patterns and underglaze blue transfer prints. In this
instance, however, the juxtaposition of the yellow
ground and the Bengal Tiger pattern seems incongruous and inconsistent with the Worcester style of the
period. Furthermore, the yellow is uncharacteristically deep in tone. In these circumstances there must
be some doubt as to whether the whole decoration is
contemporary with the porcelain. This shape, probably based upon a silver original, has long been traditionally termed a "chestnut basket." However, the sale
of Worcester porcelain at Christie's, in 1769, listed in
its catalogue "Two fine oval white and gold cream-
basons, pierced covers and plates."[1] In hindsight, it is
a little difficult to envisage this basket as being used
for cream, but the 1769 catalogue description is fairly
specific and seems not to correspond with any other
known shape. As with many of the more elaborately
modeled forms, it seems likely that this ambitious
shape coincided with the arrival at Worcester, from
Bow, of the modeler John Toulouse. Certainly, there
are similarities in the modeling of the flowers with
those on the canary candlestick (cat. no. 96).

1. J. Sandon, *The Dictionary of Worcester Porcelain, 1751–
1851*, p. 108.

110

Worcester Mask Jug, ca. 1768–70

Of pear shape, painted with exotic birds in a watery landscape, within large mirror-shaped panels upon an apple green ground.

HEIGHT: 7¼ in. (18.4 cm)
MARK: None
LITERATURE: H. Sandon, *The Illustrated Guide to Worcester Porcelain, 1751–1793*, pl. 68
ACCESSION NUMBER: 1991.40.16

The sale advertisement for Worcester porcelain to be sold by Mr. Burnsall at Christie's in May 1769 lists a range of colored grounds, including "Pea Green, French Green and Sea Green." Of these, it is the "Pea Green" that corresponds to the shade known today as apple green, a notably opaque color. Although examples of the apple green ground, in conjunction with exotic birds, are illustrated widely in reference books on Worcester porcelain, many authorities have in recent years become doubtful as to whether the decoration is contemporary with the porcelain. These reservations apply to bird painting rather than to floral decoration, though there are clearly exceptions. It also seems likely that while the majority of teawares and dessert wares are free from controversy, upright forms such as mugs, jugs, and vases should be viewed with suspicion.[1] However, despite this uncertainty, it is generally considered that no collection of Worcester is complete without an example of the apple green ground.

1. J. Sandon, *The Dictionary of Worcester Porcelain, 1751–1851*, p. 282.

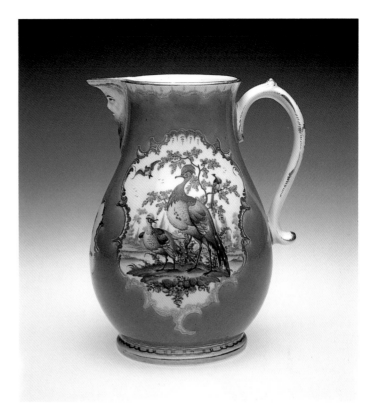

111

Worcester Mask Jug, ca. 1770

Of cabbage leaf–molded form, painted with exotic birds in landscapes, within large mirror-shaped panels upon an apple green ground.

HEIGHT: 7½ in. (19.1 cm)

MARK: None

LITERATURE: Marshall, *Coloured Worcester Porcelain of the First Period*, pl. 49, no. 1002

ACCESSION NUMBER: 1991.41.9

The apple green ground at Worcester was derived from Sèvres, where *fonds verds* were recorded as early as 1751, but they seem not to have come into production until 1756 as the *pomme vert*. The color was as well received in England as it was in France. Lady Caroline Lennox, wife of the great radical politician Charles James Fox, wrote to her sister Emily in 1759, describing her dressing room as "fitted up with a great deal of pea-green china and painted pea green."[1] This china can only have been the newly invented Sèvres *pomme vert*, suggesting that this green ground had an immediate impact on the tastes of the English aristocracy. Unlike the *bleu céleste* or turquoise, for example, the apple green ground was seldom used at the Giles atelier. A peculiarity of the apple green was that it would not take gilding, so that a narrow margin needed to be left between the green and the inner edge of the gilt decoration. The presence of this margin, however, is no guarantee that the decoration is contemporary with the porcelain, and the opaque nature of the apple green allowed it to be very successfully copied. The most revealing indication of redecoration is a blackening around the base and rim, often disguised by a very elaborate gilt border.[2] An extensive collection of Worcester decorated with colored grounds, especially the apple green, is in the Lady Ludlow Collection at Luton Hoo, in Bedfordshire. These ground colors are in many instances not contemporary with the porcelain.

1. Tillyard, *Aristocrats*, p. 148.
2. Spero and J. Sandon, *Eighteenth-Century Worcester Porcelain: The Zorensky Collection*, Appendix A.

113
Worcester Mug, ca. 1758–62

Of cylindrical form, painted with exotic birds in parkland, within rococo panels, upon an apple green ground.

HEIGHT: 3¼ in. (8.3 cm)

MARK: None

LITERATURE: Peirce, *English Ceramics: The Frances and Emory Cocke Collection,* cat. no. 182

ACCESSION NUMBER: 1991.40.17

An examination of the paste and glaze of this mug indicates that it is from a relatively early period, certainly no later than about 1762. This conclusion is strongly supported by the shape of the handle, where the upper terminal meets the body of the mug. This curve is typical of handles of the late 1750s. Furthermore, there is a slight suggestion of a flared base, which would also be consistent with this early period. Consequently, it is beyond doubt that the porcelain is in this instance at least ten years earlier than the first use of the apple green ground at Worcester. Aside from the problematic ground color itself, the style of bird painting is unusually stilted and the colors unnaturally bright and ill matched. Contentious though this issue is, all the great collections of First Period Worcester porcelain in England and North America contain representative pieces of apple green Worcester, and examples are illustrated in all of the standard reference works on the subject.[1]

1. J. Sandon, *The Dictionary of Worcester Porcelain, 1751–1851,* pp. 282–83.

114
Worcester Vase, ca. 1770

Of baluster shape, decorated with exotic birds in wooded landscapes within large rococo panels, upon an apple green ground edged in gilt.

HEIGHT: 4¾ in. (12.1 cm)

MARK: None

LITERATURE: Marshall, *Coloured Worcester Porcelain of the First Period,* pl. 34, no. 734

ACCESSION NUMBER: 1991.41.13

From a garniture set of either five or seven vases, this example would originally have been complete with a cover. The shape, derived from Sèvres, sometimes had the addition of two handles and spans a period from about 1770 to 1778. As with the green ground mug (cat. no. 113), the bird decoration on this vase lacks the rhythm and vitality of Worcester painting in this genre. For instance, by comparison with the fine yellow scale teacup and saucer (cat. no. 101), the painting is stiff and lifeless and the colors have a hint of garishness. Consequently, the same questions arise as to the period of the green ground and bird decoration. This form of vase also occurs at Worcester in conjunction with blue scale grounds and with underglaze blue patterns. The green ground was in use at Chelsea by 1760, employed principally on vases. But the color was never fully mastered and examples are scarce.

114

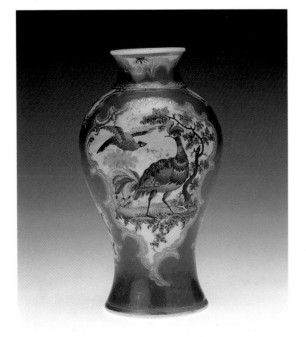

113

115

Worcester Teapot and Cover, ca. 1770

Painted with festoons of flowers trailing obliquely downward from an apple green border, edged with gilt scrolls.

HEIGHT: 6 in. (15.2 cm)
MARK: None
LITERATURE: J. Sandon, *The Dictionary of Worcester Porcelain, 1751–1851,* p. 330
ACCESSION NUMBER: 1991.41.14a–b

This pattern takes its name, the Marchioness of Huntly, from the second wife of the tenth marquess of Huntly, who sold a dessert service of this design on 16 June 1882. Occurring on both teawares and dessert and dinner services, the pattern shows a distinct Sèvres influence. Unlike the solid apple green grounds, this green-bordered pattern is free of controversy, and the flower painting on this teapot is absolutely typical of the period, though the green border on the spout is an unusual feature. This pattern appears on some miniature tea bowls and saucers in the Museum of Fine Arts, Houston.

The genteel ritual of afternoon tea was reputed to have been made fashionable by Anna, duchess of Bedford, who was accustomed to taking tea at five o'clock in order to allay the "sinking feeling" which she experienced at that hour. Alternatively, the wife of Charles II, Catherine of Braganza, has been credited with initiating the vogue for tea drinking in England. She was Portuguese, from a country that had traded with China since the early sixteenth century, and she would certainly have been accustomed to drinking tea. On her arrival in England in 1662, her dowry included chests of tea.

115

116

Worcester Teacup and Saucer, ca. 1772

Painted in a solid turquoise ground, enriched with gilding, the teacup having entwined handles.

DIAMETER OF SAUCER: 5¼ in. (13.3 cm)
MARK: Crossed swords and numeral 9
LITERATURE: Spero, *Worcester Porcelain: The Klepser Collection,* cat. no. 99, illustrates a fluted cup and saucer
ACCESSION NUMBER: 1991.40.55a–b

The turquoise ground almost certainly corresponds to the "Sky Blue" that was listed in an advertisement for a sale of Worcester porcelain held at Christie's in May 1769, by Mr. Burnsall. The ground color was probably derived from Sèvres, where it was introduced in 1752, although it appeared on Meissen nearly thirty years previously and has its origins in Chinese porcelain of the Kangxi dynasty (1662–1722). The ground occurs in conjunction with a restricted range of shapes, including faceted and plain teawares, dessert plates, and small vases. It was also used on contemporary Derby wares.

Both Giles and the Factory produced the turquoise ground, and examples are not easy to distinguish from one another. The diminishing gilt dots on the entwined handle are likely to be an indication of an attribution to the Giles studio. The handle form was derived from Vincennes and introduced at Worcester in the late 1760s. The presence of a pseudo-Meissen mark refers to the shape of the cup and saucer rather than to the origin of the turquoise ground, but it suggests that the entwined handle was also in use at Meissen. The Vincennes-Sèvres color, invented by Hellot, was devised principally as a wide border design, embellished with rich gilding, a far more imaginative and effective treatment of the turquoise ground than was adopted on Worcester porcelain.

116

117

Worcester Two-Handled Cup and Saucer,
ca. 1770–72

Of fluted shape, painted with exotic birds below a turquoise border, with a cluster of fruit at the bottom of the cup and in the center of the saucer.

DIAMETER OF SAUCER: 5¾ in. (14.6 cm)
MARK: None
LITERATURE: Marshall, *Coloured Worcester Porcelain of the First Period*, pl. 28, no. 605
ACCESSION NUMBER: 1991.41.11a–b

117

This is most likely the shape that corresponds to the caudle cups and saucers listed in the Christie's sale of Worcester held in London in December 1769. The shape was introduced at Worcester at about that date and continued in production for most of the following decade. It occurs in a variety of overglaze colors, in underglaze blue, and with overglaze transfer prints. The decoration, although somewhat in the style of the Giles workshop, cannot be convincingly attributed to that atelier. The cut fruit, normally a characteristic of Giles's work, and a motif derived from Meissen, lacks the vitality one expects, both in palette and execution. On the other hand, the decoration fits uneasily into the established Factory style, in its atypical conjunction of decorative idioms. Tea caudle, introduced in the late seventeenth century, was a hot drink made from green China tea, egg yolk, white wine, and caster sugar, with the addition of grated nutmeg.

118

Worcester Tea Bowl and Saucer, ca. 1778–80

Painted with flowers and fruit, below a richly gilded claret ground cornucopia-shaped border.

DIAMETER OF SAUCER: 4⅞ in. (12.4 cm)

MARK: None

LITERATURE: Spero and J. Sandon, *Eighteenth-Century Worcester Porcelain: The Zorensky Collection*, Appendix A

ACCESSION NUMBER: 1991.40.49a–b

The Hope-Edwardes pattern was produced at the London atelier of James Giles and is notable for the quality and exuberant style of its gilding. The shapes are confined entirely to a range of dessert wares. The teawares in this design, however, differ in both their gilding and floral decoration, and it has been suggested that many examples show indications of later decoration.[1] The flower painting on this example is reminiscent in style to that on gold anchor period Chelsea, though it lacks a certain vitality in its execution and in its palette. The pattern, which takes its name from a service reputedly made for Sir Thomas Edwardes, recurs on Derby porcelain of the 1780s.

1. J. Sandon, *The Dictionary of Worcester Porcelain, 1751–1851*, p. 199.

118

119

Pair of Worcester Plates, ca. 1770

Decorated in the atelier of James Giles with a central cluster of fruit and sprays of flowers pendant from a cornucopia-shaped pink scale border, edged in gilt.

DIAMETER: 9 in. (22.9 cm)

MARK: None

LITERATURE: Spero and J. Sandon, *Eighteenth-Century Worcester Porcelain: The Zorensky Collection*, chap. 12

ACCESSION NUMBERS: 1991.41.7.1, 2

This superb pair of plates can be firmly linked to the James Giles atelier through their close resemblance to one of the four celebrated Grubbe plates. These plates, each decorated with a different subject, are by family tradition believed to have been painted by Giles himself. In 1935 they were given to the Victoria and Albert Museum by Mrs. Dora Edgell Grubbe, a descendant of Giles. Together, these four plates form a basis from which much of the atelier's work can be identified. For instance, both the blue auricula and the spray of daisylike flowers above it, on the right-hand plate, correspond very closely to decoration on one of the Grubbe plates. Further shared similarities include the loose central arrangement of fruit and flowers and details in the leaves. The loose cluster of fruit is strongly influenced in style by Meissen decoration of the Academic Period (1763–74). Still more

119

characteristic of the Giles atelier are the sprays of flowers scattered around the border. The pink scale border itself was derived from the *Mosaik* border patterns that appeared at Meissen in about 1760. The pink scale was used first by Giles, only later being adopted by the Factory. It is associated with the finest decoration undertaken at the Giles atelier. The freedom, airiness, and sense of space conveyed by this decoration contrast strikingly with the heavier, more densely bunched fruit painting on the duke of Gloucester plates (cat. nos. 97 and 98), decorated at the Factory several years later. The Giles palette is lighter by comparison, emphasizing a more relaxed treatment of much the same idiom.

120

Worcester Coffee Cup and Saucer, ca. 1780–85

Of fluted form, decorated with trailing floral sprays pendant from a cornucopia-shaped pink scale border edged with gilt scrolls.

DIAMETER OF SAUCER: 5¼ in. (13.3 cm)
MARK: None
LITERATURE: Marshall, *Coloured Worcester Porcelain of the First Period*, pl. 18, no. 320
ACCESSION NUMBER: 1991.40.47a–b

In his book *In Search of James Giles*, Gerald Coke implied that he believed this pattern to be the work of the London atelier of Giles. Although the style of gilding around the handle is consistent with this attribution, other aspects of the decoration give rise to doubts. The tight and compressed nature of the trailing flowers and the somewhat lifeless palette are very atypical of Giles's studio. In particular, the pinkish puce and the bright tone of blue are unlike colors in the Giles palette. Alternatively, if this is Factory decoration, the painting would seem to be of a later period than the porcelain. In more general terms, the Sèvres influence, discernible in the fluted form and handle shape, is indicative of a date after about 1780. An examination of the paste, glaze, and enamel colors confirms a date of manufacture of no earlier than 1780–85, a period by which time Giles was no longer active.

Worcester Sucrier and Cover, ca. 1780–85

Of fluted form, painted with circular medallions enclosing river landscapes, with a turquoise husk border, surrounded by insects and fruit, all within a narrow royal blue border with a chain-link pattern in gilding.

DIAMETER: 4 in. (10.2 cm)
HEIGHT: 5 in. (12.7 cm)
MARK: Crescent in underglaze blue
LITERATURE: Spero and J. Sandon, *Eighteenth-Century Worcester Porcelain: The Zorensky Collection*, chap. 9
ACCESSION NUMBER: 1991.40.30a–b

Patterns of this general type, with landscapes within medallions surrounded by either fruit or flowers below narrow blue borders, occur on a variety of shapes made between about 1780 and 1785. These include dinner services, teawares, mugs, and cider jugs. The patterns are popularly associated with Lord Henry Thynne, though there are clearly far too many examples extant for one single service. The fluted shapes associated with those teawares were derived from Sèvres, as can be determined from the handle forms of coffee cups and the outlines of teapots. An examination of the yellowish toned body and the bluish tint to the glaze strongly suggests that these pieces belong to the early and middle 1780s. A small mug of this type in the Museum of Fine Arts, Houston, is inscribed on the base with the surprisingly late date of 1784. This confirms recent research which suggests that a whole range of patterns, including many with narrow blue borders, are at least ten years later in date than was previously realized.

Sugar, imported from the West Indies, was sold in large cones or loaf-shaped pieces, which were chipped away prior to use. The sugar was served in lumps necessitating a relatively capacious receptacle. On the Continent, however, sugar was taken in powdered form, and, as a consequence, sucriers were far smaller in size.

121

122

122

Pair of Worcester Plates, ca. 1780–85

Each painted with fable subjects within circular reserved panels edged in a turquoise husk and gilt border, surrounded by fruit and birds, the fluted rims decorated with blue borders and gilt scrollwork.

DIAMETER: 8½ in. (21.6 cm)

MARK: Crescent in underglaze blue on each piece

LITERATURE: Marshall, *Coloured Worcester Porcelain of the First Period,* pl. 27, no. 594; Spero and J. Sandon, *Eighteenth-Century Worcester Porcelain: The Zorensky Collection,* chap. 9

ACCESSION NUMBERS: 1991.40.13.1, 2

The fable subjects depicted are the Ox and the Hound and the Fox and the Stork. Fable subjects on First Period Worcester porcelain have long been attributed to Jefferyes Hamett O'Neale. However, there are few similarities between the hand on these plates and the *gros bleu* example that can be attributed to O'Neale with complete confidence (cat. no. 131). The palette is entirely different, lacking the strongly con-

trasted colors that help to link O'Neale's work on Worcester with his earlier decoration at Chelsea. The animal painting, though apparently influenced by O'Neale's overall style, exhibits none of the sharpness of his caricature, nor the incisive characteristics with which he imbued each animal. This is particularly evident in the treatment of the fox, an animal that recurs frequently in O'Neale's work on both Chelsea (cat. no. 21) and Worcester. O'Neale endowed his scenes with a sense of vitality and animation never evident in the more bland encounters depicted on this pair of plates. Furthermore, they appear to be at least twelve or fifteen years later in date than the *gros bleu* wares decorated by O'Neale and show an unmistakable Sèvres influence. One may therefore conclude that they were painted by an artist influenced by O'Neale's style, but who is as yet unidentified. Fidèle Duvivier has sometimes been mentioned as a possibility, but a comparison with his work on Newhall, several years later, surely precludes this theory.

123

123
Worcester Bowl, ca. 1780–85

Of fluted form, decorated with flowers and butterflies above a turquoise *caillouté* border, edged in gilt, and a blue border to the rim, outlined in gilding.

DIAMETER: 6³⁄₈ in. (16.2 cm)
MARK: Crescent in underglaze blue
LITERATURE: Spero and J. Sandon, *Eighteenth-Century Worcester Porcelain: The Zorensky Collection*, chap. 9
ACCESSION NUMBER: 1991.40.82

The substantial range of Worcester patterns incorporating narrow blue borders is generally associated with European-style patterns and with the fluted shapes that evolved from Sèvres from about 1775 onward. This decoration largely replaced the Worcester solid blue grounds, though there was a brief period of overlapping with the *gros bleu,* or "wet blue." The blue borders are generally underglaze and, in their bright vivid tone, are suggestive of the 1780s rather than the previous decade. It is noticeable that none of the Giles patterns appear upon the fluted body, principally because his business was in terminal decline prior to the period of their introduction. The crescent mark introduced at Worcester on a fairly regular basis in the mid-1760s has its origins in the coat of arms of the Warmstry family. The factory was located in Warmstry House, and the family arms, which included a cross moline between four crescents, are recorded as being carved in various places in the building.

124
Worcester Tea Cannister and Cover, ca. 1780–85

Of fluted ovoid shape, painted with a garland of flowers and apples, and a neoclassical vase, below a royal blue border, enriched in gilding, the cover with a floral finial.

HEIGHT: 5 in. (12.7 cm)
MARK: Crescent in underglaze blue
LITERATURE: Marshall, *Coloured Worcester Porcelain of the First Period,* no. 494, illustrates a teacup and saucer; Spero and J. Sandon, *Eighteenth-Century Worcester Porcelain: The Zorensky Collection,* chap. 9
ACCESSION NUMBER: 1991.40.35a–b

Introduced in its plain nonfluted form (cat. no. 99) in about 1765, this shape remained in production until about 1785. Decoration incorporating vases was a typical neoclassical motif of the 1770s and 1780s, popular at Derby and inspired by Sèvres. It represents a somewhat heavy-handed attempt to compete with the far more sophisticated Chelsea and Derby wares, all of which exhibit a greater understanding of neoclassical motifs. Fluted shapes of this type are usually marked with a crescent, often of small size. Alternatively, a script *W* mark was used, but never the fretted square, generally associated with oriental idioms. This shape, also used at Caughley, is of larger capacity than the plain version (cat. no. 99), reflecting the reduced cost of tea during the 1780s.

The popularity of tea in Britain was such that by 1784, the year of the Commutation Act, as much as thirteen million pounds of tea were being consumed each year, a tenfold increase within fifty years. With the reduction in the tax on tea that occurred that year, this figure increased dramatically, and by the end of the century tea drinking in Britain was universal. By 1797 its popularity was such that Sir Frederick Eden could write: "in poor families tea is not only the usual beverage in the morning and evening, but is generally drank in large quantities at dinner."

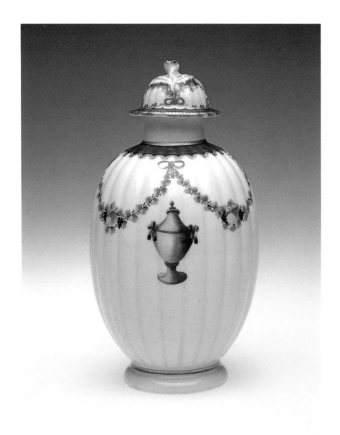

124

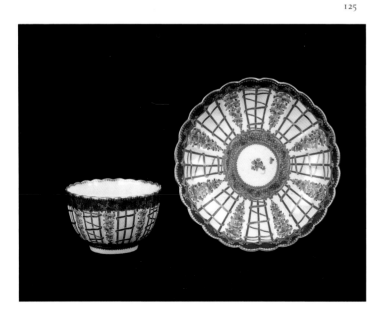

125

125

Worcester Tea Bowl and Saucer, ca. 1775–80

Of fluted form, decorated alternately with red hop trellis and garlands of berried hops, pendant from gilt scrolls on a royal blue rim and with an inner border of turquoise *caillouté*.

DIAMETER OF SAUCER: 5¼ in. (13.3 cm)
MARK: None
LITERATURE: Spero, *Worcester Porcelain: The Klepser Collection*, cat. no. 111
ACCESSION NUMBER: 1991.41.19a–b

The Hop-Trellis patterns, inspired by Sèvres, were introduced at Worcester in the mid-1770s and occur in at least ten variations with border patterns in pink, mauve, turquoise, and royal blue. This example is an adaptation of a Sèvres pattern of about 1763. The number of trellis panels has been reduced from the original, and the size of each one expanded. In place of a crenellated *bleu de roi* design, the Worcester designer has inserted a wide inner border of turquoise *caillouté*. By contrast, the version decorated in the London atelier of James Giles is far more faithful to the Sèvres, and indeed its origins are openly admitted in the catalogue of the sale of Worcester porcelain at Christie's in March 1774. This lists "Pair caudle cups ribb'd to a rich Seve pattern." This shape of tea bowl and saucer was also inspired by Sèvres, being introduced at the factory in 1753 but not appearing at Worcester until the early 1770s. The name "Hop-Trellis" associated with this range of patterns is a traditional description and, as has been pointed out,[1] reflects the long-standing history of hop growing in Worcestershire, though the design itself conveys this impression in only the most generalized manner.

1. J. Sandon, *The Dictionary of Worcester Porcelain, 1751–1851*, p. 202.

126

Worcester Coffeepot and Cover, ca. 1765–68

Decorated with exotic birds within fan-shaped reserved panels, and insects within circular panels, upon a powder blue ground enriched with gilding, the spout and handle decorated with scrolls and leaves in puce.

HEIGHT: 7½ in. (19.1 cm)

MARK: None

LITERATURE: Spero, *Worcester Porcelain: The Klepser Collection,* color pl. 33, cat. no. 125, illustrates a teapot

ACCESSION NUMBER: 1991.40.27a–b

The powder blue was the first of the underglaze blue grounds to be introduced at Worcester, initially occurring in about 1760, though it was not until some five years later that it was used in conjunction with overglaze decoration. The underglaze blue is almost invariably segmented by fan-shaped reserved panels, rather than the mirror- and vase-shaped panels of the blue scale and *gros bleu*. Originating in China, where it was known as *chui qing*, the powder blue was copied at Meissen and later at Sèvres under the name of *bleu soufflé*. In England it was used extensively at Bow (cat. nos. 64–70) and to a limited extent at Lowestoft, Caughley (cat. no. 167), and Derby. Only at Worcester did it regularly occur in conjunction

with overglaze decoration, and it is evident from this fine coffeepot that the impact of the powder blue ground was transformed by the addition of coloring. Nearly all the forms of decoration associated with the powder blue ground at Worcester — agitated and exotic birds, English and oriental flowers, and Japanese designs — were executed at the Factory rather than at the Giles atelier in London. In this instance, the palette with its free use of pink, the somewhat compressed nature of the composition, the comparatively restrained style of gilding, and the puce scrolls and leaves around the spout and handle are invariably firm indications of Factory decoration.

By the end of the seventeenth century, coffee had become England's most popular beverage. In 1652 the founder of the first coffeehouse, Pasqua Rosee, justifiably claimed that "It will prevent Drowsiness and make one fit for business." By the early 1700s London boasted two thousand coffeehouses, "penny universities," where news and opinions were exchanged over newspaper and coffee. The majority of these coffeehouses were set up in the Cornhill area of the City of London, and the preponderance of customers were merchants and men of business. Indeed, business was increasingly conducted in these shops, and both the atmosphere and the beverages available were far more conducive to successful transactions than were the surrounding taverns. Many of the coffee shops soon became associated with particular trades or professions, and from these evolved companies that would in time become institutions within the City of London. One such coffeehouse, owned by Edward Lloyd in Lombard Street, eventually developed into the celebrated marine insurance company, Lloyds of London.

127

127

Pair of Worcester Mugs, ca. 1768–70

Of cylindrical form, with grooved handles, painted with exotic birds among foliage, within asymmetrical panels, edged in gilt, upon a blue scale ground.

HEIGHT: 3¼ in. (8.3 cm)

MARK: Fretted square on each piece

LITERATURE: Spero, *Worcester Porcelain: The Klepser Collection*, cat. no. 115

ACCESSION NUMBERS: 1991.41.17.1, 2

These mugs are a standard Worcester form that was first produced in about 1756–58 and continued into the mid-1770s. Issued in three sizes, they are found in conjunction with a wide range of patterns, polychrome, transfer printed, and in underglaze blue. The basic form was copied at Derby, Caughley, and elsewhere. The blue scale ground, so closely associated with the Worcester factory, was introduced in about 1765–67, though Hobson states on the authority of a family tradition that a blue scale tea cannister illustrated in his book on the Lloyd Collection dates from 1763.[1] This would seem to be an improbably early date, both for the style of decoration and for the shape itself. Similarly, a Bow teapot in the Glynn Vivian Art Gallery, Swansea, painted with exotic birds in panels upon a blue scale ground, bears the inscription upon the base *C I. G. 1761,* a surprisingly early date for such decoration. The possibility must exist that this was deliberately predated at the time of its manufacture for reasons unknown to us today. Considering the success of the blue scale ground at Worcester in both decorative and commercial terms, it is surprising that it was not imitated to any substantial extent elsewhere. Plates in this style were made at Bow for a brief period, and an underglaze scale is known at Caughley and on the Robert Browne pattern on Lowestoft tearwares. However, these are fairly isolated instances and offered no competition to Worcester's mastery of this style of decoration.

1. Hobson, *Catalogue of the Frank Lloyd Collection of Worcester Porcelain of the Wall Period, British Museum,* p. 114.

Worcester Coffee Cup and Saucer, ca. 1770

Decorated with exotic birds and insects within vase- and mirror-shaped panels edged in gilt, upon a blue scale ground.

DIAMETER OF SAUCER: 4⅝ in. (11.7 cm)

MARK: Fretted square

LITERATURE: Spero, *The Price Guide to Eighteenth-Century English Porcelain*, p. 106, illustrates a teacup and saucer

ACCESSION NUMBER: 1991.47.24a–b

Worcester coffee cups and saucers decorated in this idiom were issued in two sizes, the larger examples possibly being intended for chocolate. The concept of exotic birds within reserved panels upon a colored ground originated at Meissen. However, these ground colors were overglaze and did not include the underglaze blue grounds that became such a speciality at Worcester. It was used on tea- and coffeewares, dessert services, and openwork baskets and is seen to great advantage on larger forms, such as bough pots and the imposing hexagonal vases. The combination of the rich underglaze, blue scale ground, and the exotic birds with their colorful plumage was very striking and proved successful at Worcester for over twenty years. The mirror- and vase-shaped panels, enriched with scrolls of gilt, which customarily surround the bird decoration, provide one of the relatively few excursions into formal rococo themes at the factory. The asymmetrical gilded panels fulfilled a twofold purpose of concealing any blurring of the underglaze blue, while offsetting the heaviness of the deep ground color.

128

129

Worcester Broth Bowl and Cover, ca. 1768–70

Of bombé form, decorated with an extensive bouquet of flowers, together with smaller sprays in mirror- and vase-shaped reserved panels, edged with gilt scrolls, upon a blue scale ground.

DIAMETER: 7½ in. (19.1 cm)
MARK: Fretted square
LITERATURE: Spero and J. Sandon, *Eighteenth-Century Worcester Porcelain: The Zorensky Collection*, chap. 8
ACCESSION NUMBER: 1991.41.21a–b

This rare form is sometimes known as a bouillon cup or a porringer. An exactly similar shape was made at Worcester with gilt shell handles replacing the conventional S-shaped form. By comparison, the somewhat similar ecuelle, also made at Worcester, tended to be earlier in date, more shallow in form, and was designed to have a stand. A Chantilly form, similar in shape, is discussed in catalogue number 173. It is possible that this piece corresponds to the "Porringers" listed in the announcement in the *Public Advertiser* for 5 May 1769, for Burnsall's auction of that year, which clearly included the finest and most opulent of the factory's production. Sadly, unlike the Christie's sale in December 1769, no catalogue has survived of the earlier auction. Curiously, the sale notice for May 1769 itemizing the colored grounds that had been successfully devised at Worcester did not mention the blue scale. The explanation for this apparent oversight may have been that whereas the "Mazarine Blue and Gold, Sky Blue, Pea Green," and so forth had been newly invented, the blue scale had been in production for some three or four years and was therefore known to the public. Alternatively, the term *Mazarine Blue* may have been intended to describe all of the underglaze blue grounds.

129

130

Worcester Plate, ca. 1770

With a scalloped edge, painted with bouquets of flowers within vase- and mirror-shaped panels edged in gilt, upon a blue scale ground.

DIAMETER: 7¾ in. (19.7 cm)
MARK: Fretted square
LITERATURE: Spero, *The Price Guide to Eighteenth-Century English Porcelain*, p. 92
ACCESSION NUMBER: 1991.40.26

The underglaze blue scale ground seems to have been a Worcester invention, although Rissik Marshall refers to a Chinese punch bowl (item 152) in the Robert Drane Collection dating from about 1723, which he describes as being "covered externally with a small downward scale blue ground with white reserves."[1] No other Chinese example has been recorded. However, a Japanese Imari pattern dating from about 1700–1710 includes as a central motif an urn decorated in an underglaze blue scale. Another possible source for this celebrated Worcester decoration are the *Mosaik* border patterns employed at Meissen and Berlin in overglaze colors from about 1755 and later imitated at Sèvres. Yet on balance, it seems reasonable to give Worcester the credit for inventing the blue scale ground, a form of decoration brought to such perfection as to become almost synonymous with the factory and its production.

1. Marshall, *Coloured Worcester Porcelain of the First Period*, p. 69.

130

130

131   *Detail p. 131*

Worcester Plate, ca. 1770

With a scalloped edge, painted by Jefferyes Hamett O'Neale with the fable of the Bear and the Beehives, enclosed within a circular panel with a gilt scroll and latticework border, upon a *gros bleu* ground.

DIAMETER: 9 in. (22.9 cm)

MARK: Fretted square

LITERATURE: Savage, *English Pottery and Porcelain,* no. 14b, illustrates a plate with the same fable subject; Spero and J. Sandon, *Eighteenth-Century Worcester Porcelain: The Zorensky Collection,* chap. 8

ACCESSION NUMBER: 1991.40.23

This fable, painted by Jefferyes Hamett O'Neale, was taken from Francis Barlow's *Aesop's Fables with His Life* (1687, p. 173):

> FABLE 86, THE BEAR AND THE BEE-HIVES
> *A Bee's keene sting a Bear didse inrage,*
> *That with the Hives a war he does ingage,*
> *The numbers joyne, and on the foe do fall,*
> *Who grieves, his private fewd prov'd nationall.*
> *Morall: So petty tumults by the Root persu'd*
>   *Have often mighty common wealths subdu'd.*

O'Neale was the chief fable painter at Chelsea from about 1753–55. He seems to have gone to Worcester at some time in 1767 or early 1768, being resident at Mr. Parson's, a watchmaker in High Street, before returning to London in March 1770. Allowing for the intervening thirteen years or so, there are many similarities between his style at Chelsea and that at Worcester. In both cases, his work has a whimsical humor, which invests his animals with facial expressions that have human characteristics. The open mouth of ·

the bear, tormented by the angry bees, shares features common to the wolf on the Chelsea saucer and especially with the chasing hound, mouth agape, on the Chelsea beaker (cat. no. 22). As may be discerned here, O'Neale's skill lay in capturing the essence of an animal humorously depicted in particular circumstances rather than in any mastery of anatomical detail, and this aspect of his style showed little advance from that on his work on Chelsea, some fifteen years earlier. Several examples of his painting on Worcester vases are signed, lending retrospective confirmation that he was the fable painter at Chelsea. The suggestion that O'Neale's work on Worcester porcelain was undertaken at the Giles atelier in London can be immediately discounted by an examination of the gilding on this plate, typical of the Factory, but quite unlike the opulent and more loosely composed style associated with Giles. Indeed, the overall effect of the "wet blue" ground and gilding may be likened to the *bleu lapis* of Vincennes and Sèvres. O'Neale's decoration in this genre was mainly inspired by versions of Aesop's fables by Francis Barlow, Croxall, and others. However, such was the skill, wit, and imagination of the artist that certain subjects were partially of his own invention and seem to have no basis in recorded fables.

O'Neale's work on Worcester is almost invariably accompanied by a wide *gros bleu* border, enriched with gilding. For this reason, he employed a much stronger palette and far fuller decoration overall, so that his scenes would not be overpowered by the heaviness of the blue ground. He had painted a version of this fable on Chelsea, some fifteen years previously. On it, the elements of the design were arranged somewhat differently, the cottage being far less prominent and the tree far more so, and, most noticeably, there was a great expanse of sky, with lighter-toned clouds.

132

132

Pair of Worcester Plates, ca. 1770

With scalloped rims, painted in the Kakiemon taste, with a long-tailed bird perched upon a turquoise rock, among flowering plants, enclosed within a circular reserved panel edged in gilt, upon a *gros bleu* ground.

DIAMETER: 8¼ in. (21.0 cm)

MARK: Open crescents on each

LITERATURE: Spero, *Worcester Porcelain: The Klepser Collection*, cat. no. 132, illustrates an openwork basket in this pattern

ACCESSION NUMBERS: 1991.40.14. 1, 2

This celebrated design, which, when on Worcester, is called the Sir Joshua Reynolds pattern, originated in a late-seventeenth-century Japanese version of a Chinese pattern. On Worcester the pattern is characterized by brilliant turquoise and yellow enamel colors and occurs on a white ground, especially on vases, in the mid-1750s, and on lobed plates and fac-

eted teawares in the late 1760s. Slightly later versions are in conjunction with either a *gros bleu* (wet blue) ground or underglaze blue panels, and the pattern reappears on Chamberlain's Worcester porcelain in about 1795–1800. The blue ground version might possibly correspond to the "fine old Japan pheasant pattern" listed in Christie's 1769 sale of Worcester porcelain.

The pattern was also utilized at Meissen, from which the Worcester version may have been adapted. Other versions of this design represented in the Bowles Collection — on an early Chelsea beaker (cat. no. 7) and a Chantilly quatrefoil saucer (cat. no. 177) — both depict the same decorative elements in a manner more faithful to their oriental origins. The puzzling connection with the painter Sir Joshua Reynolds applies only to the Worcester version and is traditional and possibly one of ownership.

133
Worcester Milk Jug, ca. 1765–68

Probably painted in the London atelier of James Giles, with Chinese figures within mirror-shaped panels, divided by vase-shaped panels enclosing floral sprays, all outlined with gilt scrolls, upon a blue scale ground.

HEIGHT: 3½ in. (8.9 cm)

MARK: None

LITERATURE: Spero, *Worcester Porcelain: The Klepser Collection*, cat. no. 158, illustrates a tea bowl and saucer

ACCESSION NUMBER: 1991.40.84

Several features of the design, called the Bodenham pattern, suggest an attribution to the Giles atelier. The combination of rose pink on the Chinaman's robe beside the orange-brown of the floral sprays would be an incongruous association of colors in the Worcester Factory's palette. Moreover, the spontaneous and slightly haphazard treatment of the floral sprays in the smaller reserved panels is strongly reminiscent of the Giles atelier. The pattern takes its name from the sale of the Bodenham Collection in 1872, which included a full service, though it appears that more than one service may originally have been made. The design is confined to tea- and coffeewares. This is one of the earliest instances at Worcester of blue scale decoration, as can be deduced from the unusually small diameter of the tea bowls and saucers, the slightly bell-shaped coffee cups, together with the low-bellied form of this milk jug (which would originally have had a cover), all characteristics of the mid-1760s in Worcester teawares. Although this milk jug is unmarked, the majority of blue ground pieces do bear underglaze factory marks. The blue scale ground is chiefly associated with the fretted square and, less often, with the crescent. The *gros bleu* ground is also usually marked with either a fretted square or a crescent. Patterns with underglaze blue borders, on the other hand, occur in conjunction with crescent and script *W* marks, but never with a fretted square.

133

134
Worcester Teapot, Cover, and Stand, ca. 1768–70

Decorated with flowering plants growing from banded hedges within vase- and mirror-shaped panels upon a blue scale ground edged with gilt scrolls.

DIAMETER OF TEAPOT: 4½ in. (11.4 cm)

DIAMETER OF STAND: 5 in. (12.7 cm)

MARK: Fretted square

LITERATURE: Spero, *Worcester Porcelain: The Klepser Collection*, cat. no. 113

ACCESSION NUMBER: 1991.40.44a–c

This may well be the design listed in the 1769 Christie's sale catalogue of Worcester porcelain as "of the very rich Mazarine Blue and Gold, fine old Wheatsheaf pattern." A teapot, formerly in the Drane Collection, painted with the same pattern on a blue scale ground, is inscribed within a gilt cartouche under the spout, *No 45*. A gold brooch attached to the finial is of the numerals *45* and the word *Liberty.* This refers to John Wilkes, the radical politician, and the celebrated issue "Number 45" of his paper, *The North Briton,* published on 23 April 1763. However, the ceramics commemorating "Wilkes and Liberty" date from five years later, at the time of the Middlesex Elections of 1768, a date that conforms more readily with the likely period of this teapot. The pattern, which was in production for at least ten years from about 1768, was also issued without the addition of gilding, presumably at a discounted price (cf. cat. no. 135). It is in the "rich Kakiemon" style, an idiom developed at Worcester that contained elements of Japanese Kakiemon, the *indianische Blumen* of Meissen, and the blue scale ground in an original manner, unique to the factory. Stands for teapots, introduced during the late 1750s, generally followed this hexagonal shape and were intended to protect the surface of furniture from the heat of the teapot. Like spoon trays, they were an optional component of tea services, and it is significant that they are relatively less common in blue and white.

134

135

135

Worcester Teacup and Saucer, ca. 1770

Decorated with flowering plants growing from banded hedges within mirror- and vase-shaped panels upon a blue scale ground.

DIAMETER OF SAUCER: 5¼ in. (13.3 cm)

MARK: Fretted square

LITERATURE: Spero, *Worcester Porcelain: The Klepser Collection,* cat. no. 113; Spero and J. Sandon, *Eighteenth-Century Worcester Porcelain: The Zorensky Collection,* chap. 8

ACCESSION NUMBER: 1991.40.43a–b

By comparison with the teapot and stand (cat. no. 134), this pattern is simplified and, even allowing for the absence of gilding, far less carefully painted. The decoration is somewhat slapdash, fitting poorly into the reserved panels and in places apparently unfinished. Such poor workmanship is highly uncharacteristic of the Worcester factory at this period. The probable explanation is that faulty or misfired pieces were often sold off prior to overglaze decoration. The purchaser, an independent decorator, anxious to avoid the costly and skillful process of gilding, outlined the panels in red enamel. The panels were then decorated in the rich Kakiemon style, employing a restricted palette. The underglaze blue ground itself would have been applied at Worcester. The early 1770s, and in particular 1772, was a period of serious economic recession in England, and it is likely that the Worcester factory sold off much of their undecorated, or partially decorated, old stock at this time. A comparison with the coffee cup and saucer (cat. no. 128) illustrates the enormous decorative impact of gilded cartouches surrounding the mirror- and vase-shaped panels, obscuring blemishes and transforming the decorative impact.

Teacups, introduced at Worcester in the mid-1750s on a very restricted scale, were not produced in large quantities until the late 1760s. Whereas tea bowls had associations with Chinese porcelain, teacups were an alternative shape, derived from Meissen and usually decorated with patterns not directly drawn from oriental sources.

135

136

Worcester Dish, ca. 1778–85

Molded in the form of two overlapping cabbage leaves, the crossed stalks forming a handle at one end, decorated in the Japanese taste, with flowers within triangular, mirror-, and vase-shaped panels upon a blue scale ground, overlaid with *caillouté* gilding.

LENGTH: 12½ in. (31.8 cm)

MARK: Fretted square

LITERATURE: Spero, *Worcester Porcelain: The Klepser Collection*, cat. no. 44, illustrates the shape

ACCESSION NUMBER: 1991.41.24

The shape, issued at Worcester in three sizes, generally spans the period from about 1756 to 1770, though, from a close examination of the hardness of its body, this example seems to be somewhat later. The form also occurs in conjunction with overglaze transfer prints and hand-painted decoration, as well as underglaze blue painting and transfer printing.

The unusual and distinctive style of gilding upon a blue ground is derived from the *lapis caillouté* at Sèvres, which first appears in the factory's records in 1756. The effect has been described as reminiscent of oriental lacquer. On English porcelain, *caillouté* gilding is rare, occurring on Worcester of the 1770s and to a lesser extent on Liverpool wares of the Pennington class, at the same period. An identical style of gilding was later copied at Minton in the early 1840s.

Gilding was the most costly process in the manufacture and decoration of porcelain, and gilders were relatively highly paid. It was not until 1765–70, with the onset of the Sèvres influence, that gilding became prominent on Worcester patterns, but thereafter it became a hallmark of the excellence of the more elaborate decoration at the factory. At first the celebrated honey gilding was used, giving a thick, grainy effect, but from about 1788–89 it was replaced by mercury gilding.

137

Worcester Teapot and Cover, ca. 1768–70

Of globular form, painted in the Japanese taste with eight radiating panels, four in underglaze blue enriched with gilt and four with flowers and diapers on a white ground with mons.

HEIGHT: 6½ in. (16.5 cm)

MARK: Pseudo-Chinese characters in underglaze blue

LITERATURE: Spero, *Worcester Porcelain: The Klepser Collection*, cat. no. 80, illustrates an openwork basket in this pattern

ACCESSION NUMBER: 1991.41.6a–b

Though principally a pattern associated with tea, coffee, and dessert services, this design, the Old *Mosaik* pattern, also occurs on vases and openwork baskets. Unlike many of the other Worcester "Japan" patterns, it seems to have been confined to a relatively brief period from about 1768 to 1772. With its complex and varied components and slightly unusual palette, it is one of the most elaborate and detailed of all the Worcester "Japan" patterns. This is one of the relatively few Worcester patterns of this period that is a direct adaptation of an oriental design, and, as with other such instances, the Chinese characters on the original have been substituted for a conventional Worcester factory mark. A somewhat similar pattern was briefly in production at Chelsea (cat. no. 12). The pattern was also in production at Meissen in the 1730s and at Vienna in the 1760s, though it seems likely that the Worcester version was inspired directly from Japanese originals.

136

137

138

138

Worcester Milk Jug and Cover, ca. 1768–70

Painted in the Japanese taste with eight radiating panels, four in underglaze blue enriched in gilt and four with flowers and diapers on a white ground with mons.

HEIGHT: 4¼ in. (10.8 cm)
MARK: Pseudo-Chinese characters in underglaze blue
LITERATURE: Spero, *Worcester Porcelain: The Klepser Collection*, cat. no. 80, illustrates an openwork basket in this pattern
ACCESSION NUMBER: 1991.40.25a–b

The pattern, called Old *Mosaik,* can be identified from a contemporary reference to the sale of "a large and elegant Assortment of the Worcester porcelaine" offered for sale at Christie's on 14 December 1769 and on the five following days (excluding Sunday), which included "Twelve beautiful plates, old mosaik japan pattern £2.15s." The same Christie's catalogue itemizes the components of a full Worcester tea service of forty-three pieces, describing the milk jug as a "milk-pot and cover." This form is seldom encountered in English porcelain until the early 1760s, though the East India Company's sales of oriental porcelain included milk pots with covers from 1706 onward. From this, it is clear that tea and coffee were often taken with milk, yet this was not an invariable custom. Writing in 1797 in a survey on the condition of the poor in Britain, Sir Frederick Eden observed, "Exclusive of beer, when he can afford it, and spirits, the quantity of water, which with tea forms a beverage which is seldom qualified with milk or sugar, poured down the throats of a labourer's family is astounding."

139
Worcester Saucer Dish, ca. 1768–70

Of circular form, painted in the Japanese taste with eight radiating panels, four in underglaze blue enriched with gilt and four with flowers and diapers on a white ground with mons.

DIAMETER: 7⅛ in. (18.1 cm)
MARK: Pseudo-Chinese characters in underglaze blue
LITERATURE: Spero and J. Sandon, *Eighteenth-Century Worcester Porcelain: The Zorensky Collection*, chap. 7
ACCESSION NUMBER: 1991.40.54

The Old *Mosaik* pattern is an adaptation of an original Japanese Imari design dating from 1720–40. Though the component parts themselves are faithfully copied, the pattern is compressed and simplified, the sixteen panels on the Imari original being reduced to eight and the Worcester panels being correspondingly larger. Various minor alterations were made to the Japanese design and also to the palette. For instance, in certain places, such as on the mons, the green in the Imari original is replaced by turquoise. Adaptations of "Japan" patterns were an important and successful element of the Worcester production in the years between the late 1760s and the mid-1770s. The importation of Japanese porcelain had ceased completely by the 1740s, and the demand for the earlier Kakiemon wares was exploited by both Chelsea and Bow in the 1750s. But it was the later "Japan" style with which Worcester was so successful. No other English factory offered serious competition in this market, although it later became a speciality at Derby.

This shape, probably intended for bread and butter or biscuits, was sometimes issued in two sizes in the same service. As with tea cannisters, spoon trays, and teapot stands, saucer dishes were not included in all services and most infrequently in the blue-and-white sets. Mainwarings, china dealers in Bath, were selling "complete Tea Services of Blue and White Worcester China, from £1.15s." in 1769, "the set consisting of 43 pieces."[1]

1. Branyan, French, and J. Sandon, *Worcester Blue and White Porcelain, 1751–1790*, p. 11.

139

140
Worcester Two-Handled Cup and Saucer, ca. 1768–70

Of double ogee shape, painted in the Japanese taste with eight radiating panels, four in underglaze blue enriched with gilt and four with flowers and diapers on a white ground with mons.

DIAMETER OF CUP: 3⅞ in. (9.8 cm)
DIAMETER OF SAUCER: 5¾ in. (14.6 cm)
MARK: Pseudo-Chinese characters in underglaze blue
LITERATURE: Spero, *Worcester Porcelain: The Klepser Collection*, cat. no. 137, illustrates the shape
ACCESSION NUMBER: 1991.40.34a–b

This form was introduced at Worcester in the mid-1760s and occurs in a wide range of patterns painted and transfer printed over the glaze and also in underglaze blue; here it is seen in the Old *Mosaik* pattern. The shape is variously described as a chocolate cup or a caudle cup. At least some examples had covers, and the Christie's sale of December 1769 describes in lot 69 on the fifth day, "Six caudle-cups covers and plates." A similar form was produced with only one handle, and it must be concluded that covers were optional.

Like chocolate, caudle was served hot. Tea caudle, for example, was a recipe invented in the late seventeenth century, soon after tea was first introduced into England from China. The tea was strained into a small saucepan and heated, with added sugar and nutmeg. Meanwhile, an egg yolk was beaten in a small basin and wine was added. The mixture was then poured into the saucepan of tea and stirred over a gentle heat. It was served hot.

140

141

Worcester Bowl, ca. 1770

Painted in underglaze blue, iron red, and rose pink and enriched with gilt, with swirling bands of stylized foliage.

DIAMETER: 5¾ in. (14.6 cm)
MARK: Painter's mark in underglaze blue
LITERATURE: H. Sandon, *The Illustrated Guide to Worcester Porcelain, 1751–1793*, pl. 50, illustrates a vase with a matching waster
ACCESSION NUMBER: 1991.47.54

One of the most popular and long-lived of all Worcester patterns, this was in production from the early 1760s until well into the nineteenth century. Now celebrated as the Queen Charlotte pattern, it was not so named until George III and Queen Charlotte visited the factory in August 1788. The pattern originated at Meissen in the 1730s, and it was imitated on Chinese porcelain made for export to the Turkish market. The Meissen version differs from the Worcester in having a spirally molded body and a more elaborate design in the central panel of the saucers. Several variants of the pattern were devised, not all of which included the use of underglaze blue. Some of these were executed outside the factory, and the orthodox version was also used at Bow. The Queen Charlotte pattern occurs on Worcester on a huge range of objects, probably greater in variety than that of any other single pattern.

141

142

Worcester Teacup and Saucer, ca. 1770

Painted in the Japanese taste with half-chrysanthemum roundels petaled alternately in underglaze blue and red and green enamels, the underglaze blue decorated with gilt trelliswork.

DIAMETER OF SAUCER: 5¼ in. (13.3 cm)
MARK: Pseudo-Chinese Ming dynasty reign mark in underglaze blue
LITERATURE: Spero, *Worcester Porcelain: The Klepser Collection*, cat. no. 81, illustrates a lozenge-shaped dish
ACCESSION NUMBER: 1991.40.74a–b

The Old Japan Fan pattern, with its prominent stylized chrysanthemums, was derived from a Japanese Imari original of about 1690 and occurs also on Chinese Imari during the first quarter of the eighteenth century. The Worcester version may possibly have been influenced by Meissen. The pattern is listed in the 1769 Worcester sale catalogue, which included "six caudle cups and saucers of the fine old Japan fan pattern £1.19s." It was utilized widely at Worcester during the early 1770s on teawares, dessert services, punch pots, vases, punch bowls, and caudle cups. The pattern was also produced at Derby and at Chamberlain's Worcester factory. At Worcester it is invariably accompanied by its own pseudo-Chinese mark. The presence of marks of this kind, some of which may have been adapted rather than imitated, tends to suggest the probability of a *direct* copy of an oriental original.

143

Worcester Tea Bowl and Saucer, ca. 1768–70

Of faceted form, decorated in the Japanese taste with alternating panels of oriental flowers and branches, and underglaze blue panels enriched in gilt with mons.

DIAMETER OF SAUCER: 4¾ in. (12.1 cm)
MARK: Fretted square
LITERATURE: Hobson, *Catalogue of the Frank Lloyd Collection of Worcester Porcelain of the Wall Period, British Museum*, pl. 11, cat. no. 63; Spero and J. Sandon, *Eighteenth-Century Worcester Porcelain: The Zorensky Collection*, chap. 7, illustrate three versions of the Queen's pattern
ACCESSION NUMBER: 1991.40.75a–b

This pattern, which was issued in both plain and faceted versions, was probably the most common of all the "Japan" patterns produced at Worcester in the 1770s, and it remained in production until the early part of the nineteenth century. An almost equally common version has orange panels in place of the underglaze blue (cat. nos. 147 and 148). The record books of Chamberlain's Worcester factory, for the 1790s, suggest that it is this rather than the Queen Charlotte pattern (cat. no. 141) that was described in the December 1769 auction catalogue as "Rich Queens."

The reason for the relatively small size of most eighteenth-century porcelain tea bowls lay in the high cost of tea. Ranging from sixteen to twenty-four shillings per pound, retail, at the beginning of the eighteenth century, the average cost had fallen to around eight shillings per pound by the 1770s. Nearly half this cost was due to taxation, which fluctuated at changing levels. However, following the Commutation Act of 1784, the average price of tea fell sharply, increasing consumption and leading indirectly to the demand for larger teapots and tea bowls. It has been calculated that immediately prior to the 1784 Act, over half of the tea imported into Britain was smuggled, thereby causing the government a significant loss of revenue. The reduction in the tax on tea was therefore a sensible measure, lessening both the incentive and the profits of the smugglers.

144

Worcester Bowl, ca. 1770

Decorated in the Japanese taste with alternating panels of oriental flowers and branches and underglaze blue panels enriched in gilt with mons.

DIAMETER: 6¾ in. (17.1 cm)
MARK: Fretted square
LITERATURE: Spero, *The Price Guide to Eighteenth-Century English Porcelain*, p. 108, illustrates a coffee cup and saucer
ACCESSION NUMBER: 1991.40.56

By the mid-1760s, a Worcester tea and coffee service comprised forty-three pieces. The Christie's sale of Worcester in December 1769 included eighty-one "complete tea and coffee equipages," each including a "Bason" or slop bowl. The full description of this pattern at Worcester was "Best Queen mosaic, blue and gold with india work." A version of this pattern designed with panels in orange rather than underglaze blue is catalogue number 147.

Although the "Japan" patterns on Worcester porcelain of the 1770s were inspired by oriental sources, some designs in this idiom had appeared on Meissen in the 1740s. The Worcester factory developed this richly decorated range of patterns, incorporating both Japanese Kakiemon motifs and Chinese themes, combining designs and palettes from diverse influences, with a liberal use of gilding. From these disparate sources, the designers created a decorative style that was in one sense derivative yet, in another, completely original.

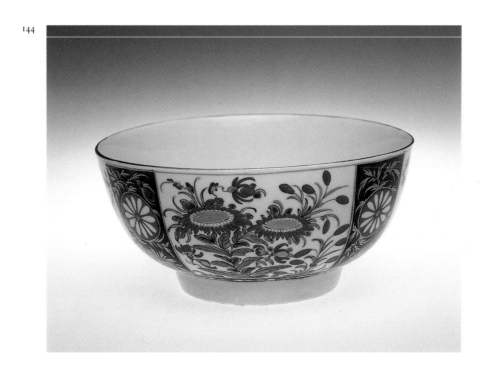

144

145

Worcester Cream Jug, ca. 1768–70

Decorated in the Japanese taste with alternating panels of oriental flowers and branches and underglaze blue panels with mons.

HEIGHT: 3¼ in. ((8.2 cm)
MARK: Fretted square
LITERATURE: Marshall, *Coloured Worcester Porcelain of the First Period*, pl. 23, no. 501, illustrates a molded cream jug of this shape
ACCESSION NUMBER: 1991.47.12

By comparison with the Kakiemon-inspired patterns that were introduced at Worcester by the mid-1750s, the designs derived from Chinese and Japanese Imari porcelain did not appear until the late 1760s, coinciding with the first widespread use of underglaze blue grounds and panels. No other European porcelain factory approached the size of the Worcester output in this genre, or indeed their output of patterns incorporating underglaze blue grounds. In this instance, the indifferent quality of the decoration, together with the red-line border, suggests the hand of an independent decorator, working on a "second." This shape, relatively uncommon in color, was suggested by an earlier silver original. Introduced in the late 1750s, it occurs only in conjunction with relief-molded and faceted bodies.

This cream jug was made by "press-molding." The other main method of manufacture was by the "throwing and turning" process, using a potter's wheel. This was utilized for such wares as mugs, teapots, bowls, and cups.

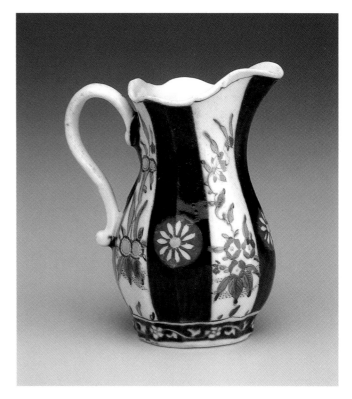

145

146

146

Worcester Tea Bowl, Saucer, and Coffee Cup, ca. 1770

Decorated in the Japanese taste with alternating panels of oriental flowers and branches and underglaze blue panels with mons.

DIAMETER OF SAUCER: 4 in. (10.2 cm)
MARK: Fretted square on each piece
LITERATURE: J. Sandon, *The Dictionary of Worcester Porcelain, 1751–1851*, color pl. 67
ACCESSION NUMBERS: 1991.40.11.1a–b, 40.12

The pattern is a simplified version of that on the faceted tea bowl and saucer (cat. no. 143), lacking the gilding and being painted with less care. Wares of this type, characterized by the distinctive narrow red-line border, were possibly the work of an independent decorator who bought up stocks of faulty blue ground pieces, put aside at the factory as "seconds." More than thirty variants of this basic design are known, alternating a ground color, most often underglaze blue or orange, with white panels, all radiating from a circular white reserve with a central mons. Many of these are factory patterns, but a large proportion, including this example, would seem to have had their overglaze decoration executed elsewhere. At this period a Worcester tea and coffee service would include twelve coffee cups, twelve tea bowls, and twelve saucers, there being no reason for the cups and tea bowls to be in use at the same time.

147

Worcester Bowl, ca. 1770

Painted with alternating panels of oriental flowering plants and narrower orange panels, painted with gilt trelliswork and containing a mons.

DIAMETER: 6¼ in. (15.9 cm)

MARK: None

LITERATURE: Spero, *Worcester Porcelain: The Klepser Collection*, cat. no. 165, illustrates a teapot and cover; Spero and J. Sandon, *Eighteenth-Century Worcester Porcelain: The Zorensky Collection,* chap. 7

ACCESSION NUMBER: 1991.40.24

This pattern, derived from eighteenth-century Chinese porcelain, was widely used on Worcester porcelain of the 1770s, both at the Factory and at the James Giles atelier in London. It occurs on a wide range of shapes including plain, fluted, and faceted teawares and dessert services. The orange tone in the panels may well have been that described in the advertisement for the Christie's sale of Worcester porcelain in May 1769 as "Scarlet," a color not otherwise associated with Japan patterns. The design was employed with great versatility, being adapted for use on an extensive range of forms including "Dutch Jugs," vases, mugs, teawares, dessert wares, and many other shapes. The function of this piece might have been as a slop bowl, or an alternative to the sucrier and cover of the "compleat" service.

148

Worcester Coffee Cup and Saucer, ca. 1770

Painted with alternating panels of oriental flowering plants and narrower orange panels, painted with gilt trelliswork and each containing a mons.

DIAMETER OF SAUCER: 5⅛ in. (13.0 cm)

MARK: Crossed swords and numeral 9

LITERATURE: Spero, *Worcester Porcelain: The Klepser Collection*, cat. no. 165

ACCESSION NUMBER: 1991.47.55a–b

An almost identical version of this "Japan" pattern was done at Richard Chaffers's Liverpool factory in the mid-1760s, and other designs employing orange panels with mons, utilized in this way, were issued at Derby, West Pans, Caughley, and on Chinese porcelain painted in London. The pattern itself strongly resembles another popular Worcester design of the period, in which underglaze blue panels were used in place of the orange ones (cat. no. 144). Some specimens of this "scarlet Japan" pattern were decorated outside the factory, and, intriguingly, these appear to predate the factory's own version.

Described by Samuel Pepys in earlier days as the "bitter black drink," coffee was by the 1770s often taken with milk and sometimes sugar. During the period of its introduction into England, in the second half of the seventeenth century, some coffee drinkers had added candy, powdered cinnamon, and, almost incredibly, mustard to improve upon the flavor, but this fashion was, unsurprisingly, short-lived.

147

148

149

Worcester Teapot and Cover, ca. 1768–70

Of faceted form, decorated in the Chinese taste with panels of fabulous animals and Precious Objects, within a green border with black dots and cell diaper.

HEIGHT: 4½ in. (11.4 cm)

MARK: Fretted square

LITERATURE: Spero, *Worcester Porcelain: The Klepser Collection*, cat. no. 87, illustrates a tea bowl and saucer; Spero and J. Sandon, *Eighteenth-Century Worcester Porcelain: The Zorensky Collection*, chap. 4

ACCESSION NUMBER: 1991.40.38a–b

The Bengal Tiger or Dragon in Compartments was exactly copied from an early-eighteenth-century Chinese famille verte design from the Kangxi period and was produced on a wide range of Worcester, including teawares, dessert services, and many larger forms, such as vases. It was first issued in the late 1760s and remained popular for many decades. It was also utilized at Plymouth, Caughley, Coalport, and at Chamberlain's Worcester factory, where it was known as the "draggon in compartments." An alternative name at Worcester was the "Kylin" pattern. Tea services in this pattern occur in plain, fluted, and faceted shapes. The wider fluting, exemplified by this teapot, is generally associated with the fretted-square mark. Faceted teawares were first introduced at Worcester in the late 1750s, but the shape had been discontinued by the mid-1770s, being replaced by the round form of fluting seen on the saucer dish (cat. no. 150) also painted in the Bengal Tiger pattern.

150

150

Worcester Saucer Dish, ca. 1778–82

Of fluted form, decorated with panels of fabulous animals and Precious Objects within a green border, dotted in black and cell diaper.

DIAMETER: 8½ in. (21.6 cm)

MARK: None

LITERATURE: Spero, *Worcester Porcelain: The Klepser Collection*, cat. no. 87, illustrates a tea bowl and saucer

ACCESSION NUMBER: 1991.41.27

The lobed fluting, seen here on a saucer dish decorated in the Bengal Tiger pattern, was introduced in the late 1770s, replacing the faceted shape on the teapot (cat. no. 149), and occurs mainly in conjunction with shapes influenced by Sèvres. These forms were in production at Worcester until the late 1780s. The cross-fertilization in English porcelain of this period is once again evident in a Chinese pattern, derived from Japanese porcelain, decorating a Worcester dish in a shape influenced by French porcelain. However, the great popularity of this pattern in the late eighteenth and early nineteenth century suggests that the public was not in the least deterred by any apparent incongruity of this mélange of diverse styles. Indeed, even the Worcester designers themselves would hardly have been aware of the rich mixture of idioms and influences evident in this saucer dish. Decorative effect would have been their sole priority.

149

151

151

Worcester Sucrier and Cover, ca. 1778–82

Of cylindrical form, painted in the Kakiemon taste with two quail under a flowering tree, within a border of iron red scrolling foliage.

HEIGHT: 6 in. (15.2 cm)

MARK: None

LITERATURE: J. Sandon, *The Dictionary of Worcester Porcelain, 1751–1851,* p. 332, illustrates a matching teapot

ACCESSION NUMBER: 1991.41.28a–b

This version of the Quail pattern is a reissue of an earlier version produced at Worcester in the mid-1760s, though the teaware shapes upon which it appears are completely different. In place of the widely fluted or faceted forms of the earlier version are flared cylindrical shapes, resembling those associated with the Duchess of Kent pattern. This Worcester pattern conforms quite closely to the Bow version (cat. nos. 57–63), from which the border design originated, though it is far removed from the simplicity and subtlety of the Meissen and Kakiemon prototypes. A crescent mark, in either red or gilt, is usually found in conjunction with the Quail pattern when it appears on these cylindrical shapes.

Sugar was a great luxury in the early eighteenth century, and the West Indian islands from which it came, Grenada in particular, were prized possessions of the British empire. However, by the later part of the century sugar had become relatively inexpensive and the poorer classes in particular often drank their tea heavily sweetened. Sugar bowls in England were larger than on the Continent, where powdered sugar was customary. In England, the sugar lumps, chipped from large cones, necessitated larger vessels, and, as the price of sugar fell, so sugar boxes progressively expanded in size.

152

Worcester Teapot, Saucer Dish, and Sucrier,
ca. 1772–78

Of fluted form, decorated in the Kakiemon taste with two quail, one blue and the other red, beneath a flowering prunus tree, within a shaped turquoise border, edged with scrolls and pendant flowers.

HEIGHT OF TEAPOT: 4½ in. (11.4 cm)
DIAMETER OF SAUCER DISH: 8¼ in. (21.0 cm)
DIAMETER OF SUCRIER: 4 in. (10.2 cm)
MARKS: None
LITERATURE: Spero, *Worcester Porcelain: The Klepser Collection*, cat. no. 89, illustrates a coffee cup and saucer
ACCESSION NUMBERS: 1991.40.8a–b, 40.9a–b, 40.10

These three pieces are decorated in one of the ten versions of the Quail or Partridge pattern that occur on Worcester, spanning the period about 1758–80. Some of these were decorated at the Worcester factory, while others were devised at the London studio of James Giles. This Factory version is one of the most elaborate of all, with its rococo overtones, far removed from the simpler patterns of the 1760s, which echoed their Bow and Meissen counterparts and were more or less faithful to the spirit of the Kakiemon original. It presents an illuminating contrast with the many versions of the Quail pattern in the Bowles Collection. The border pattern, with its combination of rococo scrolls and rich Kakiemon foliage, is entirely an invention of Worcester, echoing the "blue *Celeste* borders" listed in the 1769 Worcester sale catalogue. The fluted form of teapot, introduced at Worcester in the late 1770s, was inspired by Sèvres, as can be

discerned from the ear-shaped handle, which first appeared at the French factory in 1764. Thus, an Anglicized adaptation of a Meissen pattern, derived from Japanese porcelain, adorns a shape that originated in France. Further versions of the Quail pattern were used at Chelsea, Bow, Longton Hall, Lowestoft, West Pans, Plymouth, Chaffers's Liverpool factory, and on the mysterious unidentified "A mark" class. (See cat. nos. 57–63, 71, and 173 and 178 for versions of the Quail pattern on Bow, Lowestoft, and Chantilly.)

153   *Detail p. 148*

Worcester Mug, ca. 1765–68

Of cylindrical form, transfer printed in black with *La Diseuse d'Aventure* and on the reverse with *The Whitton Anglers.*

HEIGHT: 4¾ in. (12.1 cm)
MARK: None
LITERATURE: Handley, *Eighteenth-Century English Transfer-Printed Porcelain and Enamels*, no. 2.25
ACCESSION NUMBER: 1991.47.22

The two prints by Robert Hancock on this mug are generally found in tandem. The design for *La Diseuse d'Aventure* was taken from a painting of the same name by Watteau, and the Hancock print was probably derived from an engraving by Laurent Cars. The source for *The Whitton Anglers* was an engraving by William Woollett entitled *A View of the*

Canal and of the Gothick Tower and the Garden of His Grace the Duke of Argyle at Whitton. This was printed by Robert Sayer, the publisher of *The Ladies Amusement*. Both prints were introduced at Worcester in the early 1760s and remained in production until about 1770. They are confined to mugs of various sizes and sometimes jugs and do not appear upon teawares. This conforms to the widely accepted practice at Worcester for overglaze transfer prints to be associated with specific wares: mugs, jugs, and vases, or teawares, or dinner and dessert services. The source print for *The Whitton Anglers* is illustrated by Joseph Handley (see Literature) on page 73.

154

Worcester Bowl, ca. 1772–75

Transfer printed in black with a version of *The Tea Party*, after Robert Hancock, *The Maid and Page*, and *Gardener Grafting Tree*.

DIAMETER: 6 in. (15.2 cm)
MARK: None
LITERATURE: Handley, *Eighteenth-Century English Transfer-Printed Porcelain and Enamels*, no. 2.43; Spero and J. Sandon, *Eighteenth-Century Worcester Porcelain: The Zorensky Collection*, chap. 13
ACCESSION NUMBER: 1991.47.18

The Tea Party was the most popular and widely used of all the overglaze transfer prints produced at Worcester over a period of some twenty years, and

this popularity echoed the fashion for tea drinking. The design clearly caught the imagination of the public and was confined, appropriately enough, mainly to teawares. It is therefore understandable that the detailed depiction of this social ritual, enjoyed in the open air, in the manner of a conversation piece, should have had so enduring an appeal. Lot 21 in the sale of Worcester porcelain on 20 December 1769 was "A compleat tea and coffee equipage, with twisted handles, jet enamelled with a tea-table, forty three pieces." This sold for 1 pound 16 shillings, which was approximately seven times the weekly wage of a country laborer in 1759–60 and just under twice the weekly salary of a country clergyman.[1]

Three versions of this print were done by Robert Hancock at Worcester, but this example seems to have been the work of another engraver. This can be discerned by the dark-toned printing, the yellowish paste, and the arrangement of the tea-drinking scene, which differs considerably from Hancock's versions of the subject.

The fashion for tea drinking, introduced by Charles II's wife in the 1660s, had steadily grown in popularity by the middle of the eighteenth century, despite its high cost. Within a further thirty years, tea drinking in England was universal.

1. Porter, *English Society in the Eighteenth Century*, pp. 386–87.

154

155

Worcester Bowl, ca. 1768

Transfer printed in black with three designs by
Robert Hancock, including *The Three Fishers.*

DIAMETER: 6 in. (15.2 cm)

MARK: None

LITERATURE: Handley, *Eighteenth-Century English
Transfer-Printed Porcelain and Enamels*, no. 6.7

ACCESSION NUMBER: 1991.47.17

The Three Fishers is one of a group of designs by the
engraver Robert Hancock that echo the influence of
seventeenth-century Dutch landscape painting. The
detail and perspective afforded by the engravings, beyond the scope of landscape painting, was especially
appropriate to landscape and genre subjects. Most
often appearing in black, as here, this print also occurs in lilac. The technique of transfer printing over
the glaze was used for the first time on English porcelain at Worcester, where the earliest examples date
from about 1753–54. By about 1756–57, the process
had reached a high degree of perfection and in the
following decade was to contribute crucially to the
commercial success of the Worcester factory. Robert
Hancock was responsible for the majority of the designs on Worcester, but the earliest engravings were
by another hand, and Hancock probably did not arrive at the factory until about 1756. He subsequently
became a partner at Worcester on the sale of the factory in 1772, at the end of its lease. Whether Hancock
was at any time actually employed at Worcester,
or whether he operated independently, is an open
question.

The evolution of Worcester shapes is evident here
in the slightly more rounded contours of this bowl, by
comparison with catalogue number 154, several years
later in date.

155

156

Lund's Bristol Mug, ca. 1750

Of globular form, with a turned neck and foot,
painted in underglaze blue with a detailed
continuous Chinese riverscape.

HEIGHT: 4⅜ in. (11.1 cm)

MARK: None

LITERATURE: Watney, *English Blue and White Porcelain of
the Eighteenth Century*, pl. 22C

ACCESSION NUMBER: 1991.40.40

Only five examples of this distinctive shape are
known in early English porcelain. This example and
a similar Lund's Bristol mug painted in a slightly different pattern were both formerly in the J. W. Jenkins
Collection. The shape was probably derived from
seventeenth-century German stoneware, although
somewhat similar forms were made in English pottery, Chinese blanc de chine, and in Japanese Arita,
for the export market. The underglaze blue, a
brighter tone than that of Worcester, shows none of
the blurring or unfocused effects that so often characterize pieces of Lund's Bristol. Indeed, the river landscape, closely copying Chinese porcelain, is far more
detailed and ambitious than was usually attempted,
and the overall effect, far more successful, suggesting
intriguing parallels with Bow decoration in this
genre. Three further examples of this shape are
known in Worcester porcelain of the "Scratch Cross"
class, bearing incised marks, one in the Cormorant
pattern and the two others in the Zigzag Fence
pattern.

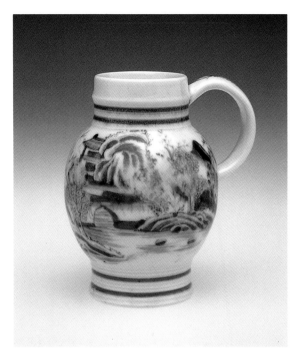

156

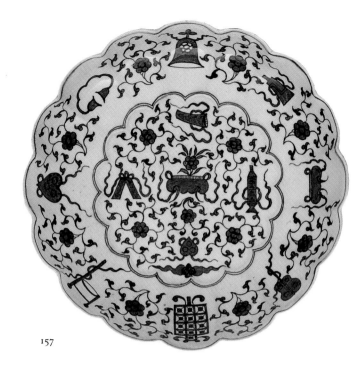

157

By comparison with Limehouse, the only class of English blue-and-white porcelain that predates Lund's Bristol, this mug shows a considerable improvement in potting, a far more translucent body, and a sophistication of decoration rarely equaled at the London factory. The shape, too, is relatively ambitious for this early period, demonstrating the skill of the potters, possibly learned from their experience in the delftware or Staffordshire salt-glaze industries. Indeed, potting of a notably high standard is a feature of Limehouse porcelain though, curiously, less so of contemporary Bow wares.

157
Worcester Junket Dish, ca. 1772
Of lobed shape, painted in underglaze blue with the Hundred Antiques joined by scrolling stylized flowers.

DIAMETER: 10 in. (25.4 cm)
MARK: Pseudo-Chinese characters
LITERATURE: Spero and J. Sandon, *Eighteenth-Century Worcester Porcelain: The Zorensky Collection*, chap. 15
ACCESSION NUMBER: 1991.40.50

The pattern is a modification of the Kangxi Hundred Antiques, or *po ku*, a collection of precious objects depicted in a stylized manner and derived from Chinese famille verte porcelain. At Worcester, the pattern was confined to dessert wares of the 1770s and 1780s, and it was used at no other eighteenth-century English factory. As with several other designs incorporating underglaze blue decoration and directly copied from Chinese sources, the pseudo-oriental mark invariably accompanies the pattern. This is one of several shapes variously described as a junket dish or salad dish, though the exact purpose is unknown. A junket dish would probably have required a more heavily molded surface in order to allow the soured cream and curd mixture to set. The shapes were introduced in the late 1750s and continued in production until the early 1780s.

158

159

158

Worcester Tea Bowl and Saucer, ca. 1765

Painted in underglaze blue with two figures on a galloping horse, accompanied by attendants on foot, some carrying canopies and lances.

DIAMETER OF SAUCER: 4¼ in. (10.8 cm)

MARK: Pseudo-Chinese characters

LITERATURE: Spero, *Worcester Porcelain: The Klepser Collection*, cat. no. 203

ACCESSION NUMBER: 1991.40.76a–b

One of the most celebrated of all underglaze blue patterns on Worcester, the Eloping Bride was adapted from a late-seventeenth-century Chinese Kangxi original, simplifying and clarifying the oriental design. Although certain elements of the design have been misinterpreted, a horseman omitted and replaced by two more figures on foot, the overall atmosphere has been skillfully re-created, especially in such features as the delicate shading, the postures of the figures, and the oriental mien of the galloping horse. It occurs only in conjunction with tea services, and the tea bowls and saucers are invariably of smaller than average size for their period. The painting is always accomplished with great care and precision, which supports the contention that the pattern is a direct modification of a specific Chinese design rather than a chinoiserie pattern. It spans the period from about 1765 to 1772, and examples tend to be thinly potted and small in size, echoing their Chinese counterparts. The eighteenth-century expression "a dish of tea" probably refers to the custom of drinking tea out of a handleless cup, a habit derived from the use of Chinese porcelain, which was later imitated at the English factories.

159

Worcester Spoon, ca. 1765–68

Of Chinese rice-spoon form, with a tapering oval bowl and straight handle, painted in underglaze blue with a central flower head, surrounded by scrolling foliage.

LENGTH: 5 in. (12.7 cm)

MARK: Crescent

LITERATURE: Spero, *Worcester Porcelain: The Klepser Collection*, cat. no. 205

ACCESSION NUMBER: 1991.40.51

Both the shape and the pattern were derived from Chinese porcelain, though neither is unique to the Worcester factory. The shape ranges in period at Worcester from about 1765 to 1780 and occurs in three other patterns. Biscuit fragments of this form were excavated on the site of the Worcester factory. Spoons of this shape were also made at Lowestoft and Bow, though examples are scarce.

As with so many utilitarian forms in eighteenth-century English porcelain, this shape occurs only in underglaze blue. Its purpose is not clear, though some Worcester examples are pierced for use as sifter spoons for sugar.

160

Worcester Cream Jug, ca. 1765–68

Of "sparrow beak" form, painted in underglaze blue with a Chinese landscape.

HEIGHT: 3⅛ in. (7.9 cm)

MARK: Crescent

LITERATURE: Spero, *The Price Guide to Eighteenth-Century English Porcelain*, p. 120

ACCESSION NUMBER: 1991.47.25

This is a classic Worcester form loosely adapted from English silver, painted with a pattern that ranged in date from the late 1750s until the mid-1770s. The Blue Rock pattern was copied at several other factories, including Bow, Derby, Plymouth, Caughley, and the Liverpool factories of Christian and Seth Pennington. At Worcester it occurs also in conjunction with painter's and script *W* marks. A relatively simple pattern, it required no great experience to copy, and this accounted for its comparative longevity. It occurs in association with a wide range of shapes including teawares, mustard pots, potting pots, small vases, and coffee cans. A Worcester teapot in this pattern, inscribed *W M 1766*, is in the Dyson Perrins Museum, Worcester, and a saucer, similarly decorated and bearing the same inscription, is in the British Museum.

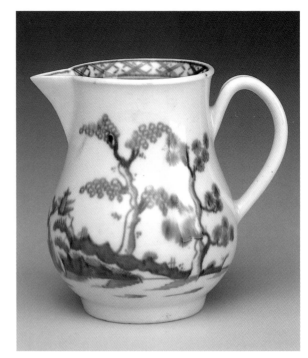

160

161

161

Worcester Coffee Cup and Saucer, ca. 1768–70

Painted in underglaze blue with flowers and branches and a prunus root, with a hovering insect.

DIAMETER OF SAUCER: 4¾ in. (12.1 cm)

MARK: Crescent

LITERATURE: Branyan, French, and J. Sandon, *Worcester Blue and White Porcelain, 1751–1790*, I.D.27

ACCESSION NUMBER: 1991.40.73a–b

The Prunus Root pattern occurs in conjunction with a very wide range of shapes and over a period from about 1756 until the mid-1770s. In teawares alone, it is seen on fluted, faceted, octagonal, and plain shapes, as well as on miniature pieces. The pattern also occurs in monochrome reddish brown, though examples are scarce. Other factories utilizing the design include Bow, Lowestoft, Longton Hall, Derby, and Richard Chaffers's Liverpool factory. It shares with the popular Dragon pattern a pleasing feature whereby portions of the design are continued onto the undersides of saucers and into the interiors of cups and tea bowls. Its popularity and longevity are probably due to its adaptability on diverse shapes and to the relative ease of its execution.

162

162

Worcester Sauceboat, ca. 1775–78

Of fluted shape with a strap handle, painted with floral sprays below an elaborate diaper border.

LENGTH: 6 in. (15.2 cm)

MARK: None

LITERATURE: Spero, *The Price Guide to Eighteenth-Century English Porcelain*, p. 331

ACCESSION NUMBER: 1991.47.13

This form, derived from an earlier Chinese Qianlong original, was confined at Worcester to the 1770s, the earlier examples having more detailed decoration and a thumb rest on top of the handle. Unusually for a sauceboat, the weight of decoration is principally sustained by the very elaborate scroll border, both interior and exterior. This was perhaps deemed necessary by the absence of the relief molding, associated with sauceboats of the 1750s and 1760s. Similar shapes were made at Derby, Lowestoft, and Caughley. However, in all instances, the shape was confined to underglaze blue decoration, with the single exception of Derby. The basic shape was used extensively in Chinese export porcelain, intended for the European market, and examples were imported into England in great numbers during the 1770s and 1780s.

163

163

Worcester Coffee Cup and Saucer, ca. 1780–82

Painted in underglaze blue with stylized flowers and scattered sprigs below a gilt line border.

DIAMETER OF SAUCER: 5 in. (12.7 cm)
MARK: "Hunting horn" in underglaze blue
LITERATURE: Branyan, French, and J. Sandon, *Worcester Blue and White Porcelain, 1751–1790,* I.E.52
ACCESSION NUMBER: 1991.47.19a–b

Both the painted Chantilly Sprig pattern and the distinctive "hunting horn" mark were derived directly from the Chantilly factory, source of so many Worcester, Derby, and Caughley shapes and patterns of the 1780s. This comparatively late pattern, also used at Caughley, did not come into production until about 1780. It is associated with this French form of coffee cup and with teapots echoing its conical shape. At this period, floral patterns in the French taste had largely superseded the hand-painted Chinese designs, though the tradition of oriental landscapes was maintained through the transfer-printed patterns at Caughley, Lowestoft, and Worcester. A pair of custard cups and covers, illustrating the origins of this pattern on Chantilly porcelain, are catalogue number 182.

Worcester Mug, ca. 1768–70

Of cylindrical form, transfer printed in underglaze blue with an oriental building, bamboo, trees, and rocks, enclosed by a fretted fence.

HEIGHT: 4⅝ in. (11.7 cm)
MARK: Crescent in underglaze blue
LITERATURE: Spero and J. Sandon, *Eighteenth-Century Worcester Porcelain: The Zorensky Collection,* chap. 16
ACCESSION NUMBER: 1991.47.31

The printed version of this pattern, The Plantation Print, introduced in about 1760, was closely derived from a hand-painted design associated with the "Scratch Cross" class of Worcester (1754–56). It was one of the first underglaze blue transfer prints to be utilized in large quantities, and although the overall pattern remained unaltered throughout the 1760s, minor changes, especially to the fretted fence, were made from time to time. The pattern occurs on teawares and bowls, but it is particularly frequent on cylindrical and bell-shaped mugs.

This cylindrical shape evolved from the earliest Worcester tankards and became a standard form at the factory by about 1756–58, remaining in production into the 1780s. Sizes ranged from "coffee cans" of no more than 2½ inches in height to quart mugs of substantial proportions, though the full range of sizes would not have been available in every pattern. As with cider jugs, a high proportion of Worcester mugs were decorated in underglaze blue.

165

Pair of Worcester Baskets, ca. 1772–78

Of oval form, with branch handles and openwork sides, transfer printed in underglaze blue with flowers, scattered sprays, and insects.

LENGTH: 8 in. (20.3 cm)
MARK: Script *W* in underglaze blue on each piece
LITERATURE: Branyan, French, and J. Sandon, *Worcester Blue and White Porcelain, 1751–1790,* 11.C.22
ACCESSION NUMBERS: 1991.47.29 1, 2

The Gilliflower, which occurs in both transfer-printed and hand-painted versions, is one of a small group of patterns derived from Continental porcelain, in this instance, Chantilly. The pattern was introduced at Worcester in about 1770 and was continued into the mid-1780s. A cylindrical mug bearing this print is inscribed *S L 1778* and was formerly in the collection of Stanley Fisher. Named after a French term for a carnation, this pattern also occurs on Derby, Pennington Liverpool, and Caughley. A pair of Chantilly custard cups and covers illustrate the origin of this style of decoration (cat. no. 182).

165

166

166

Worcester Cream Jug, ca. 1775–82

Transfer printed in underglaze blue with European landscape scenes within an intricate border design.

HEIGHT: 3½ in. (8.9 cm)
MARK: Hatched crescent in underglaze blue
LITERATURE: Branyan, French, and J. Sandon, *Worcester Blue and White Porcelain, 1751–1790,* 11.B.16
ACCESSION NUMBER: 1991.47.27

The two patterns on this cream jug form part of a class designated by Branyan, French, and Sandon as "The European Landscape Group." They are distinguished by the use of European subjects rather than the more common oriental themes, and a slightly violet or indigo tone to the underglaze blue, a change introduced in the mid-1770s. Wasters of pieces decorated with this group of patterns were found on the factory site during excavations. The vast majority of wares from this class in underglaze blue are transfer printed rather than hand painted. By comparison with the hand-painted cream jug (cat. no. 160), some ten years earlier in period, the overall shape has altered, becoming more bulbous. In addition, the upper terminal of the handle is set further down the body.

· CAUGHLEY ·

1772–1799

THE CAUGHLEY FACTORY, located in Shropshire, some sixty-four kilometers up the River Severn from Worcester, began production in 1772. It utilized a soapstone recipe very similar to that of Worcester, and indeed, one of the partners, Thomas Turner, had previously been employed there. The output was principally of blue-and-white wares, initially in imitation of Worcester patterns and shapes, and later copying the styles of Chantilly and Tournai. Later still, Caughley made a speciality of competing with the densely decorated "Nankin" porcelain, imported from China.

the vast quantities of Chinese porcelain being imported at that time. Yet although much of the English porcelain was transfer printed it could still not compete successfully with the low cost of the hand-painted Chinese wares. At Caughley, the pattern was produced in a vast range of shapes, and in many cases, records of original prices have been preserved. For instance, the teapots in the "Pleasure Boat" pattern, when sold singly, cost about two to three shillings each, according to size. By contrast, some thirty years before, the Worcester factory's wholesale price list quoted their smallest size of plain round teapot at fifteen shillings per dozen, apparently indicating a fairly substantial rise in porcelain prices over the period. Inflation, unknown in the 1750s, increasingly affected prices from the 1770s onward.

167   *Detail left*

Caughley Tea Bowl and Saucer, ca. 1785

Transfer printed in underglaze blue with the Fisherman and the Cormorant pattern.

DIAMETER OF SAUCER: 4¾ in. (12.1 cm)
MARK: *S* in underglaze blue, on the saucer
LITERATURE: Godden, *Caughley and Worcester Porcelain, 1775–1800*, color pl. 1
ACCESSION NUMBER: 1991.47.26a–b

Known in the eighteenth century as the "Pleasure Boat," this pattern was also produced at Worcester, Derby, and at Seth Pennington's Liverpool factory, though it can be readily distinguished by several variations in the print. It is representative of the range of oriental patterns being produced in England during the 1770s and 1780s, in an attempt to compete with

167

168

168

Caughley Plate, ca. 1775–80

Painted in underglaze blue with a central pattern showing an insect hovering above a flowering oriental shrub, the rim with six radiating panels, enclosing stylized flowers and Buddhistic emblems in reserve, upon a powder blue ground.

DIAMETER: 7⅞ in. (20.0 cm)

MARK: SALOPIAN, impressed

LITERATURE: Fisher, *English Blue and White Porcelain of the Eighteenth Century,* pl. 39, illustrates a lozenge-shaped dish

ACCESSION NUMBER: 1991.40.65

The powder blue ground, derived from Chinese porcelain, was used principally at Bow and Worcester, where it was introduced about 1760. It was also utilized at Lowestoft and occasionally at Derby. The Caughley versions occur only on dessert wares and are known in three different patterns. They are confined to the first ten years of the factory and tend to be of consistently good quality.

An identical plate, illustrated in *Worcester Blue and White Porcelain, 1751–1790,* is marked with an open crescent and attributed to Worcester by the authors, Lawrence Branyan, Neal French, and John Sandon.

169

169

Caughley Mustard Pot and Cover, ca. 1775

Painted in underglaze blue with meandering flowers and leaves.

HEIGHT: 3½ in. (8.9 cm)

MARK: *C* in underglaze blue

LITERATURE: Godden, *Caughley and Worcester Porcelain, 1775–1800,* pl. 156

ACCESSION NUMBER: 1991.40.57a–b

Here, both the shape and the pattern were derived from Worcester. The shape was the model used for "wet" mustard at such factories as Lowestoft and Derby, while the Mansfield pattern was utilized at Bow, Lowestoft, Derby, Plymouth, and at the Liverpool factories of Chaffers, Christian, and Pennington. Mustard pots of this form adapted from silver were first issued in the late 1760s and continued into the 1780s. They were adapted from silver and occur in Caughley porcelain in conjunction with four main patterns, three of which are transfer prints. An alternative baluster form with a domed cover, intended for "dry" mustard, was also made at Caughley, though examples are very scarce. As with many utilitarian shapes in English porcelain, the vast majority of mustard pots were issued in underglaze blue.

170

170

Caughley Egg Drainer, ca. 1785

Of circular form, pierced and with a shell-molded handle, transfer printed in underglaze blue with the Fisherman and the Cormorant pattern.

DIAMETER: 3¼ in. (8.3 cm)

MARK: None

LITERATURE: Godden, *Caughley and Worcester Porcelain, 1775–1800,* pl. 119

ACCESSION NUMBER: 1991.47.23

This shape is sometimes described as a "tea strainer," but a listing in 1789 of Caughley porcelain supplied to Robert Chamberlain refers to "Egg cups & strainers" and "Egg stands & drainers, Pleasure Boat," making their general function clear. The listing goes on to mention that the egg drainers cost fourpence "each in the white," prior to decoration. It has been suggested that drainers were used for serving poached eggs, but their exact purpose remains the subject for debate.

Egg drainers occur with two styles of handle and were also made at Worcester, Derby, Lowestoft, and James Pennington's Liverpool factory. As with so many of the utilitarian forms in the eighteenth century, egg drainers were never decorated in polychrome, though some examples were gilded.

· CHANTILLY ·

ca. 1725–1800

*Chantilly Sugar Bowl
and Cover*
Cat. no. 176

THE CHANTILLY FACTORY was established in about 1725, under the direction of Cicaire Cirou, at Petit Chantilly, and under the patronage of duc Louis-Henri de Bourbon, prince de Condé. Condé had enjoyed a brief but meteoric political career, becoming chief minister in 1723 at the age of thirty-one, before falling from power three years later and being exiled to his estate at Chantilly. Thereafter he pursued his varied interests, which included the study of chemistry and natural history and the collecting of oriental porcelain. In this enthusiasm he followed the example of other French and German princes and noblemen who not only collected porcelain but were involved in the promotion of factories under their patronage. As a consequence, these factories were guaranteed a substantial period of prosperity, as the prestige of their patrons depended upon the success of the enterprise. No such advantage was enjoyed by the English factories, with the partial exception of Chelsea, and their economic survival hinged upon more or less immediate commercial success in an extremely competitive market. In this distinction is rooted the essential differences — technical, aesthetic, and commercial — between early French porcelain and its English counterparts.

Like his illustrious contemporary Augustus Rex, Elector of Saxony, who housed his collection in the Johanneum, or Japanese Palace, in Dresden, Condé collected on a substantial scale and had a marked preference for Japanese porcelain. At the time of his death, in 1740, an inventory was drawn up that listed nearly two thousand pieces of porcelain, the majority of which were Japanese. From this it is clear that from the inception of the factory there was a significant collection of Japanese porcelain at the Château de Chantilly. These pieces were principally a type imported from Arita, in Hizen province, and associated in their decoration with the potter Sakaida Kakiemon. And it was these wares that were to inspire the production for the first twenty or more years at Chantilly and to lend to the factory its particular and indeed unique character.

Although the letters patent were not granted by Louis XV until 1735, it can be safely deduced from their wording that production of porcelain at Chantilly had begun by about 1725, at least on an experimental scale. "Our well-beloved Ciquaire Cirou has informed us that he has for more than ten years applied himself to the manufacture of porcelain similar to that which was formerly made in Japan; that his pains and the expenses he has lavished on it have achieved so favourable a success that there is no room for doubt that his porcelain is superior to that of Saxony, which had none the less achieved a great reputation in France and in the rest of Europe."

A further extract emphasizes the intention to imitate Japanese wares, rather than the Chinese idioms favored by the firmly established factory at St. Cloud: "we permit and grant to the said Ciquaire Cirou, his heirs and assigns, to make in the factory he has established at Chantilly fine porcelain in all colours, types, styles, and sizes in imitation of the porcelain of Japan, and this, during the space of the following twenty years."[1]

Cirou acquired the premises for his factory in 1730, and it is reasonable to assume that full production began at this date, probably following several years of experimentation. For the next fifteen years or so the entire production was devoted to porcelain decorated in the Japanese Kakiemon style, known at that time as *décor Coreen*, in the erroneous assumption that it derived from Korea. Unlike the English factories at Chelsea and Bow, which were largely dependent on copying Meissen versions of Japanese patterns, Cirou and his designers had direct access to Condé's collection of Kakiemon wares, which served as a source of inspiration and instruction.

Yet other diverse influences were interleaved in such a way as to set Chantilly porcelain apart from all other wares decorated in the Kakiemon style. Shapes were by no means invariably derived from Japanese sources: some echoed French silver forms, others were reminiscent of contemporary faience, and others still, unique to the Chantilly factory. Nor was the painted decoration confined to direct imitation of Japanese porcelain. Among Cirou's collaborators were Robert Dubois, who later moved to Vincennes, where he founded a factory in 1738; Grémy, who also worked at the faience factory at Sinceny; and the painter and engraver Jean-Antoine Fraisse. In 1735 Fraisse published a book of engraved designs under the title *Livre de Desseins Chinois*, and, as his dedication to Condé makes clear, many of the motifs used were inspired by pieces in Condé's own extensive collection. Fraisse's models from the collection in the Château de Chantilly were both Chinese and Japanese and many of his most detailed and inventive designs incorporate a combination of idioms from both countries, creating an effect that might be termed "Japanese chinoiserie," seasoned with a Gallic sense of style. These witty and playful designs often included domestic scenes, children's games, Chinese figure subjects, birds, and animals, painted in the Chantilly version of the Kakiemon palette. While they successfully conveyed the illusion of being Japanese, many of the motifs employed were never actually used on Kakiemon porcelain. By contrast, the patterns drawn directly from Condé's collection of Japanese wares were for the most part basically abstract, consisting of banded hedges (*haie fleurie*), wheat sheaf (*gerbe*), floral branches, and meandering plants, animated by the inclusion of such birds and animals as quail, cranes, fighting cocks, squirrels, and dragons, and further augmented by an exotic assortment of insects. Several of these patterns were exact copies of Kakiemon originals.

The Chantilly palette was very distinctive, both in terms of the colors used and the manner in which they were arranged. They included a notably matte reddish orange and a brilliant tone of green, together with more subdued shades of blue, brown, and pale yellow, all perfectly fused into the soft, whitened glaze. The fine outlines around these characteristically flat unshaded colors, usually in black but sometimes in other tones, served to restrict the freedom and fluidity of the decoration, setting it apart from the Meissen versions in this idiom. In this respect, it is evident that an overall factory style overrode the individual mannerisms of the painters. Yet the aesthetic effect of the palette and decorative style which it conveys cannot be separated from the impact of the glaze, whitened by the addition of tin oxide, which sealed the paste entirely. This served the dual purpose of obscuring both the true color of the paste and its flaws, and imitating the white body of the Japanese porcelain.

This opacified glaze made its own contribution to the Chantilly compositions, the white areas being used as a positive and integral element in the overall design. This sense of the value of the space within the composition is accentuated by the formal and stylized nature of the decoration, placed with great deliberation and invariably delineated from the areas around it. An overall feeling of restraint and simplicity pervades these patterns, their colors restricted in range but always beautifully matched, both to complement and to contrast with one another. No two similar tones were ever aligned beside one another.

Perhaps it is this that lends Chantilly decoration the almost indefinable quality of assuredness, which so draws the eye. The colors interact with one another, their static and enclosed motifs accentuated by the whitened glaze, and the asymmetry created is counterpoised by the rhythmic contours of the subtle and inventive overall shapes. This unerring sense of style, understated yet sophisticated, is typically French and imbues Chantilly decoration with a timeless quality, which defies passing fashions.

A comparison with the contemporary factory at St. Cloud is revealing. The smooth, milky whiteness of the Chantilly glaze contrasts with the translucent, creamy tone of St. Cloud, and the light airiness of the Kakiemon themes is completely absent. The more heavily potted St. Cloud is generally baroque, rather than rococo, in feeling, and Chinese designs were favored, rather than those from Japan.

As with the Bow section of their collection, it was these Kakiemon patterns that so attracted Mr. and Mrs. Bowles to Chantilly porcelain. The transitional phase of the factory, from the mid-1740s until the early 1760s, when European themes replaced the oriental, is represented by a single piece, the fine tureen, cover, and stand (cat. no. 180). This excellent example of the factory's versatility demonstrates its rococo vitality, with its elements derived from both faience and contemporary silver. Yet for an embodiment of the elegance, restraint, wit, and sheer sense of style that characterize Chantilly porcelain, one need look no further than the marvelous melon tureen (cat. no. 171).

1. Quoted by Mallet, in Ayers, Impey, and Mallet, *Porcelain for Palaces*, p. 50.

171

171

Chantilly Tureen and Cover, ca. 1735–45

Of melon shape, with a twig handle and a branch applied with leaves, extending toward a pomegranate finial, painted in the Kakiemon taste with stylized insects.

LENGTH: 8½ in. (21.6 cm)
HEIGHT: 6 in. (15.2 cm)
MARK: Hunting horn in red
EXHIBITED: The Metropolitan Museum of Art, New York, *Masterpieces of European Porcelain*, 1949, cat. no. 119
LITERATURE: *Porcelaines tendres françaises, du XVIIIe siècle provenant de la collection Gilbert Levy*, cat. no. 18
ACCESSION NUMBER: 1986.34a–b

The melon is a form that has stimulated ceramic imitations from many countries. It was popular in French faience and in English pottery and inspired modelers at both Chelsea and Longton Hall. At Chantilly, a graceful teapot was designed in a horizontally lobed shape, drawn out so as to form a spout. Like the teapot, this superb melon tureen was probably suggested by a Japanese model from the prince de Condé's collection of oriental porcelain at the Château de Chantilly. Yet the gnarled branches, applied with leaves, and the finial, fashioned as a bursting

pomegranate, known as a *grenade*, were surely of Chantilly invention, and they add a playful informality to this substantial form.

The array of insects and birds, laid out like flattened specimens, may also have been loosely inspired by the decoration on Japanese porcelain, but their stylized coloring and static placing evoke an effect that has strayed far from the spirit of oriental porcelain. This delightful composition, arranged with such humor and formality, may have been pleasing to Condé, whose catholic tastes in his enforced retirement from public life included the study of chemistry, natural history, textiles, *toiles peintes*, lacquer, and chintz wall coverings.

172

Chantilly Tureen, Cover, and Stand, ca. 1735–45

Of quatrefoil-lobed form, painted in the Kakiemon taste with floral sprays, foliage, and a brown beetle, the finial formed as three nasturtium flower heads.

LENGTH OF STAND: 9⅜ in. (23.8 cm)
LENGTH OF TUREEN: 6¼ in. (15.9 cm)
MARK: Hunting horn in red
LITERATURE: Savage, *Seventeenth- and Eighteenth-Century French Porcelain,* pl. 19a
ACCESSION NUMBER: 1987.30.1a–c

The quatrefoil-lobed form is particularly associated with Chantilly and remained in production into the 1750s; it occurs in association with European patterns as well as purely Kakiemon motifs. Adapted at several smaller French factories, this shape possibly had its origins in early-eighteenth-century French silver. A slightly simplified version was used at Bow and Derby in the 1760s, in underglaze blue decoration, though the elegance and subtlety of contour and curve eluded the English potters.

The inventive and capricious designs of figures, children playing games, Japanese landscapes, and exotic insects, devised by Jean-Antoine Fraisse, were for the most part reserved for much larger, more imposing forms as tureens, vases, and cachepots. On this tureen, the floral decoration shares components with Meissen in the same idiom, but the effect is more stylized and lacks the fluidity of the German factory. Yet in this very static quality, it remains more faithful to its Japanese origins.

172

173

173

Chantilly Ecuelle, ca. 1735–45

Of circular form, applied with two handles and decorated in the Kakiemon taste with two quail between flowering plants.

DIAMETER: 5½ in. (14.0 cm)
MARK: None
LITERATURE: Dallot-Naudin and Jacob, *Porcelaines tendres françaises,* pp. 38, 40, and 41, illustrate this form
ACCESSION NUMBER: 1990.51.5

This shape would originally have been complete with a cover and stand and known as a *bouillon couvert.* It was also made in faience and at Mennecy, Tournai, Sèvres, and Vincennes, where the first example was recorded in a 1751 inventory.[1] An earlier reference to an "écuelle de porcelaine du Japon," belonging to a Mlle Desmares in 1746, may have been of Chantilly

manufacture. Bouillon, a broth, was served in a covered ecuelle, in the boudoir or bedroom, the distance from kitchen to bedroom necessitating a cover in order to keep the broth warm. The stand, or plateau, was used for bread.

Both the shape and perhaps the function were very much a Continental custom, and although ecuelles occur in German and Italian porcelain, its production in England was restricted to the red and gold anchor periods at Chelsea, and to Worcester of the 1760s (cat. no. 129). In England the form was sometimes described as a "porringer." The shape itself was almost certainly derived from a silver or pewter original. Many other Chantilly shapes, including sauceboats, *bordaloux*, and covered jugs also echo silver, faience, or Meissen, while others are exact replicas of Japanese porcelain, presumably copied from pieces in Condé's collection.

1. Savill, *The Wallace Collection Catalogue of Sèvres Porcelain*, pt. III.

174

Chantilly Mustard Pot and Cover, ca. 1735–45

Modeled in the form of a barrel, with a twisted-branch handle applied with leaves, decorated in the Kakiemon taste with a pair of quail, flowering foliage, and, on the cover, a pair of dancing cranes.

HEIGHT: 3⅛ in. (7.9 cm)
MARK: Hunting horn in red
LITERATURE: Spero, "Eighteenth-Century French Porcelain," color pl. 2
ACCESSION NUMBER: 1987.30.2a–b

The barrel shape was a traditional form for ceramic mustard pots, or *moutardiers*, in France, whether in porcelain or faience. Mustard had been kept in small barrels made from wood, stoneware, or salt-glazed earthenware since the Middle Ages, and the eighteenth-century French porcelain vessels clearly reflected this custom. Many examples have silver mounts linking the handle to the cover, in the manner of the silver originals. However, the early Chantilly examples, invariably echoing the form of a wooden barrel, do not have silver mounts. Nor do they have the indentation for a spoon customary in St. Cloud, Mennecy, Tournai, and English mustard pots. The covers are entirely flat, with a shallow rim, simulating a wooden lid. These rustic overtones are delightfully accentuated by the fragile branch handle, naturalistically designed to adorn the barrel, with an apparent disregard for practicality.

The dancing cranes, which are depicted with such wit and rhythm, are sometimes described as storks, or *cigognes*. In Chinese mythology, cranes were symbolic of happiness, an emotion certainly embodied by these prancing birds. Although the overall decoration and palette were inspired by Kakiemon porcelain, this piece conveys a supple airiness and a teasing sense of caprice which is entirely French in feeling.

175

Chantilly Teapot and Cover, ca. 1735–45

Applied with a flattened strap handle and a rigid spout, the finial formed by three nasturtium heads, and decorated in the Kakiemon taste with flowering branches and a beetle.

HEIGHT: 5½ in. (14.0 cm)
MARK: Hunting horn in red
LITERATURE: Dallot-Naudin and Jacob, *Porcelaines tendres françaises*, p. 24, illustrate two slightly differing teapot forms
ACCESSION NUMBER: 1987.30.4a–b

This teapot is of a plain globular form that differs from the majority of Chantilly teapots, most of which are fluted, lobed, octagonal, or indented in shape. The flattened strap handle and cluster of three flower heads are recurring potting characteristics on Chantilly of this period, and peculiar to the factory.

A verse accompanying an engraving by P. Filloeul of 1735, after Jean-Baptiste-Siméon Chardin's painting entitled *A Lady Taking Tea*,[1] suggests that boiling water was employed, but as at Chelsea, Bow, and Derby, it is unlikely that the fragile soft-paste French teapots could have survived the impact of boiling liquid.

The Chantilly factory was the first to attempt a large-scale production of porcelain in the Kakiemon taste, in soft-paste, or artificial, porcelain. The letters patent, granted in 1735, specify the decoration in this idiom and imply that Cirou had been experimenting for some years beforehand. By the late 1740s the fashion for Japanese patterns had been replaced by European idioms, leaving a span of some twenty years during which the Kakiemon style held sway. However, the dating of individual pieces cannot be adduced with the confident precision appropriate to Chelsea, Bow, and Worcester. Vessels such as teapots were issued in at least nine different shapes, but the whitened glaze completely masks the various clues that might assist their chronology. Furthermore, the overriding factory style, evolved with such success, lends the whole output a consistently uniform standard of sophistication, from which it is impossible to detect a coherent development of styles, patterns, and shapes. However, it is feasible that the small minority of pieces *not* marked with the hunting horn date from before the letters patent were granted in 1735. Prior to that date, Cirou was certainly making porcelain, but, being forbidden to market it, may have felt it unwise to use a factory mark. Alternatively, the possibility exists that Cirou was endeavoring to pass off his wares as Japanese, prior to the letters patent, in which case he would most certainly have omitted a factory mark.

1. Savill, *The Wallace Collection Catalogue of Sèvres Porcelain*, pp. 490–91.

175

176   *Ill. p. 160*

Chantilly Sugar Bowl and Cover, ca. 1735–45

Decorated in the Kakiemon taste, with flowering plants and a beetle, the finial modeled in the form of three nasturtium flower heads.

HEIGHT: 3¼ in. (8.3 cm)

MARK: Hunting horn in red

LITERATURE: Williams, *The Kakiemon Influence on European Porcelain*, cat. no. 54

ACCESSION NUMBER: 1987.30.3a–b

The Kakiemon style of decoration, derived from late-seventeenth-century Japanese porcelain, was copied and adapted widely, on Chinese, French, and English porcelain, Chinese wares decorated in Holland, at Meissen, and at the various delft and faience factories throughout Europe. The individual styles evolved at each factory are more remarkable for their differences in interpretation than for their similarities.

This sugar bowl exemplifies the distinctive Chantilly approach to this decorative idiom, which was completely unlike that of any other factory. The colors stand out boldly against the whitened glaze and they are delineated from one another by fine outlines, rather in the manner of a pen-and-ink drawing. The decoration is placed with great deliberation, conveying a stylized effect, yet the contrasting juxtaposition of the colors, their clarity, and the subtle use of the undecorated areas around the composition create an effect of great sophistication. An illuminating contrast to this formal and assured interpretation of Kakiemon motifs is revealed by a comparison with the Chelsea coffee cup (cat. no. 8). Beside the Chantilly, the Chelsea decoration looks haphazard in its layout and disorganized in the arrangement of the pattern. The Chelsea painting has great vitality and the palette is bright and vivid, yet the contrast with the solid, delineated Chantilly colors could hardly be greater.

177

Chantilly Saucer, ca. 1735–45

Of indented quatrefoil shape, painted in the Kakiemon taste, with a bird perched upon a rock, flanked by flowering branches, below a phoenix in flight.

WIDTH: 4¾ in. (12.1 cm)

MARK: Hunting horn in red

ACCESSION NUMBER: Promised gift

This pattern, which has come to be known as the Ho-Ho Bird, underwent a series of variations as it was passed from one country to another. Originating in Chinese porcelain, it was adapted onto Japanese wares in the late seventeenth century. A version at Meissen, in about 1730, seems to hark back to the Chinese original, while the Chantilly and Chelsea designs are superficially very similar to one another. That version was also used at Worcester in the early 1750s, in a slightly altered palette, reappearing at the same factory some fifteen years later, more fully absorbed into the Worcester "Japan" style, and somewhat incongruously named the Sir Joshua Reynolds pattern (cat. no. 132).

In the Chelsea version (cat. no. 7) the bird is given far greater emphasis than on the Chantilly, though the composition as a whole is less compact and more informally laid out. In both instances the glaze has been whitened by the addition of tin oxide, to a greater degree with the Chantilly saucer, creating a more densely white canvas for the colors. The enclosed outlines of the Chantilly pattern heighten its greater sense of sophistication and assuredness, although in some instances the Chelsea design too was outlined.

177

178

178

Chantilly Saucer, ca. 1735–45

Of indented octafoil form, decorated in the Kakiemon taste, with a pair of quail, a banded hedge, and two dancing cranes.

DIAMETER: 5 in. (12.7 cm)

MARK: None

LITERATURE: Eriksen, *The David Collection: French Porcelain*, pl. 14, illustrates a tea bowl and saucer

ACCESSION NUMBER: 1987.30.2c

The delightful shape of this saucer typifies the cursive fluidity of so many Chantilly forms, some echoing Japanese porcelain or French silver, others being designed at the factory. The contours of these outlines, so often balanced and symmetrical, are in unexpected and exhilarating juxtaposition with the characteristic asymmetry of the painted decoration.

Quail were employed in many variations on Chantilly porcelain, of which this is the most typical. Their delineated outlines and plump, sharp-beaked appearance is faintly reminiscent of a pair of hedgehogs, and the effect is utterly different from either the Japanese original or the Chinese and Meissen versions. The pattern also occurs on English porcelain, on Chelsea, Bow (cat. nos. 57–63), Worcester (cat. no. 151), and several other factories. By contrast, the charming pair of dancing cranes, which often appear in association with this version of the Quail pattern, seem not to be motifs on either Meissen or Japanese porcelain. It is tempting to speculate that these playfully animated birds may have been invented at Chantilly, possibly by Jean-Antoine Fraisse, the painter who also acted as an artistic adviser to Cirou.

179

179

Chantilly Bourdaloue, ca. 1735–45

Of slipper shape, with a loop handle, decorated on
each side with dragons.

LENGTH: 7 in. (17.8 cm)

MARK: None

LITERATURE: Honey, *French Porcelain*, pl. 22, illustrates a
plate in this pattern

ACCESSION NUMBER: 1988.45.3

Bourdaloux, or chamber pots, were produced at Chantilly in at least three entirely different shapes, of
which this example is the simplest in outline. First
known in Dutch delftware, in about 1710, *bourdaloux*
were made at Meissen, Mennecy, Sèvres, and in
French faience, the Sinceny factory issuing this exact
form. They were also produced, complete with
covers, in Chinese porcelain, for the export market
from the 1720s onward. Yet the shape was not introduced into England until the mid-1760s, and the porcelain examples from Bow, Derby, and Caughley are
very scarce. Evidently the form was considered more
suited to creamware, for a far greater number of
Wedgwood and Leeds examples have survived.

Known at Chantilly as the Prince Henri pattern,
this design originated in Meissen, where it was ordered for the Hofsilberkammer in Dresden, between
1731 and 1734, as the *rote Drache* (red dragon). As the
Japanese version seems to date from no earlier than
1740, it seems likely that in this instance Meissen
served as the source for the Chantilly pattern. At the
time of his death in 1740, an inventory of the duc
de Bourbon's collection listed many pieces decorated
"avec une bande rouge a dragons." Unlike the Meissen and Japanese versions, the Chantilly pattern omitted the use of gilding to highlight elements in the
pattern, because gilding was prohibited by royal de-
cree at all porcelain factories other than Vincennes
and Sèvres. The pattern was introduced at Chelsea
during the raised anchor period and occurs on octagonal and fluted tewares and on plates, from about
1750 to 1753. A large representation of this pattern, including Japanese, Meissen, and Chelsea, is on view at
Castle Howard in Yorkshire.

180

Chantilly Tureen, Cover, and Stand, ca. 1745–50

Of oval form, elaborately fluted and scroll-molded, the finial on the cover in the form of an elongated bud, and painted with a large bouquet of flowers and scattered sprays.

LENGTH OF STAND: 9¼ in. (23.5 cm)

DIAMETER OF TUREEN: 7 in. (17.8 cm)

MARK: Hunting horn in red

LITERATURE: Atterbury, *European Pottery and Porcelain,* p. 107

ACCESSION NUMBER: 1988.45.1a–c

This is a fine example of the rococo style that emerged at Chantilly for a brief period, as one of the European themes that replaced the purely oriental idioms of the factory's first twenty or so years. The fluid shape, rippling with rhythmic energy, is influenced both by contemporary silver and by Meissen, while the inner portion of the stand, with its asymmetrical scroll molding, shares stylistic similarities with motifs on Niderviller faience. There are indeed many parallels between Chantilly and faience, both in terms of shape and decoration. Forms such as *bourdaloux,* *seaux,* and some covered jugs are of common shape, while intriguing similarities exist between the Kakiemon style and palette at Chantilly and that developed with such humor and panache at the Sinceny faience factory. No doubt the presence of the painter Antoine Grémy, at Chantilly by 1734, and at Sinceny thirteen years later, contributed to this cross-fertilization.

181

Chantilly Plate, ca. 1755–65

Painted with a hunting scene within a circular reserved panel and with wild animals, within six quatrefoil panels, all upon a blue diaper ground, enriched with gilt.

DIAMETER: 9⁵⁄₈ in. (24.4 cm)
MARK: Hunting horn in blue and incised letter *R*
LITERATURE: Dallot-Naudin and Jacob, *Porcelaines tendres françaises,* p. 56
ACCESSION NUMBER: 1988.45.2

This plate features a distinctive Chantilly ground color, diapered with quatrefoils within squares, forming a mosaic pattern. It occurs in conjunction with a range of subjects including birds, flowers, fruit, and fables. Although painted on-glaze, the blue can sometimes resemble an underglaze tone in its decorative effect, and the ground color was also used as a border design and, more rarely, as an overall ground on tea services. This decoration, with its echoes of Sèvres, is associated with Pierre Peyrard, who managed the factory from 1760 to 1776 and provided services in this style for the various residences of the prince de Condé, son of the factory's patron and father of the unfortunate duc d'Enghien.

At various times between the mid-1740s and the mid-1760s, attempts were made to enforce a royal monopoly, in order to protect the interests of Vincennes and Sèvres, the French royal factory, by prohibiting the manufacture of porcelain at rival establishments. These successive edicts, designed to maximize profitability and emulate the success and stature of Meissen, were only partially effective, and factories such as Chantilly and Mennecy were able to continue in production, though on a restricted scale.

182

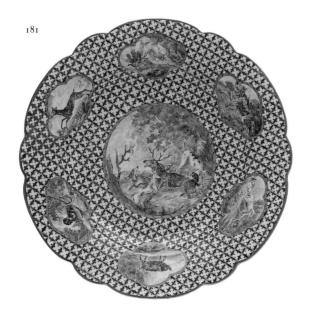

181

182

Pair of Chantilly Custard Cups and Covers, ca. 1760–65

Of spirally fluted form, painted in underglaze blue with floral sprigs.

HEIGHT: 2¹⁄₂ in. (6.4 cm)
MARK: Hunting horn in underglaze blue on each piece
LITERATURE: *Les porcelainiers du XVIIIe siècle français,* p. 114, illustrates a group of Chantilly domestic wares decorated in this pattern
ACCESSION NUMBERS: 1991.40.89.1a–b, 89.2a–b

Custard cups and covers, known in France as *pots à crèmes,* were produced in great quantities, from the 1750s onward, at Chantilly, Sèvres, Mennecy, and Tournai. Prior to about 1755, examples are scarce. They were intended to be used in a set, *en suite,* accompanied by a serving tray. In England the shape was not introduced until the late 1760s, and it was in production at Worcester, Caughley, Derby, and, on a more restricted scale, at Bristol and Lowestoft.

This simple underglaze blue pattern, termed *à la brindille,* is strongly associated with the Chantilly factory, though it was later adapted at Tournai, Caughley, and Derby. From the 1760s onward underglaze blue decoration formed an increasingly prominent element in the Chantilly factory's production and occurs on a wide range of domestic shapes. The output as a whole, beginning with this period, in terms of both decoration and marketing priorities, might be likened to that of Caughley during the 1780s.

· GLOSSARY ·

atelier (Fr., workshop): artist's studio.

blanc de chine (Fr., China white): French name given in 18th century to unpainted white-glazed Chinese porcelain made in factories at Dehua, in Fujian province, in southeastern China.

bleu de roi (Fr., king's blue): a blue color first developed at Vincennes and later used at Sèvres.

bleu lapis (Fr., lapis blue): a blue streaked with veins, similar in effect to lapis lazuli stone.

bleu soufflé (Fr., blown blue): blue color applied in tiny drops, in effect as if color had been blown onto the piece.

blue and white: underglaze blue decoration.

bocage: a leafy background; used in connection with figures.

caillouté/lapis caillouté (from Fr., *caillou*, "pebble"): a decorative motif of meshed oval forms, devised at Sèvres in about 1752.

camaïeu (Fr., like a cameo): decoration resembling a cameo in monochrome.

chinoiserie: European interpretation of Middle and Far Eastern shapes and decorative motifs.

ciselé (Fr., chiseled): gilding tooled into decorative patterns.

ecuelle (Fr.): porringer, bowl, basin.

faience (Fr. name of Faenza, in Italy): tin-glazed earthenware.

famille rose/verte (Fr., rose/green family): Chinese porcelain of the 17th and 18th century decorated in enamel colors, named for predominating color. Famille rose and famille verte are the most common. Famille verte uses iron red, yellow, purple, and violet blue. Famille rose uses these same colors, with the addition of a rose pink, introduced to China from Europe.

finial: ornamental top, usually of a teapot or coffee pot cover.

fluted shape: molded with parallel grooves.

gros bleu: solid blue ground derived from Sèvres; also known as "wet blue."

hard-paste porcelain: extremely hard, translucent ceramic made with kaolin and silica and fired at a high temperature (1,250°–1,350° C). First made in China in the 7th or 8th century, it was not made in Europe until 1709, at Meissen.

ho-ho bird: a phoenix incorporated into several Kakiemon patterns.

"in the white": lacking colored decoration.

Imari (Jap.): richly decorated porcelain made at Arita for the export market and shipped to Europe from the port of Imari. Dating from the late 17th century, it features underglaze blue with chiefly red overglaze enamel and gold. Chinese Imari ware was made to compete with the Japanese ware.

Kakiemon (Jap.): style of decoration derived from the work of the Kakiemon family of Japanese potters; high-quality Japanese porcelain, sparsely and asymmetrically decorated with overglaze enamels and sometimes gold. Imitated at European factories, including Chantilly, Chelsea, Bow, and Worcester.

mirror-shaped panel: oval or round panel in a decorative asymmetrical scrolled form.

mons: area raised above surrounding material.

moons: circular areas of greater translucency when viewed by transmitted light.

Mosaik: border pattern with areas of ground color overpainted with a diaper pattern.

palette: a group of colors peculiar to an artist or a factory.

prunus: a white plum blossom.

saucer dish: a shallow dish of saucer shape; component of a tea service.

scale ground: a ground pattern composed of overlapping scales, either in underglaze blue or overglaze colors.

silver shape: a shape in the style of silver or directly influenced by silver.

soft-paste porcelain: European imitation of true porcelain, usually made of mixture of white clay and glass and fired at a comparatively low temperature (less than 1,250° C).

sparrow beak: a pouring lip resembling the beak of a sparrow; associated with cream jugs.

spoon tray: a narrow tray used to hold hot or wet spoons when not in use; a component of a tea service.

strawberry-leaf molding: decoration in relief, suggested by strawberry leaves.

sucrier (Fr.): sugar bowl or sugar box.

tea-plant decoration: spiraling decoration in relief of applied blossoms.

transfer printing: process in which a design is transferred from a copperplate inked with ceramic colors to a piece of paper or other intermediary medium, which, while still wet, is pressed onto the ceramic surface.

underglaze blue: painted blue decoration, applied before the glaze, and permanently fixed when the glaze is fired. *See* blue and white.

waster: a broken or defective pot, cast aside on a waster heap at some stage during the process of manufacture.

· BIBLIOGRAPHY ·

CHELSEA

Adams, Elizabeth. *Chelsea Porcelain*. London: Barrie & Jenkins, 1987.

Austin, John C. *Chelsea Porcelain at Colonial Williamsburg*. Williamsburg, Va.: Colonial Williamsburg Foundation, 1977.

Ayers, John, Oliver Impey, and J. V. G. Mallet. *Porcelain for Palaces: The Fashion for Japan in Europe, 1650–1750*. London: Oriental Ceramic Society, 1990.

Clarke, T. H. "Sir Charles Hanbury Williams and the Chelsea Factory." *English Ceramic Circle Transactions* 13, pt. 2 (1988).

Cushion, John, and Margaret Cushion. *A Collector's History of British Porcelain*. Woodbridge: Antique Collectors' Club, 1992.

Dragesco, Bernard. *English Ceramics in French Archives*. London: Dragesco, 1993.

Ehret, George Dionysius, and Christopher James Trew. *Plantae selectae quarum imagines*. After paintings by George Dionysius Ehret. Nuremberg: Christopher James Trew; Augsburg: B. C. Vogel, 1750–92.

Gardner, H. Bellamy. "Silvershape in Porcelain." *English Ceramic Circle Transactions* 2, no. 6 (1939): 27ff.

Hillier, Bevis. *Pottery and Porcelain, 1700–1914*. London: Weidenfeld and Nicolson, 1968.

Ilchester, earl of. "A Notable Service of Meissen Porcelain." *Burlington Magazine* 55 (October 1929): 18.

Legge, Margaret. *Flowers and Fables*. Melbourne: National Gallery of Victoria, 1984.

Le Rougetel, Hazel. *The Chelsea Gardener: Philip Miller, 1691–1771*. Portland, Oreg.: Sagapress, 1990.

Lippert, Catherine Beth. *Eighteenth-Century English Porcelain in the Indianapolis Museum of Fine Arts*. Indianapolis: Indianapolis Museum of Fine Arts, 1984.

MacKenna, F. Severne. *Chelsea Porcelain: The Triangle and Raised Anchor Wares*. 1948; Leigh-on-Sea: F. Lewis, Publishers, 1969.

———. *Chelsea Porcelain: The Red Anchor Wares*. Leigh-on-Sea: F. Lewis, Publishers, 1951.

———. *Chelsea Porcelain: The Gold Anchor Wares*. Leigh-on-Sea: F. Lewis, Publishers, 1952.

Peirce, Donald C. *English Ceramics: The Francis and Emory Cocke Collection*. Atlanta, Ga.: High Museum of Art, 1988.

Savage, George. *English Pottery and Porcelain*. New York: Universe Books, 1961.

Spero, Simon. *"A Taste entirely new": Chelsea Porcelain, 1744–1754*. London: Simon Spero, 1988.

———. "Chelsea Porcelain, 1744–1769." *The Magazine Antiques* 135, no. 1 (January 1989): 260–71.

———. *Twenty-five Years' Exhibition*. London: Simon Spero, 1989.

———. *English Porcelain and Enamels, 1745–1785*. London: Simon Spero, 1990.

BOW

Adams, Elizabeth, and David Redstone. *Bow Porcelain*. London and Boston: Faber and Faber, 1981.

Ayers, John, Oliver Impey, and J. V. G. Mallet. *Porcelain for Palaces: The Fashion for Japan in Europe, 1650–1750*. London: Oriental Ceramic Society, 1990.

Corson, Margaret. *Variety in Lowestoft Porcelain*. Cambridge: Lilac, 1992.

Finer, Ann, and George Savage. *The Selected Letters of Josiah Wedgwood*. London: Cory, Adams & Mackay, 1965.

Gabszewicz, Anton, with Geoffrey Freeman. *Bow Porcelain: The Collection Formed by Geoffrey Freeman*. London: Lund Humphries, 1982.

Honey, W. B. *Old English Porcelain*. 1928. 3d ed. rev. by Franklin A. Barrett. London, 1972.

Hurlbutt, Frank. *Bow Porcelain*. London: G. Bell and Sons, 1926.

Le Rougetel, Hazel. *The Chelsea Gardener: Philip Miller, 1691–1771*. Portland, Oreg.: Sagapress, 1990.

Peirce, Donald C. *English Ceramics: The Francis and Emory Cocke Collection*. Atlanta, Ga.: High Museum of Art, 1988.

Porter, Roy. *English Society in the Eighteenth Century*. Harmondsworth: Penguin, 1982.

Spelman, W. W. R. *Lowestoft China*. London: Jarrold, 1905.

Spero, Simon. *The Price Guide to Eighteenth-Century English Porcelain*. London: Antique Collectors' Club, 1970.

———. *"A Taste entirely new": Chelsea Porcelain, 1744–1754*. London: Simon Spero, 1988.

LONGTON HALL

Peirce, Donald C. *English Ceramics: The Francis and Emory Cocke Collection*. Atlanta, Ga.: High Museum of Art, 1988.

Watney, Bernard. "A Study of Longton Hall Teapots." *Antique Collector* (February 1955).

———. *Longton Hall Porcelain*. London: Faber and Faber, 1957.

WORCESTER

Amor, Albert, Ltd. *James Giles: China Painter, 1718–1780*. London: Albert Amor, 1977.

Ayers, John, Oliver Impey, and J. V. G. Mallet. *Porcelain for Palaces: The Fashion for Japan in Europe, 1650–1750*. London: Oriental Ceramic Society, 1990.

Barrett, Franklin A. *Worcester Porcelain and Lund's Bristol*. 2d ed. London: Faber and Faber, 1966.

Branyan, Lawrence, Neal French, and John Sandon. *Worcester Blue and White Porcelain, 1751–1790*. 2d ed. London: Barrie & Jenkins, 1989.

Coke, Gerald. *In Search of James Giles, 1718–1780*. Wingham, Kent: Micawber Publications, 1983.

Fisher, Stanley W. *English Blue-and-White Porcelain of the Eighteenth Century*. London: B. T. Batsford, 1947.

Godden, Geoffrey A. *Caughley and Worcester Porcelain, 1775–1800*. London: Herbert Jenkins, 1969.

Handley, Joseph. *Eighteenth-Century English Transfer-Printed Porcelain and Enamels*. Carmel, Calif.: Mulberry Press, [1991].

Hobson, R. L. *Catalogue of the Frank Lloyd Collection of Worcester Porcelain of the Wall Period, British Museum*. London: British Museum, 1923.

Marshall, H. Rissik. *Coloured Worcester Porcelain of the First Period*. Newport and London: Ceramic Book Company, 1954.

Peirce, Donald C. *English Ceramics: The Francis and Emory Cocke Collection*. Atlanta, Ga.: High Museum of Art, 1988.

Pietsch, Ulrich. *Early Meissen Porcelain*. Lübeck: Museum für Kunst und Kulturgeschichte, 1993.

Porter, Roy. *English Society in the Eighteenth Century*. Harmondsworth: Penguin, 1982.

Sandon, Henry. *The Illustrated Guide to Worcester Porcelain, 1751–1793*. London: Herbert Jenkins, 1969.

———. *Coffee Pots and Teapots*. Edinburgh: John Bartholomew & Son, 1973.

Sandon, John. *The Dictionary of Worcester Porcelain*. Vol. 1. *1751–1851*. Woodbridge: Antique Collector's Club, 1993.

Savage, George. *English Pottery and Porcelain*. New York: Universe Books, 1961.

Spero, Simon. *The Price Guide to Eighteenth-Century English Porcelain*. London: Antique Collectors' Club, 1970.

———. *Worcester Porcelain: The Klepser Collection*. Minneapolis: Minneapolis Institute of Arts; London: Lund Humphries, 1984.

———. *English Porcelain and Enamels, 1745–1785*. London: Simon Spero, 1990.

Spero, Simon, and John Sandon. *Eighteenth-Century Worcester Porcelain: The Zorensky Collection*. Woodbridge: Antique Collectors' Club, forthcoming.

Tilley, Frank. *Teapots and Tea*. Newport: The Ceramic Book Co., 1957.

Tillyard, Stella. *Aristocrats*. London: Chatto & Windus, 1994.

Watney, Bernard. *English Blue-and-White Porcelain of the Eighteenth Century*. 2d ed. London: Faber and Faber, 1973.

Wills, Geoffrey. *English Pottery and Porcelain*. London: Guinness Signatures, 1969.

CHANTILLY

Atterbury, Paul, ed. *European Pottery and Porcelain*. N.p.: Mayflower, 1979.

Ayers, John, Oliver Impey, and J. V. G. Mallet. *Porcelain for Palaces: The Fashion for Japan in Europe, 1650–1750*. London: Oriental Ceramic Society, 1990.

Dallot-Naudin, Yvonne, and Alain Jacob. *Porcelaines tendres françaises: Rouen, L. Poterat, St-Cloud, Mennecy, Chantilly, Bourg la Reine, Vincennes*. Paris: C.P.I.P., 1983.

Honey, W. B. *French Porcelain*. London: Faber, 1950.

Les porcelainiers du XVIII siècle français. Paris: Librairie Hachette, 1964.

Savage, George. *Seventeenth- and Eighteenth-Century French Porcelain*. London: Hamlyn, Spring Books, 1960.

Savill, Rosalind. *The Wallace Collection Catalogue of Sèvres Porcelain*. London: Trustees of the Wallace Collection, 1988.

Spero, Simon. "Eighteenth-Century French Porcelain." *Antique Collecting* (April 1992).

Svend, Eriksen. *Davids Samling, fransk porcelaen* (The David Collection: French Porcelain). Copenhagen: Davids Samling, 1980.

Williams, Winifred. *The Kakiemon Influence on European Porcelain*. London, 1974.

· INDEX OF PATTERNS ·

· GENERAL INDEX ·

tureens and stands
Chelsea, cos lettuce, 77
Longton Hall, 10, **77**
Worcester, cauliflower, **103**
Turner, Thomas, 157
turquoise (*bleu céleste*), 86, 118, 120
two-handled cup and saucer, Worcester, **121**
Old *Mosaik*, 20, **138**, *139*

underglaze blue
à la brindille, 173
at Bow, 54–55, 65, 70
at Caughley, 158
at Chantilly, 173
at Chelsea, 17, 20
and Chinese shapes, 153
at Longton Hall, 75, 79
at Lowestoft, 73
at Worcester: 86–87; with
birds, 129; introduction of,
127, 142; landscapes and, 155;
marks associated with, 134;
Mazarine Blue as, 130, 135;
molding and, 109; patterns in,
133, 139, 151; transfer prints
and, 115, 154, 155; for wall pockets, 96

vase
as decoration, 125
Worcester, **119**
Vauxhall, porcelain from, 15, 22, 43,
62, 92, 96
vegetables. *See* naturalistic forms
Vienna, Old *Mosaik* from, 136
*A View of the Canal and of the Gothick
Tower and the Garden of His
Grace the Duke of Argyle at Whit-
ton* (Woollett), 146–47
Vincennes
Clostermann at, 14
influence of: on Chelsea, 24, 29,
49; on Worcester, 86, 120, 132
porcelain from, 162, 166, 173
Vivares, Francis, 110
Vogel, B. C., 37

wages, compared with prices for porcelain, 63, 67, 68, 147
wall pocket, Worcester, cornucopia, *x,
82*, 85, **96**
Walpole, Horace, 11
Warmstry House, Worcester, 83,
125
Watney, Dr. Bernard, 80
Watteau, Jean-Antoine, 146

Weatherby, John, 53
Wedgwood factory, 43, 69, 171
Wedgwood, Josiah, 54
Welsh, James, 62
West, James, 11
West Pans factory, porcelain from, 63,
69, 79, 81, 143, 146
White, Gilbert, 42
Wilkes, John, 134
"Wilkes and Liberty," ceramics com-
memorating, 134
William Augustus, duke of Cumber-
land, 3
Williamsburg, Virginia, porcelain col-
lection in, 34
wine funnel, Worcester, x, 79, 85, **88**
wine tasters
Worcester, ix, 80, 85, **90**
Longton Hall, pair, ix, **80**, 90
Woollett, William, 146
*Worcester Blue and White Porcelain,
1751–1790* (Branyan, French,
and Sandon), 158
Worcester, 82–155 and passim

yellow ground. *See* ground, colored
yellow scale. *See* scale
Young, Arthur, 107